AN ENTITY OBSER[...]   S

BOX BRO[...]

RETROFIT/*BIG PLANET*

MEMOREXIA®

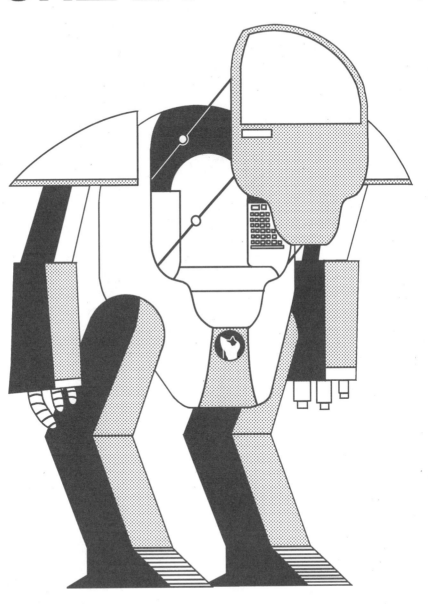

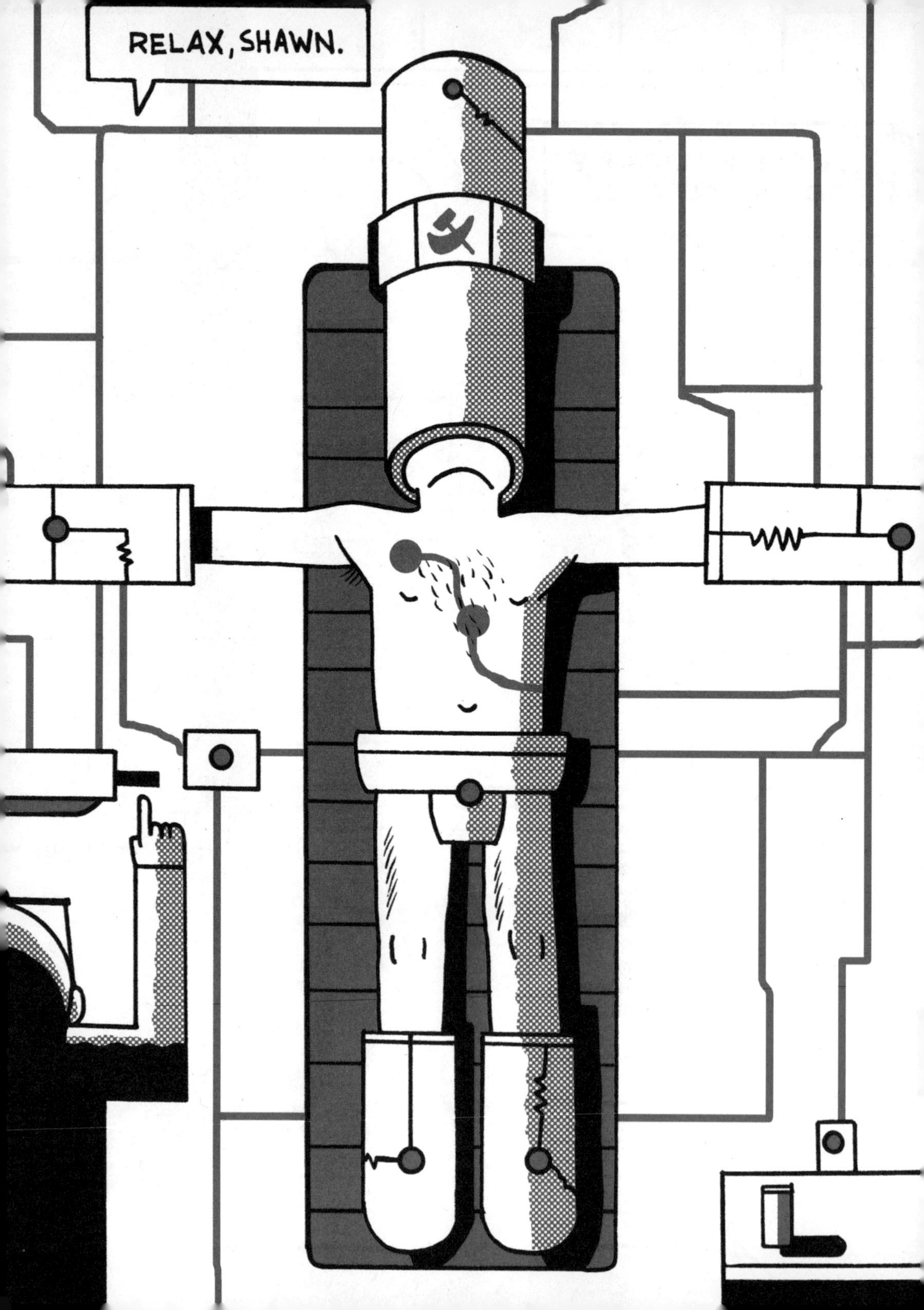
RELAX, SHAWN.

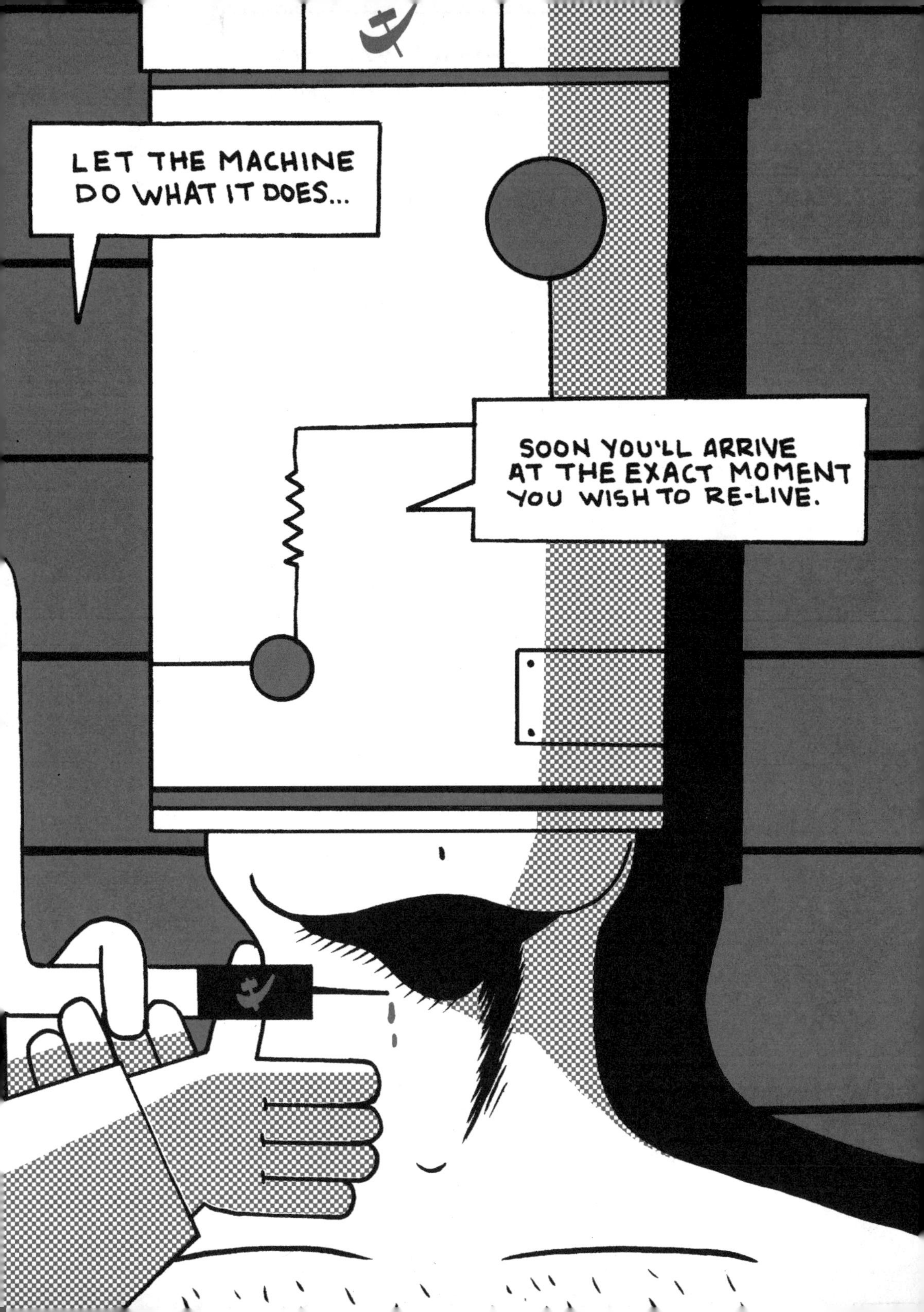
LET THE MACHINE DO WHAT IT DOES...
SOON YOU'LL ARRIVE AT THE EXACT MOMENT YOU WISH TO RE-LIVE.

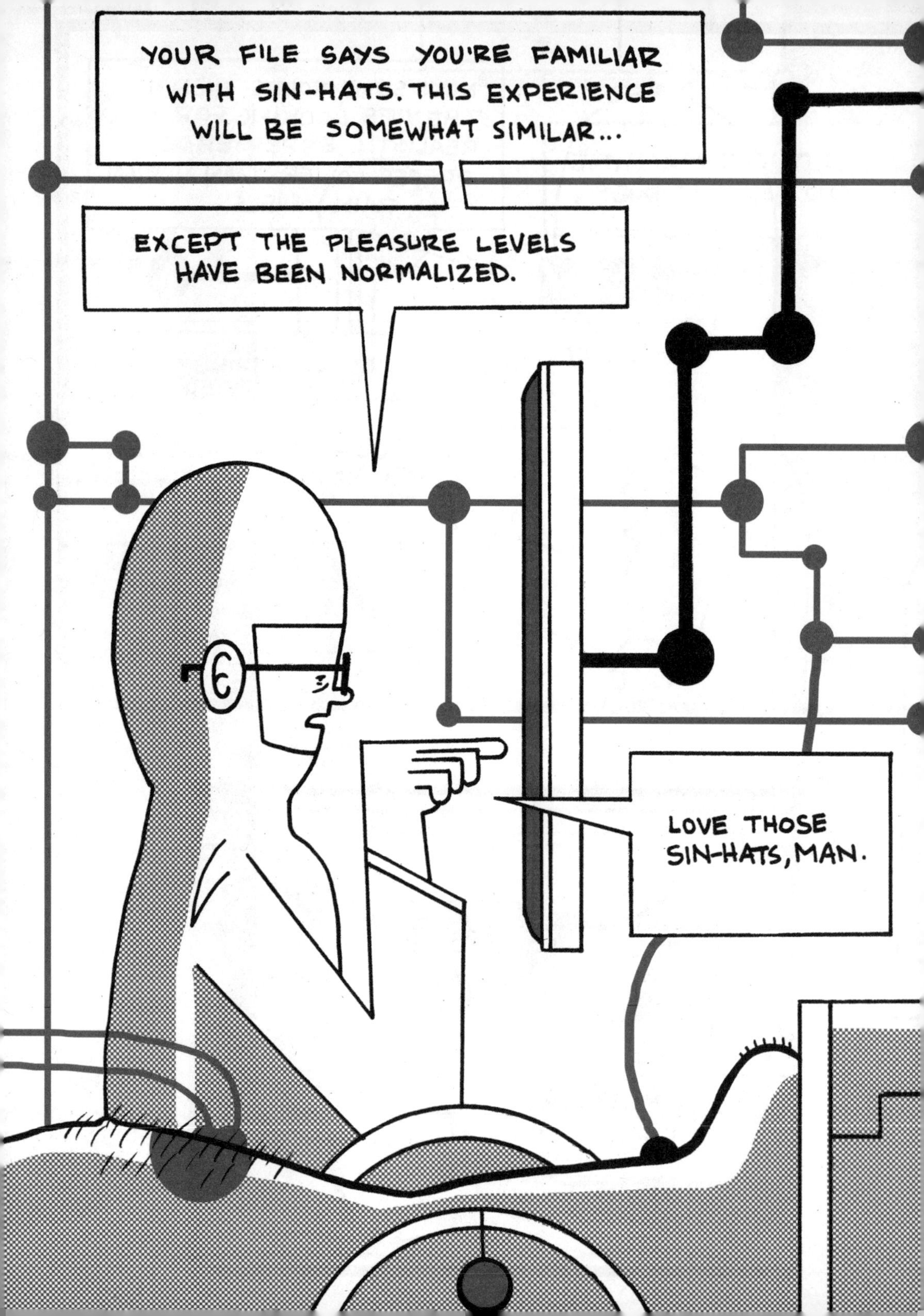
YOUR FILE SAYS YOU'RE FAMILIAR WITH SIN-HATS. THIS EXPERIENCE WILL BE SOMEWHAT SIMILAR...
EXCEPT THE PLEASURE LEVELS HAVE BEEN NORMALIZED.
LOVE THOSE SIN-HATS, MAN.

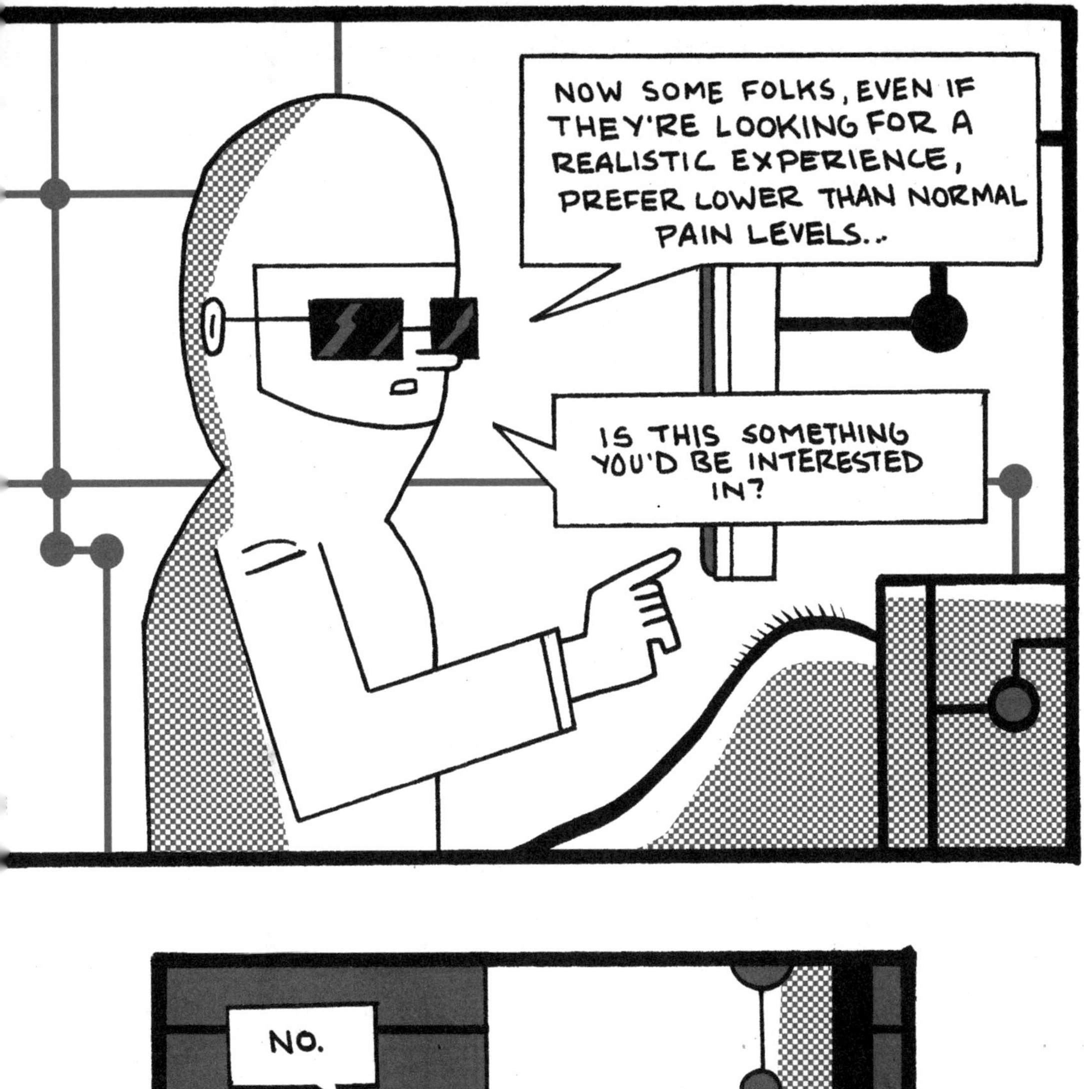
NOW SOME FOLKS, EVEN IF THEY'RE LOOKING FOR A REALISTIC EXPERIENCE, PREFER LOWER THAN NORMAL PAIN LEVELS..
IS THIS SOMETHING YOU'D BE INTERESTED IN?

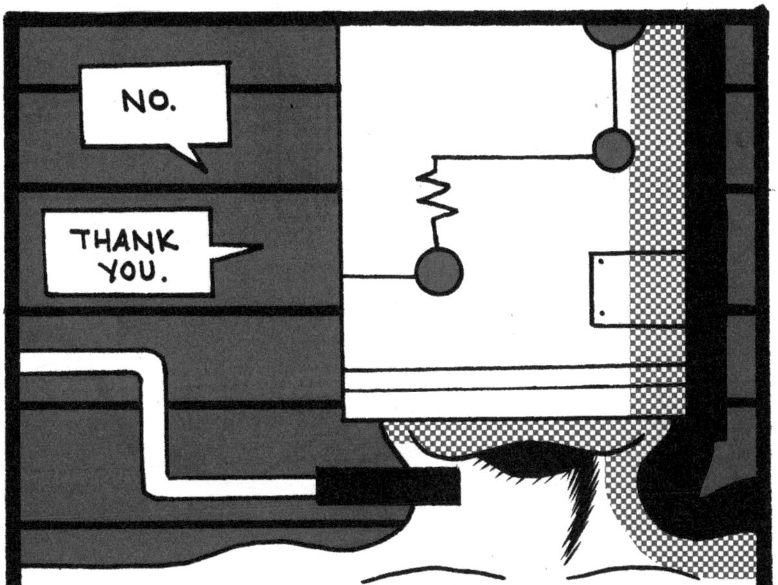
NO.
THANK YOU.

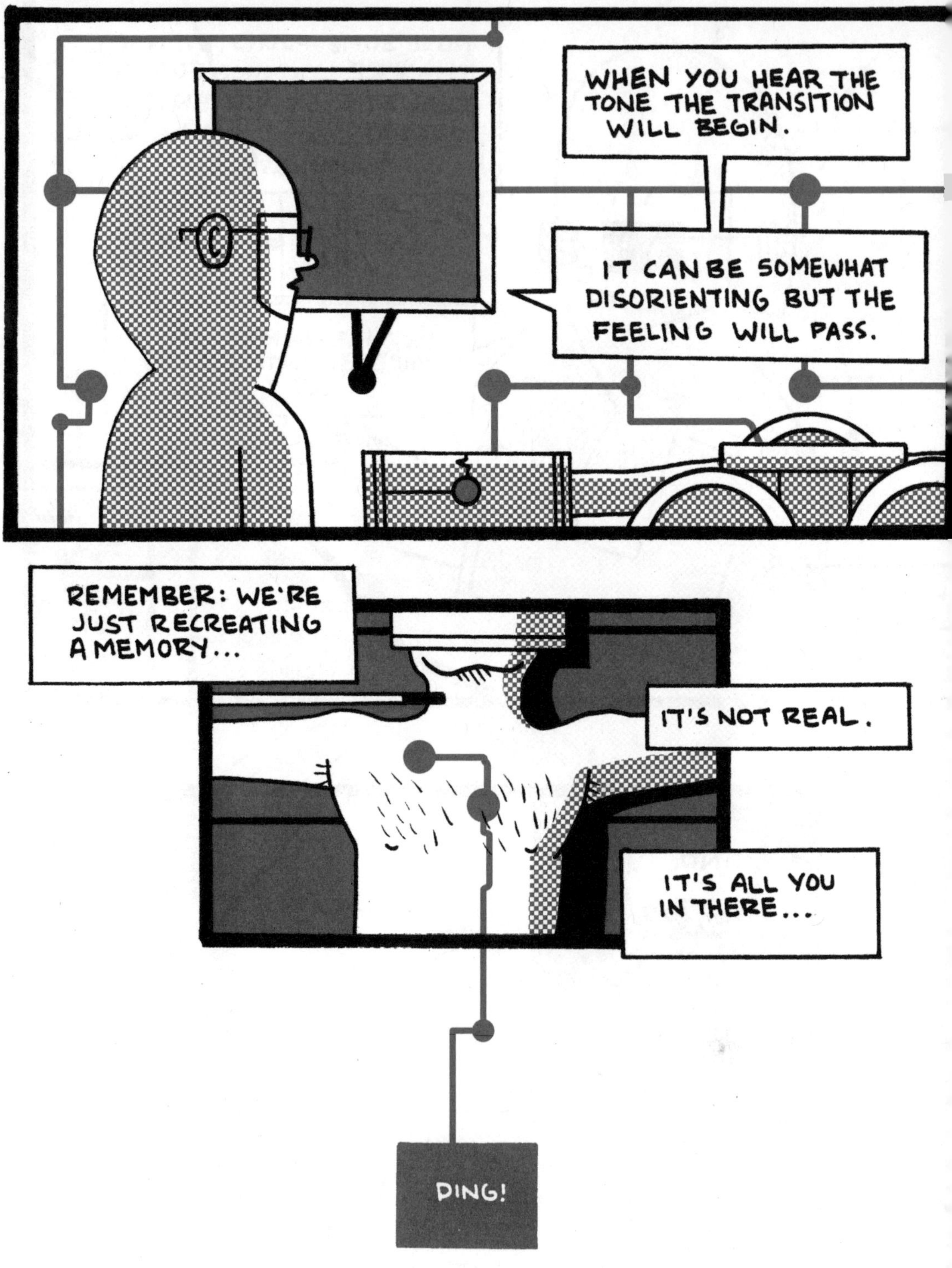
WHEN YOU HEAR THE TONE THE TRANSITION WILL BEGIN.
IT CAN BE SOMEWHAT DISORIENTING BUT THE FEELING WILL PASS.
REMEMBER: WE'RE JUST RECREATING A MEMORY...
IT'S NOT REAL.
IT'S ALL YOU IN THERE...
DING!

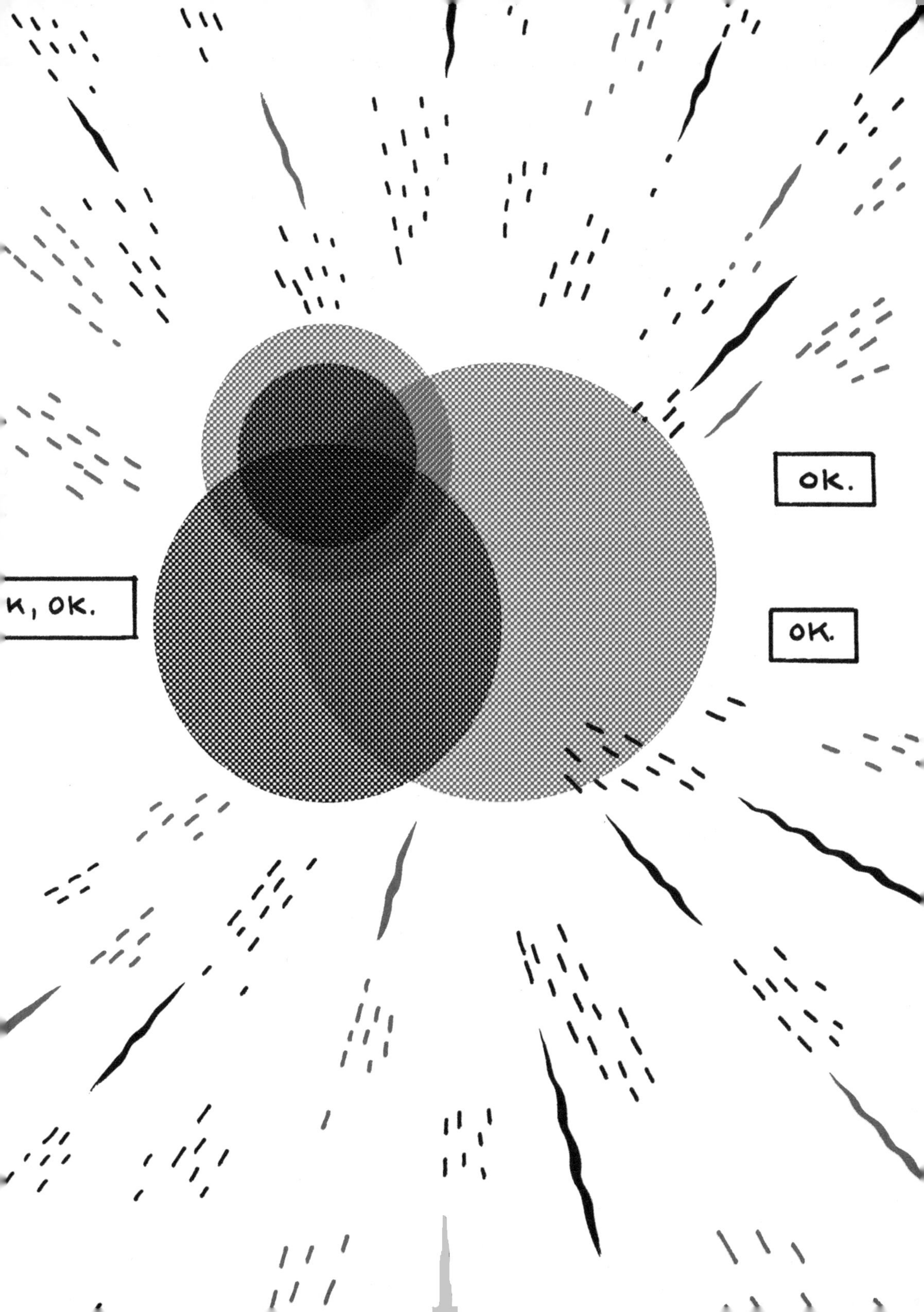
K, OK.
OK.
OK.

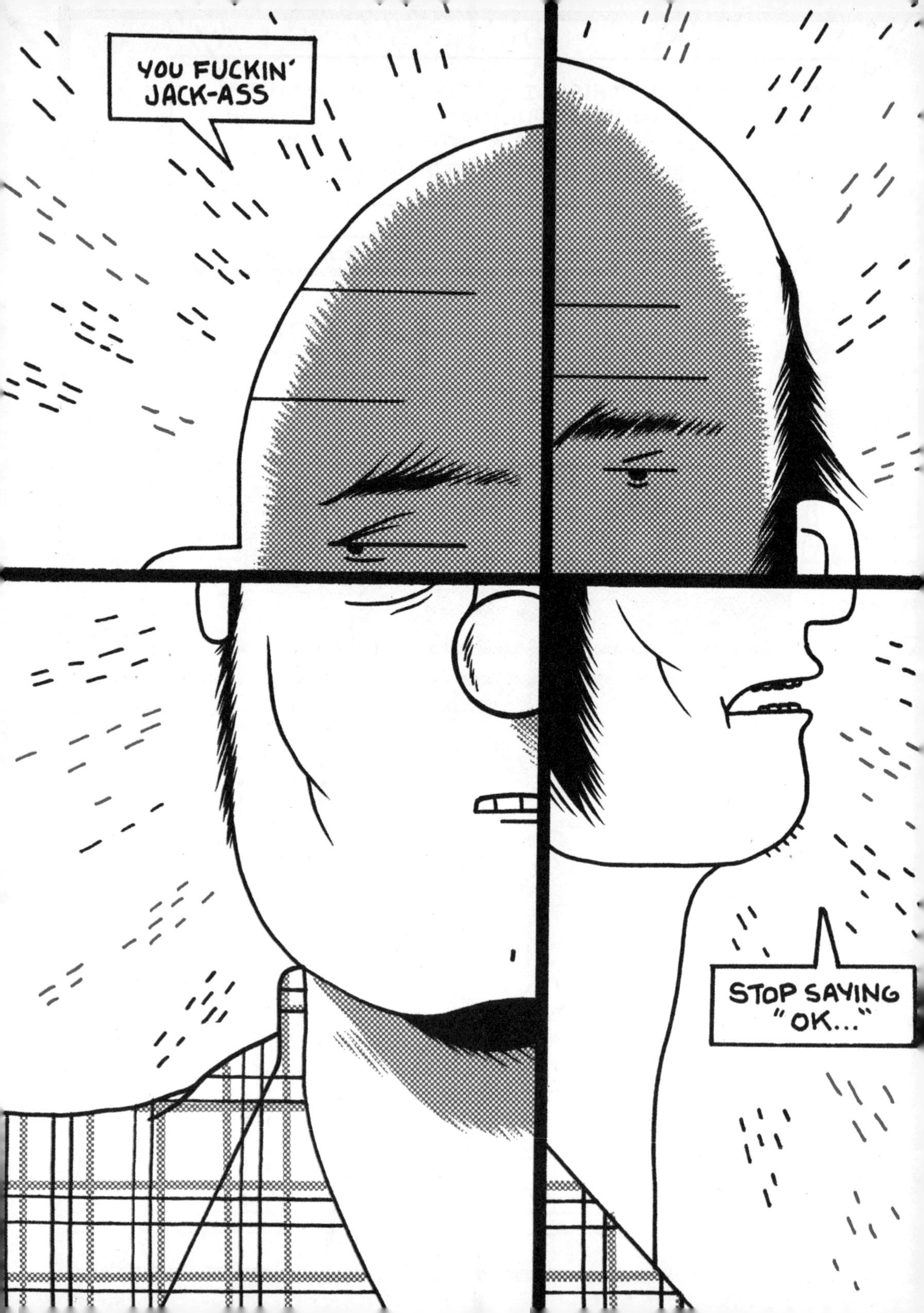
YOU FUCKIN' JACK-ASS
STOP SAYING "OK..."

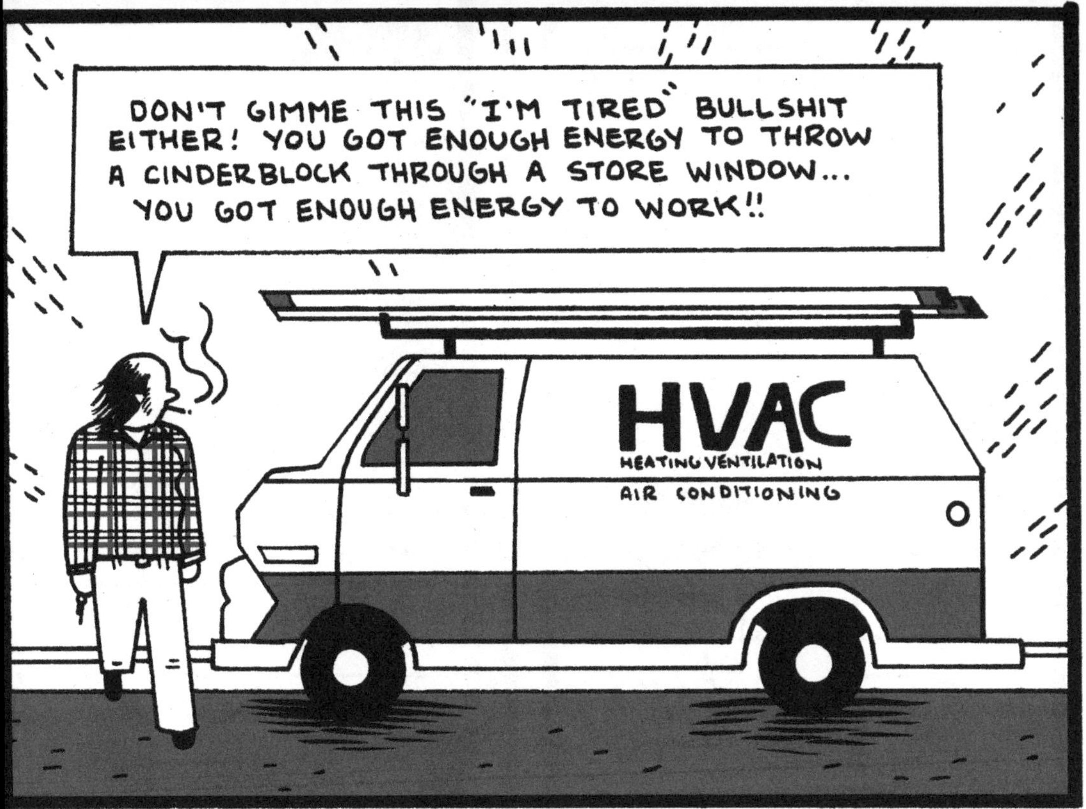
DON'T GIMME THIS "I'M TIRED" BULLSHIT EITHER! YOU GOT ENOUGH ENERGY TO THROW A CINDERBLOCK THROUGH A STORE WINDOW... YOU GOT ENOUGH ENERGY TO WORK!!
HVAC
HEATING VENTILATION
AIR CONDITIONING

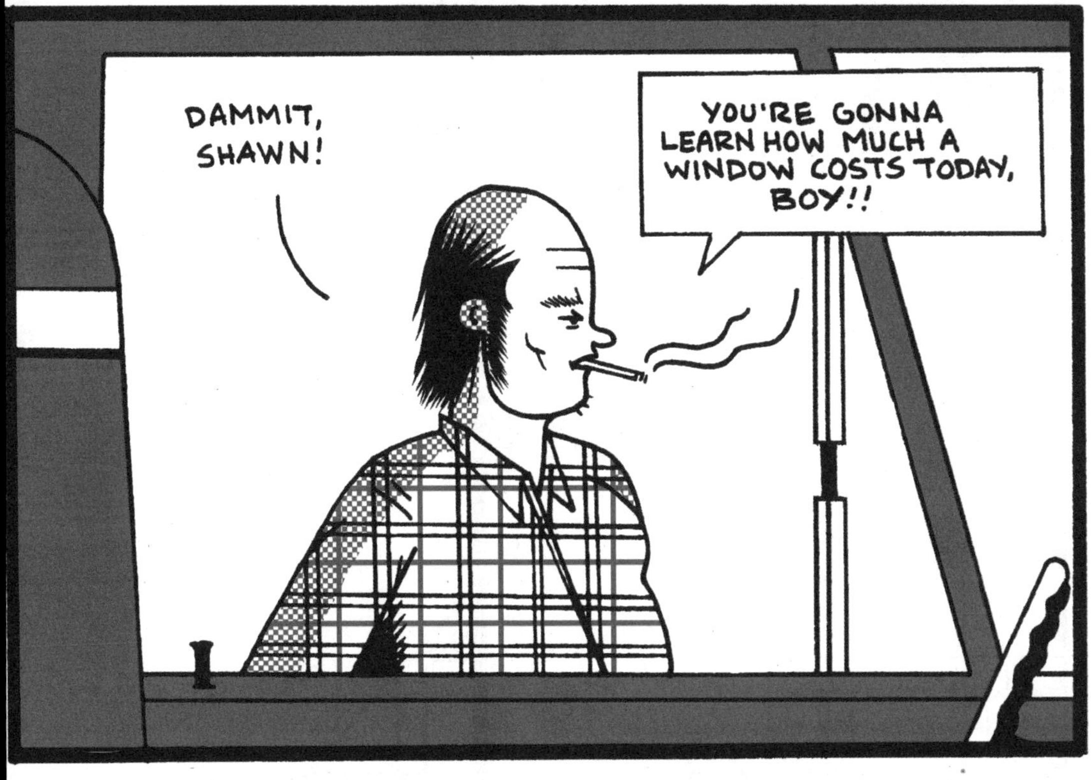
DAMMIT, SHAWN!
YOU'RE GONNA LEARN HOW MUCH A WINDOW COSTS TODAY, BOY!!

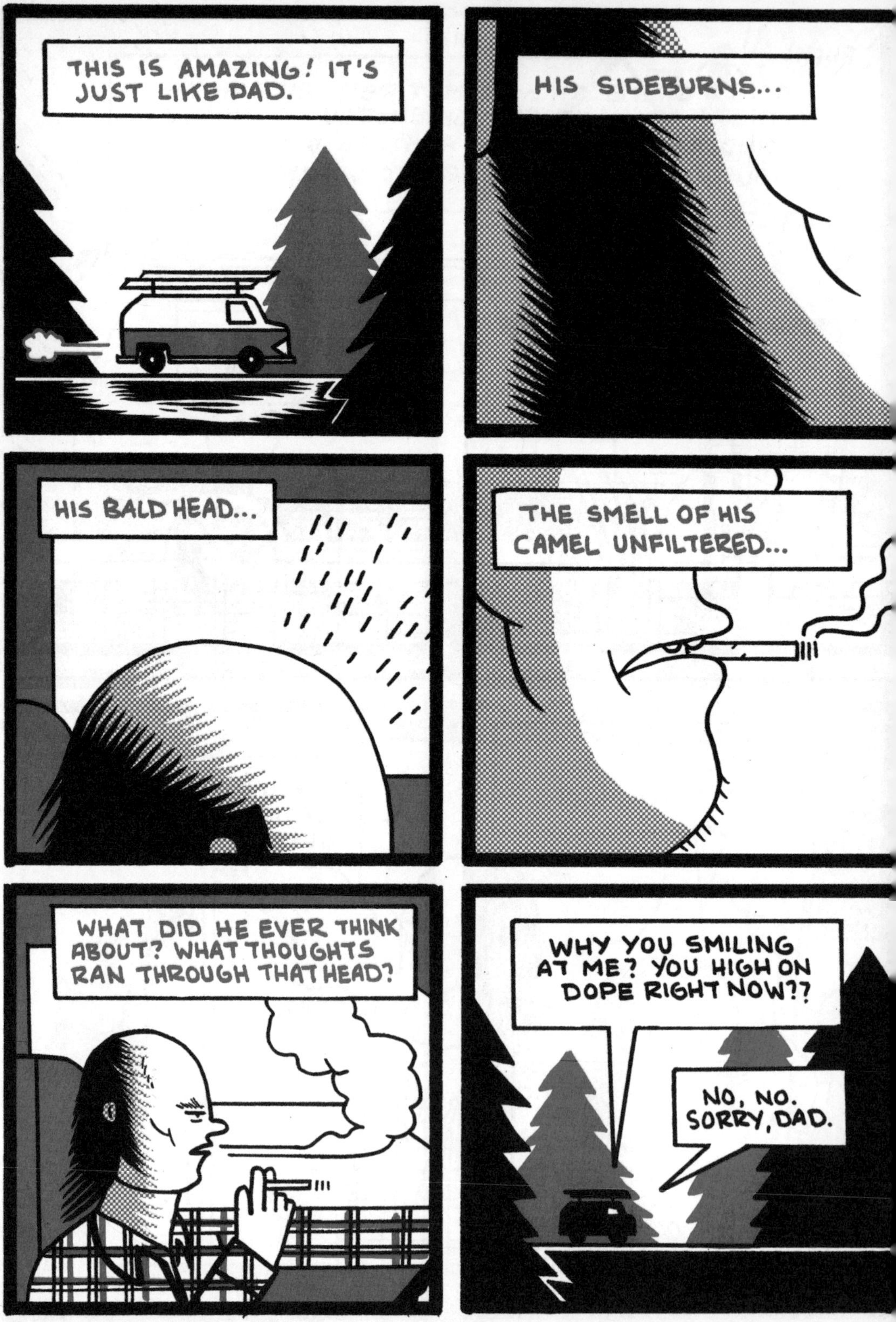
THIS IS AMAZING! IT'S JUST LIKE DAD.
HIS SIDEBURNS...
HIS BALD HEAD...
THE SMELL OF HIS CAMEL UNFILTERED...
WHAT DID HE EVER THINK ABOUT? WHAT THOUGHTS RAN THROUGH THAT HEAD?
WHY YOU SMILING AT ME? YOU HIGH ON DOPE RIGHT NOW??
NO, NO. SORRY, DAD.

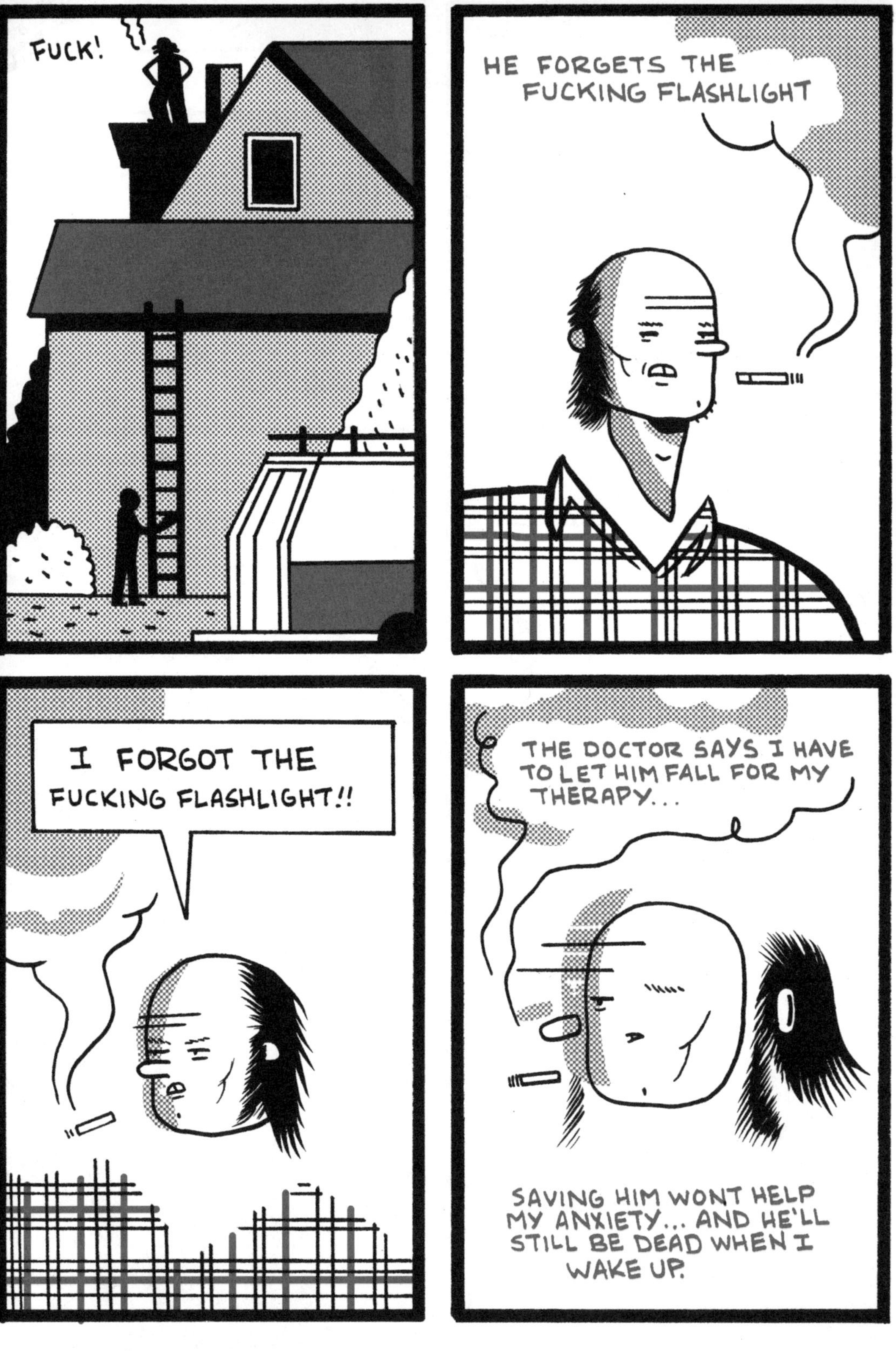
FUCK!
HE FORGETS THE FUCKING FLASHLIGHT
I FORGOT THE FUCKING FLASHLIGHT!!
THE DOCTOR SAYS I HAVE TO LET HIM FALL FOR MY THERAPY...
SAVING HIM WONT HELP MY ANXIETY... AND HE'LL STILL BE DEAD WHEN I WAKE UP.

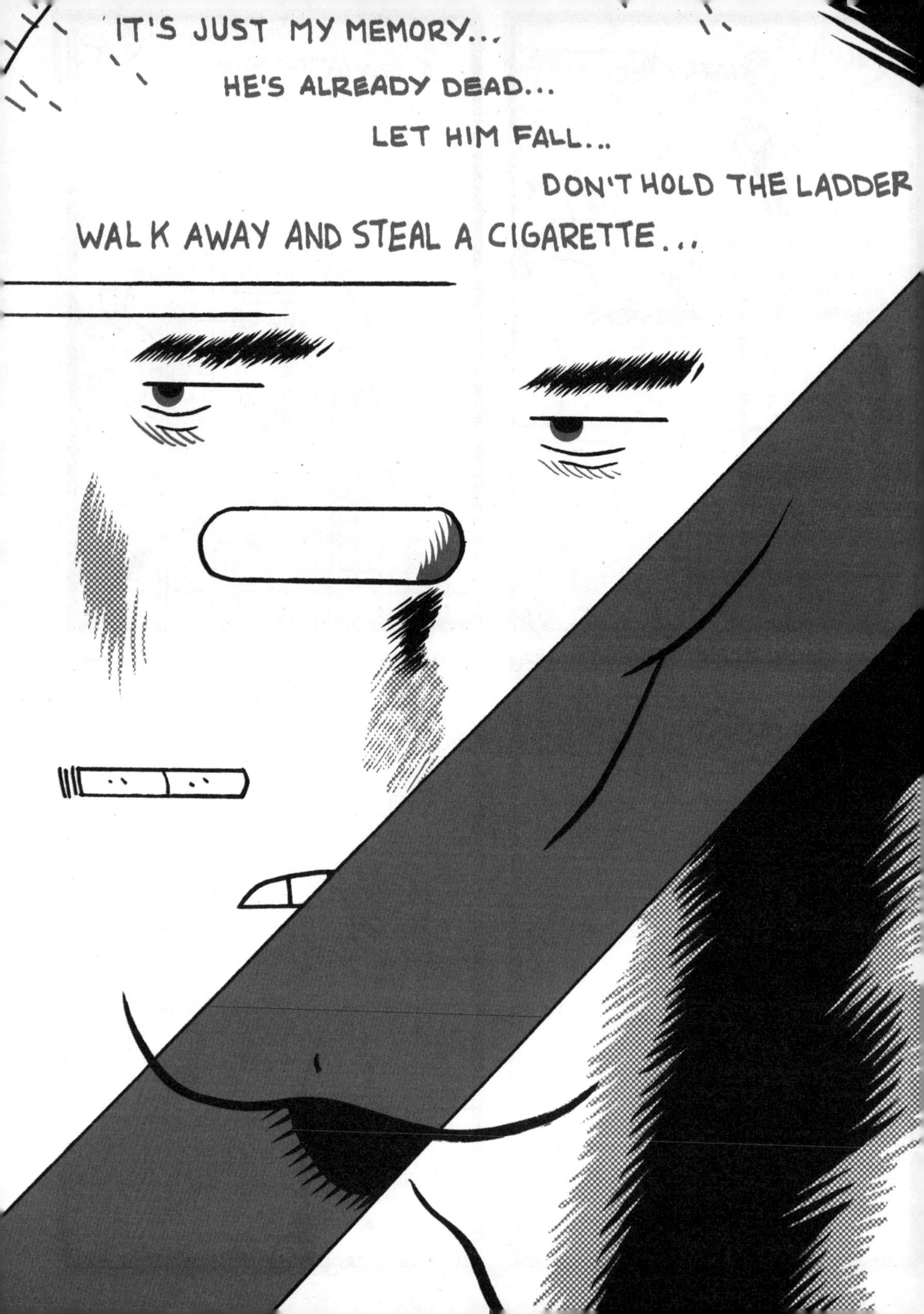
IT'S JUST MY MEMORY...
HE'S ALREADY DEAD...
LET HIM FALL...
DON'T HOLD THE LADDER
WALK AWAY AND STEAL A CIGARETTE...

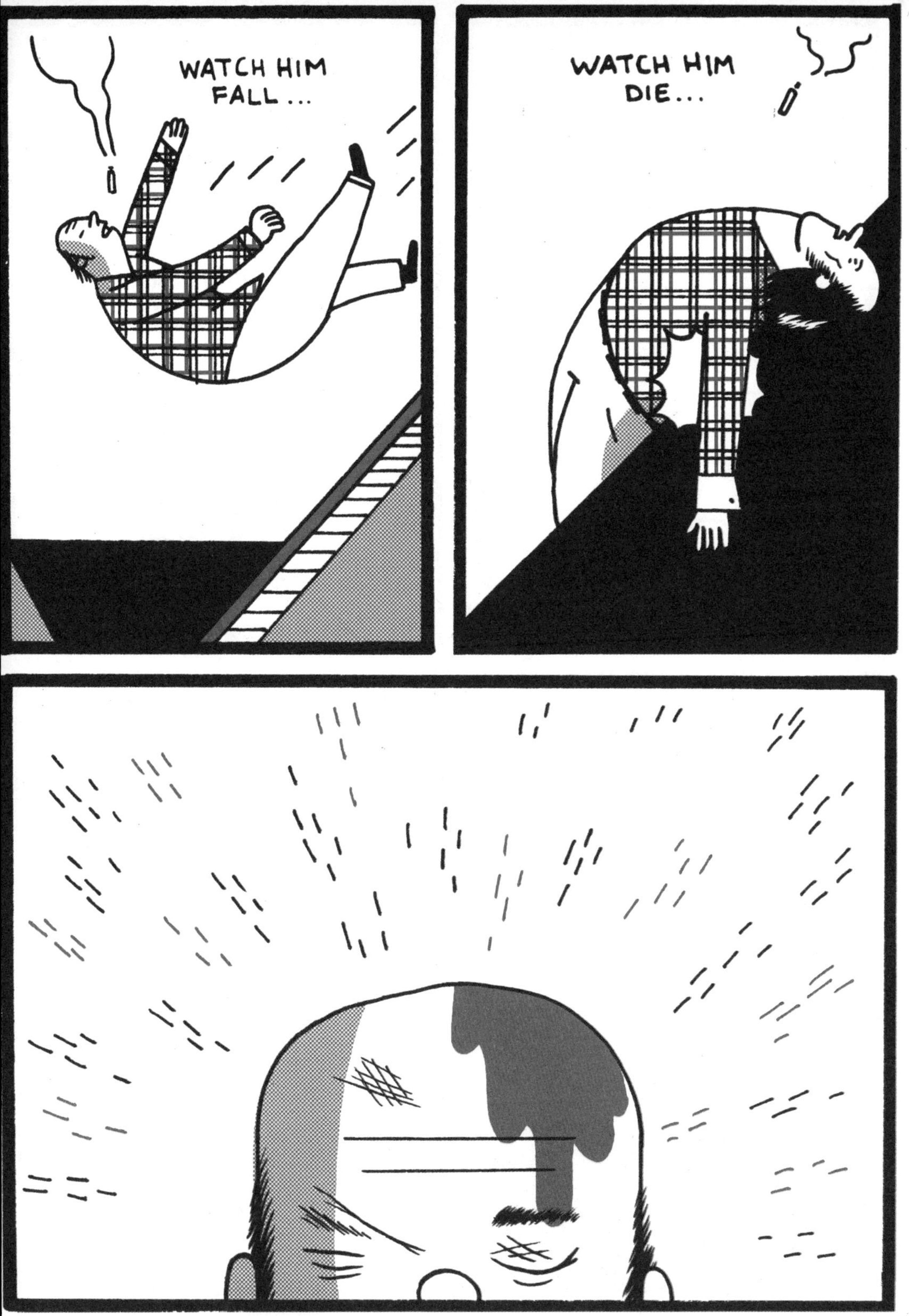
WATCH HIM FALL...
WATCH HIM DIE...

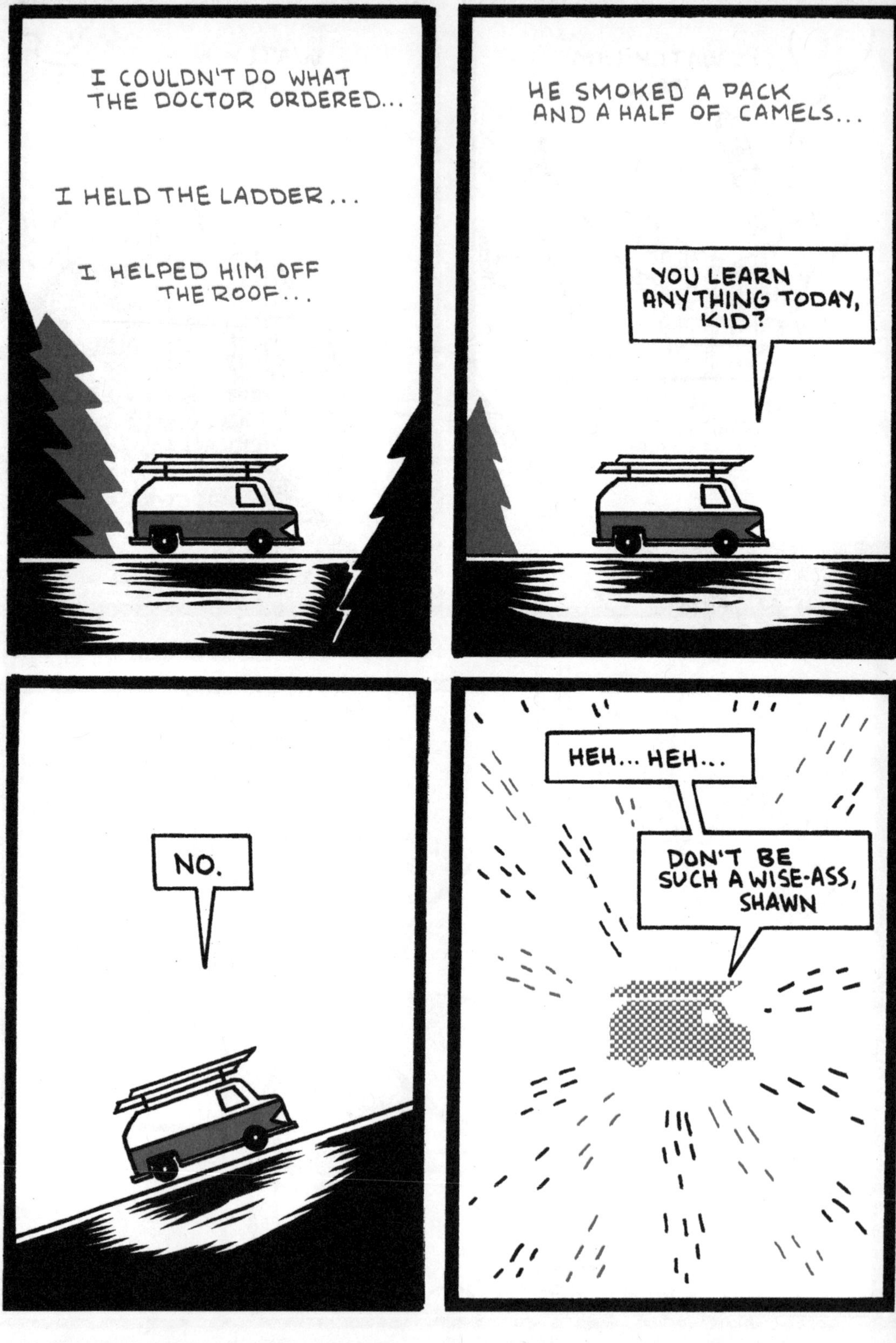
I COULDN'T DO WHAT THE DOCTOR ORDERED...
I HELD THE LADDER...
I HELPED HIM OFF THE ROOF...
HE SMOKED A PACK AND A HALF OF CAMELS...
YOU LEARN ANYTHING TODAY, KID?
NO.
HEH... HEH...
DON'T BE SUCH A WISE-ASS, SHAWN

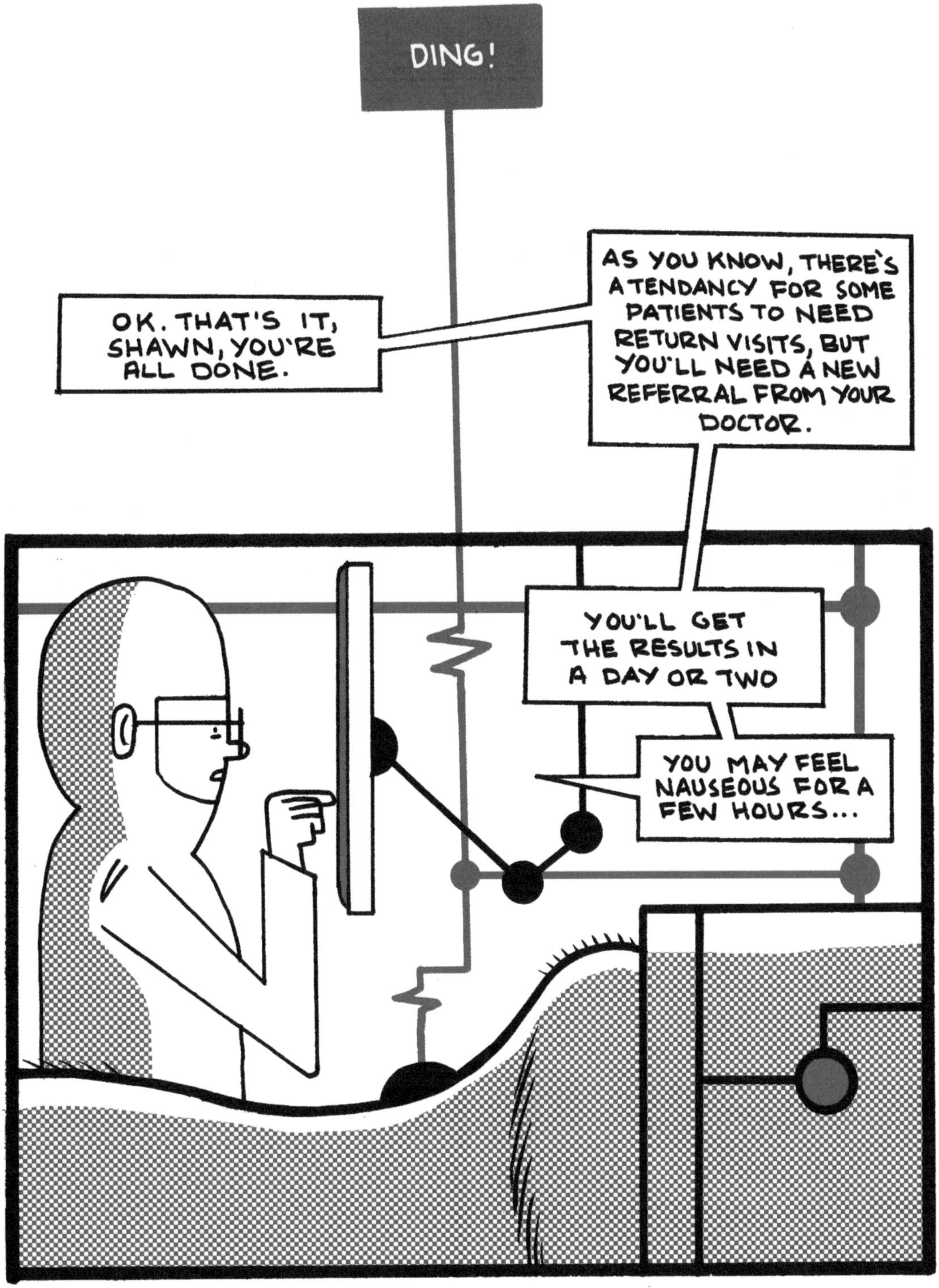
DING!
OK. THAT'S IT, SHAWN, YOU'RE ALL DONE.
AS YOU KNOW, THERE'S A TENDANCY FOR SOME PATIENTS TO NEED RETURN VISITS, BUT YOU'LL NEED A NEW REFERRAL FROM YOUR DOCTOR.
YOU'LL GET THE RESULTS IN A DAY OR TWO
YOU MAY FEEL NAUSEOUS FOR A FEW HOURS...

MUNDO JELLY

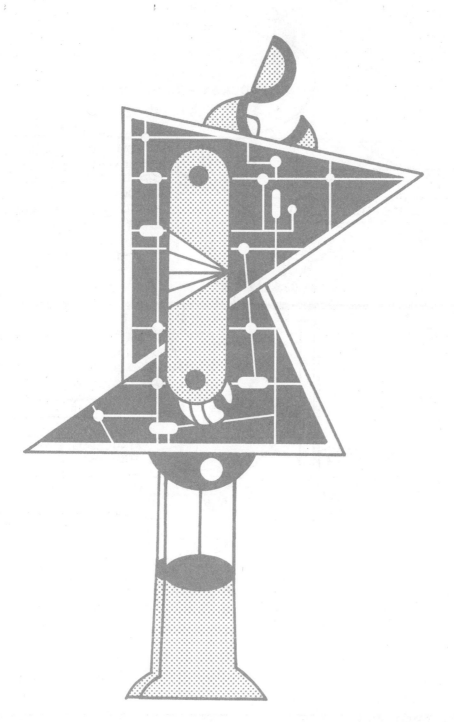

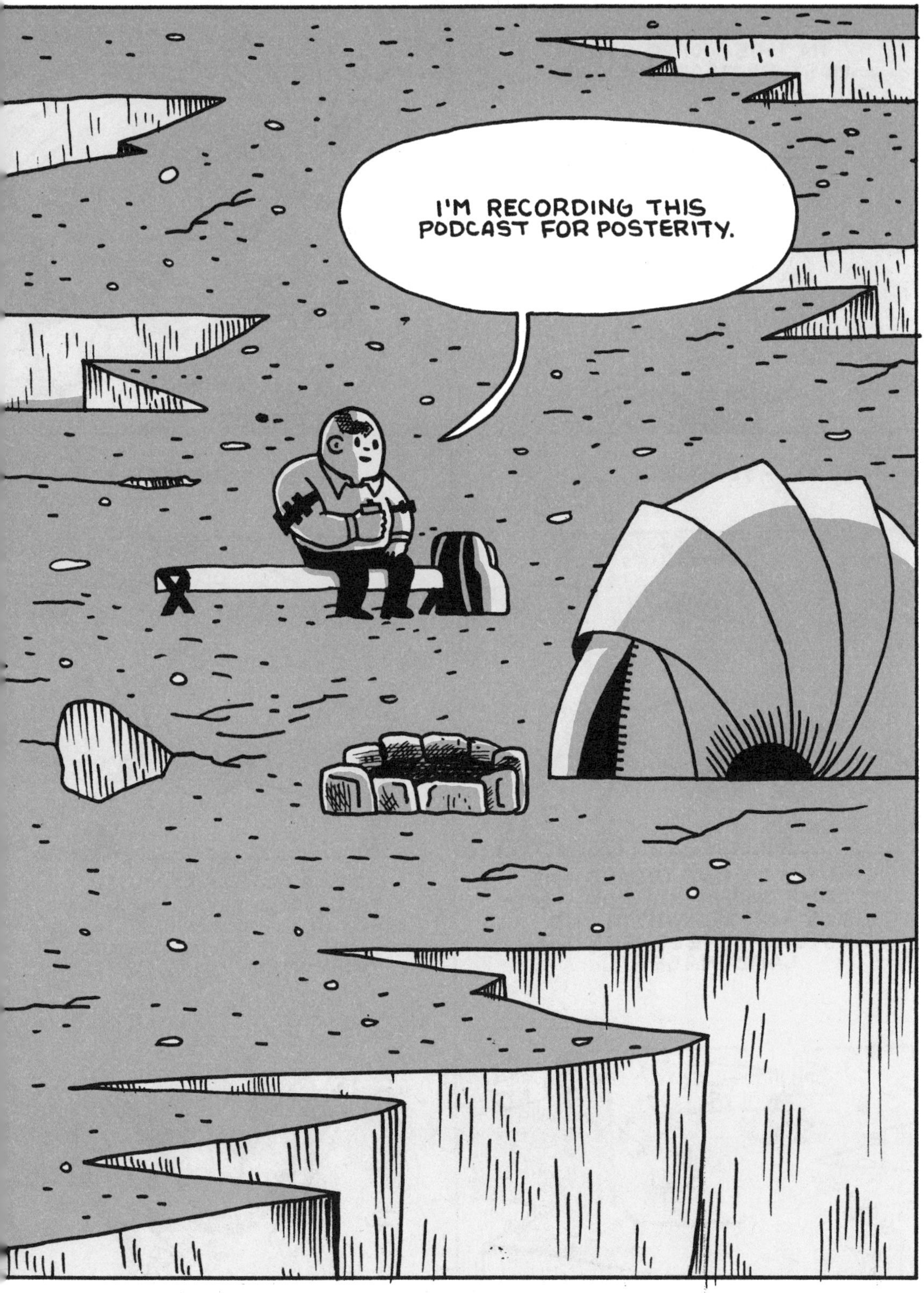
I'M RECORDING THIS PODCAST FOR POSTERITY.

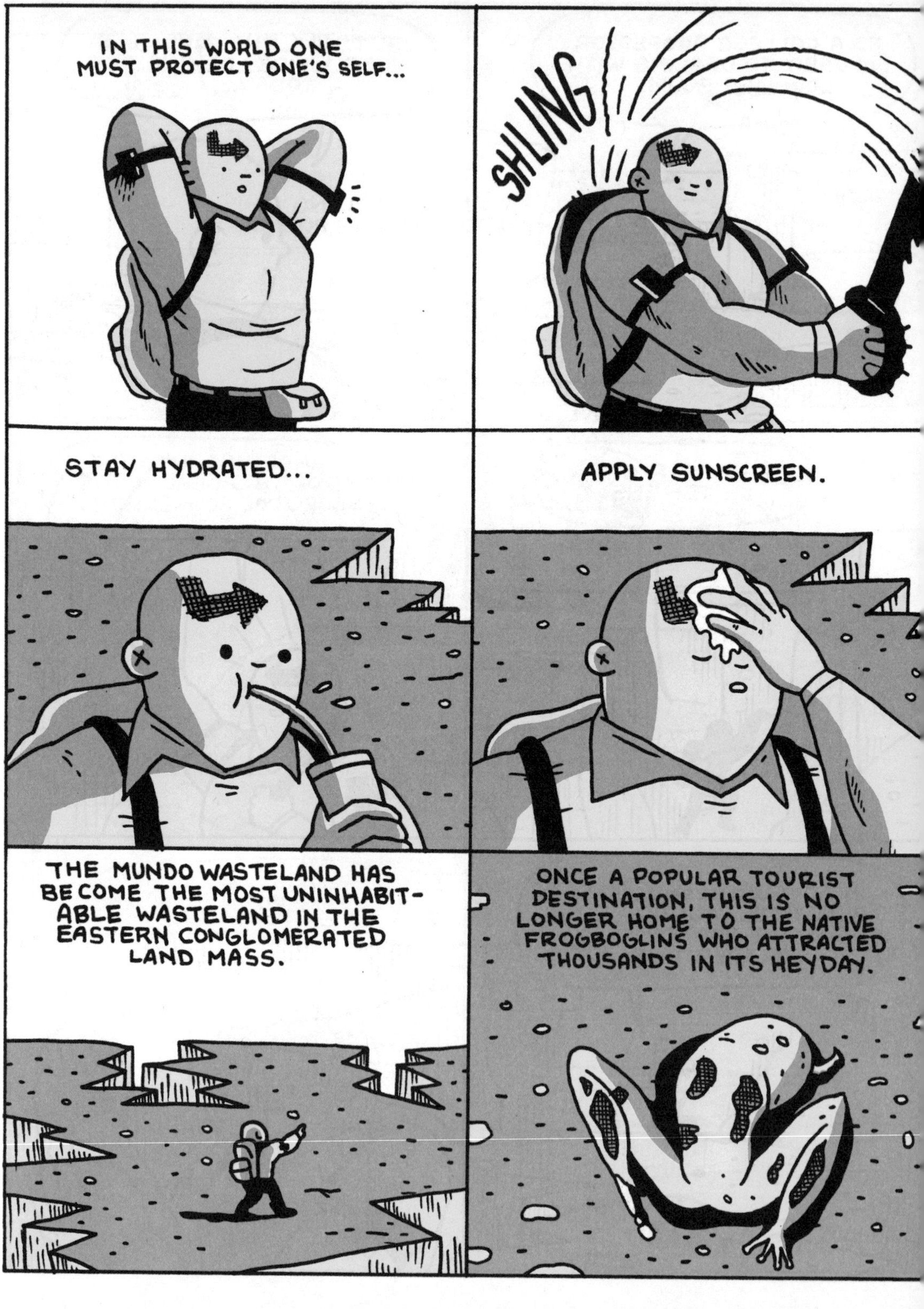
IN THIS WORLD ONE MUST PROTECT ONE'S SELF...
SHLING
STAY HYDRATED...
APPLY SUNSCREEN.
THE MUNDO WASTELAND HAS BECOME THE MOST UNINHABIT-ABLE WASTELAND IN THE EASTERN CONGLOMERATED LAND MASS.
ONCE A POPULAR TOURIST DESTINATION, THIS IS NO LONGER HOME TO THE NATIVE FROGBOGLINS WHO ATTRACTED THOUSANDS IN ITS HEYDAY.

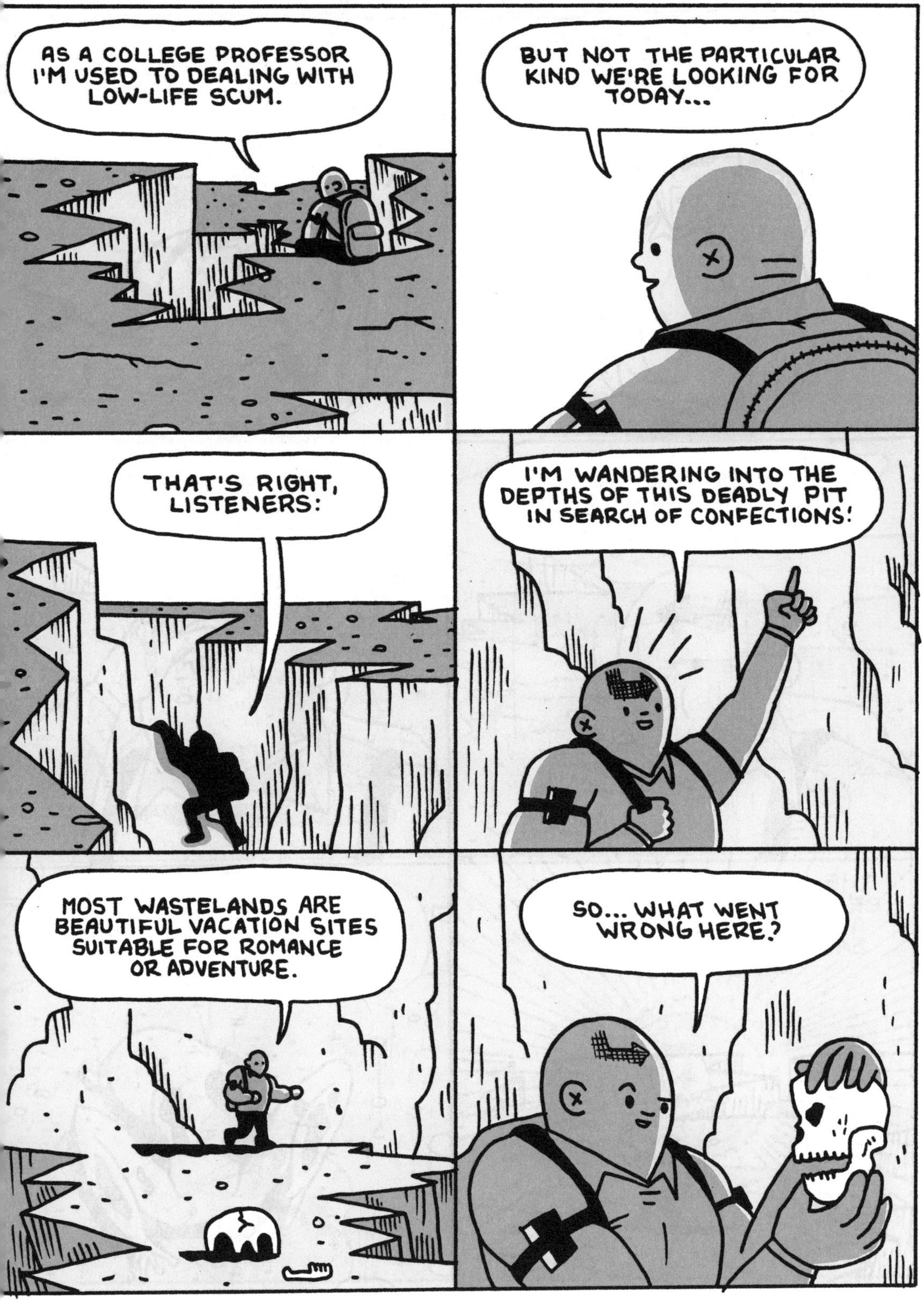
AS A COLLEGE PROFESSOR I'M USED TO DEALING WITH LOW-LIFE SCUM.
BUT NOT THE PARTICULAR KIND WE'RE LOOKING FOR TODAY...
THAT'S RIGHT, LISTENERS:
I'M WANDERING INTO THE DEPTHS OF THIS DEADLY PIT IN SEARCH OF CONFECTIONS!
MOST WASTELANDS ARE BEAUTIFUL VACATION SITES SUITABLE FOR ROMANCE OR ADVENTURE.
SO... WHAT WENT WRONG HERE?

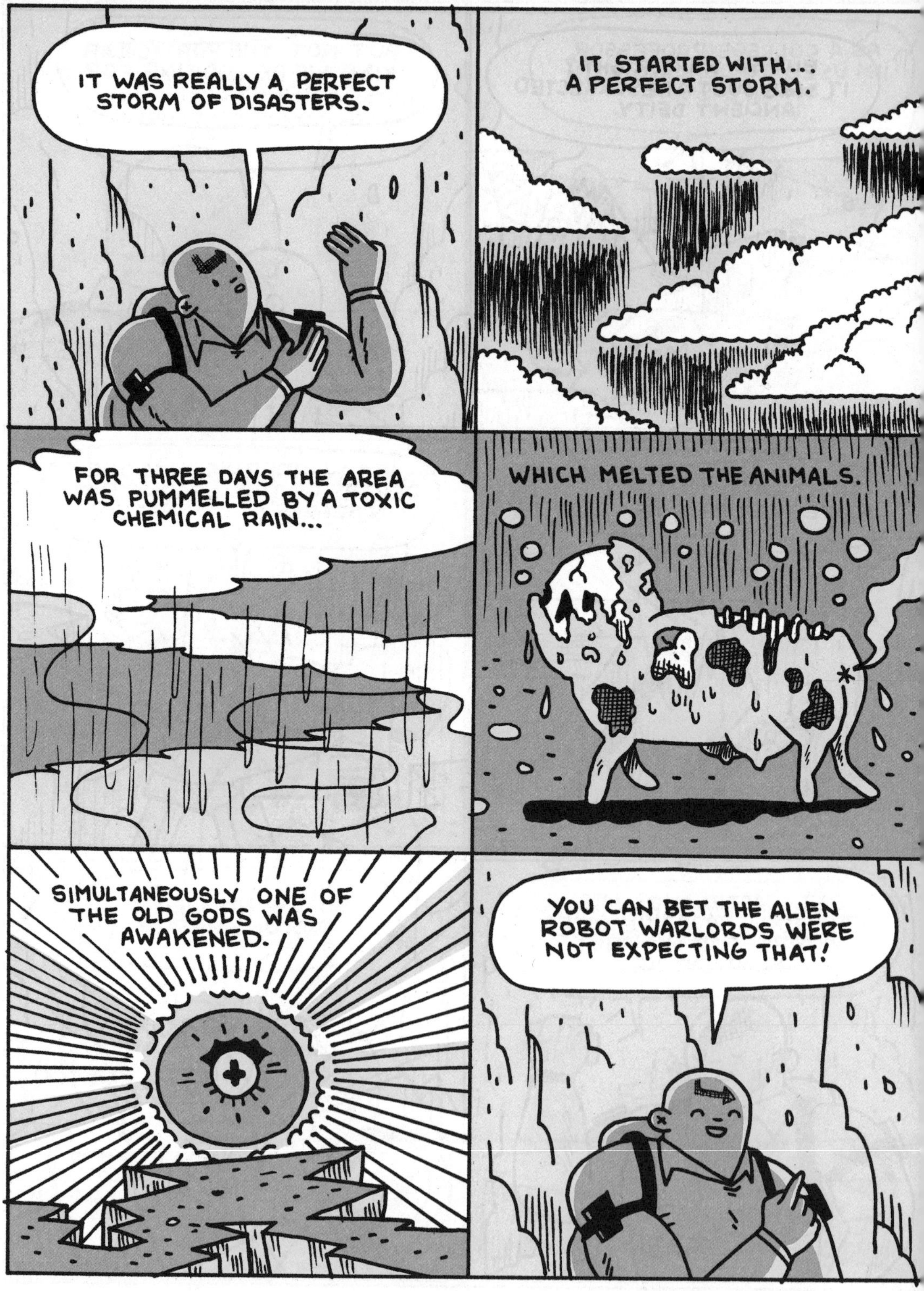
IT WAS REALLY A PERFECT STORM OF DISASTERS.
IT STARTED WITH... A PERFECT STORM.
FOR THREE DAYS THE AREA WAS PUMMELLED BY A TOXIC CHEMICAL RAIN...
WHICH MELTED THE ANIMALS.
SIMULTANEOUSLY ONE OF THE OLD GODS WAS AWAKENED.
YOU CAN BET THE ALIEN ROBOT WARLORDS WERE NOT EXPECTING THAT!

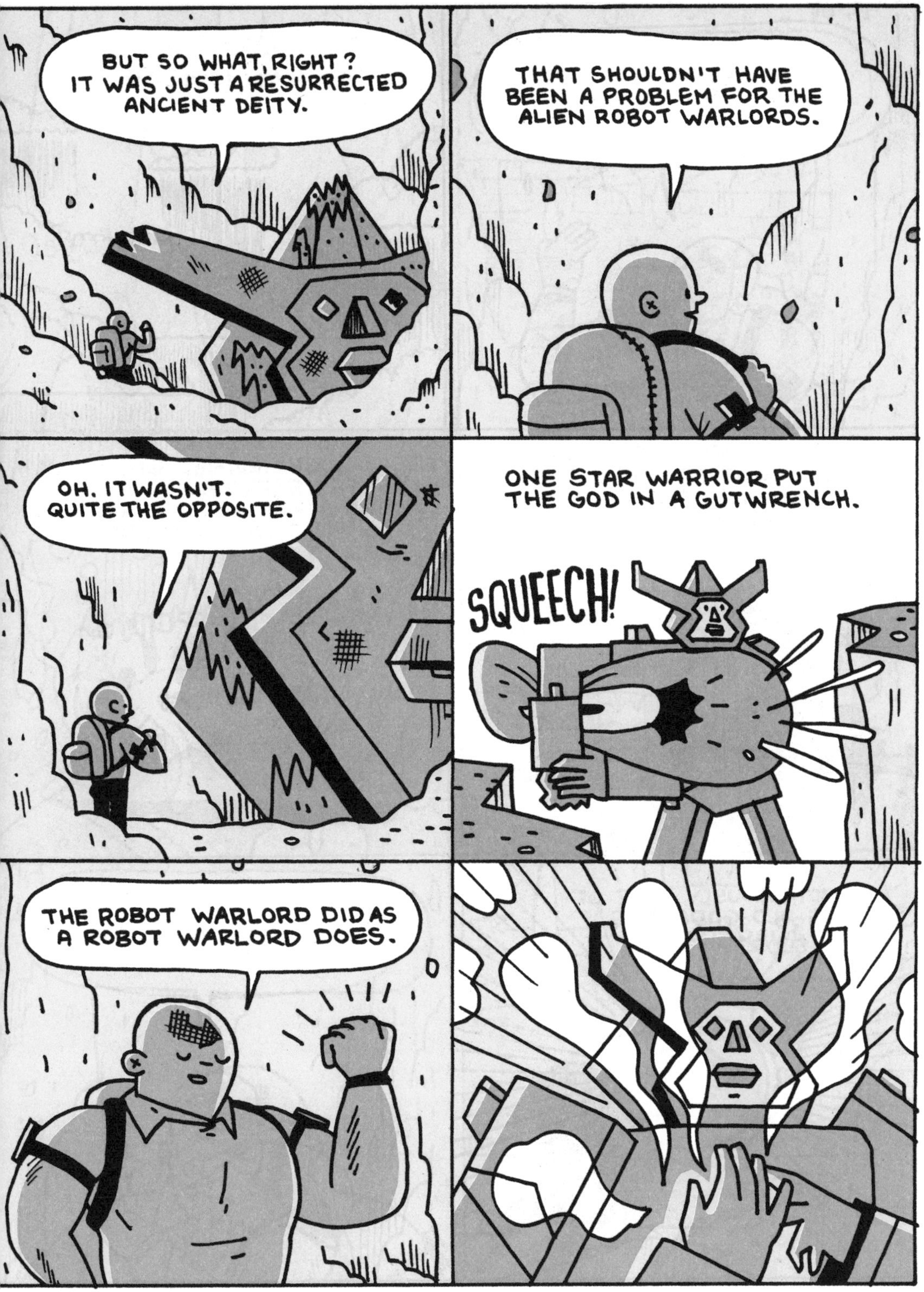
BUT SO WHAT, RIGHT? IT WAS JUST A RESURRECTED ANCIENT DEITY.
THAT SHOULDN'T HAVE BEEN A PROBLEM FOR THE ALIEN ROBOT WARLORDS.
OH. IT WASN'T. QUITE THE OPPOSITE.
ONE STAR WARRIOR PUT THE GOD IN A GUTWRENCH.
SQUEECH!
THE ROBOT WARLORD DID AS A ROBOT WARLORD DOES.

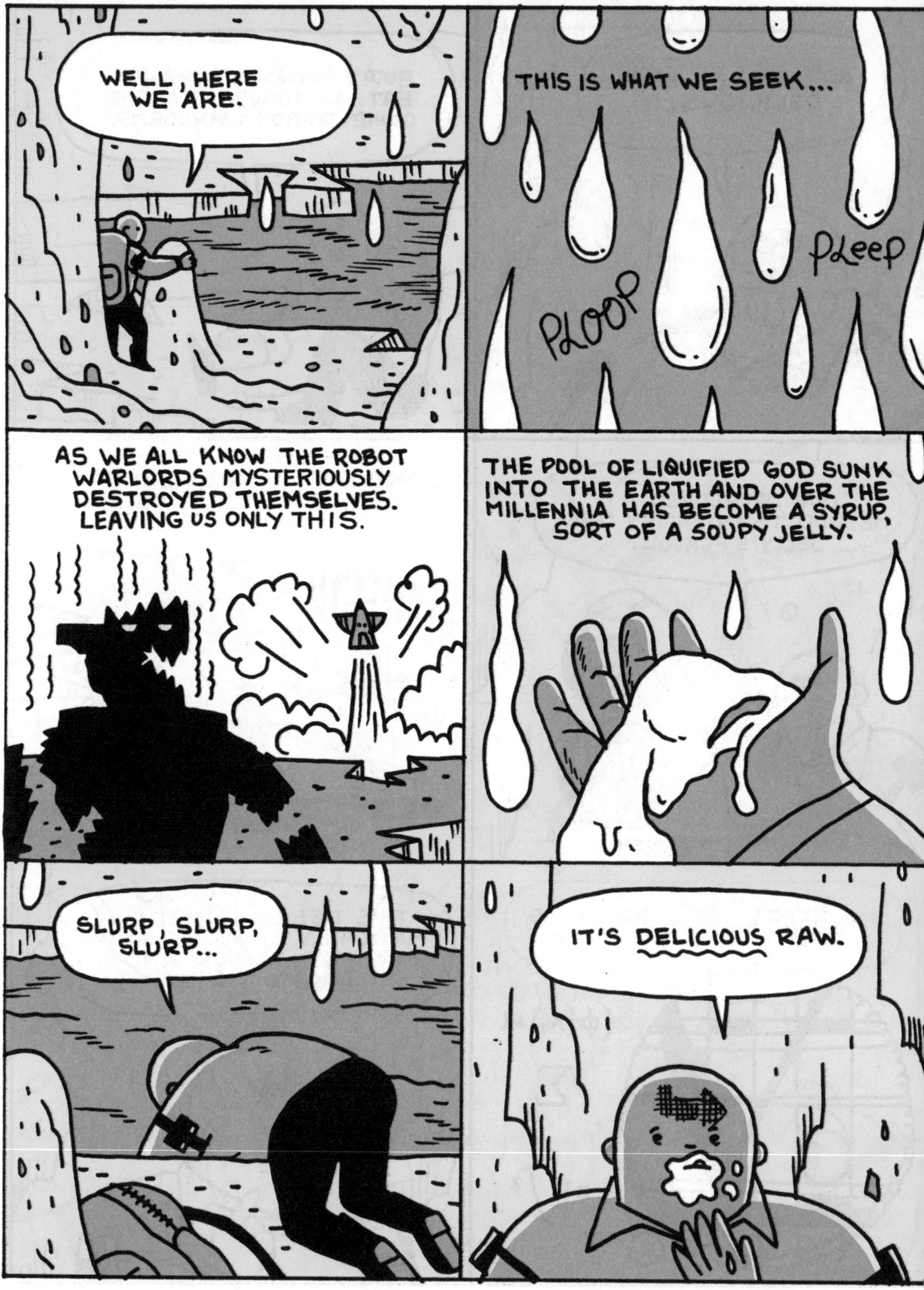
WELL, HERE WE ARE.
THIS IS WHAT WE SEEK...
PLOOP
PLEEP
AS WE ALL KNOW THE ROBOT WARLORDS MYSTERIOUSLY DESTROYED THEMSELVES. LEAVING US ONLY THIS.
THE POOL OF LIQUIFIED GOD SUNK INTO THE EARTH AND OVER THE MILLENNIA HAS BECOME A SYRUP, SORT OF A SOUPY JELLY.
SLURP, SLURP, SLURP...
IT'S DELICIOUS RAW.

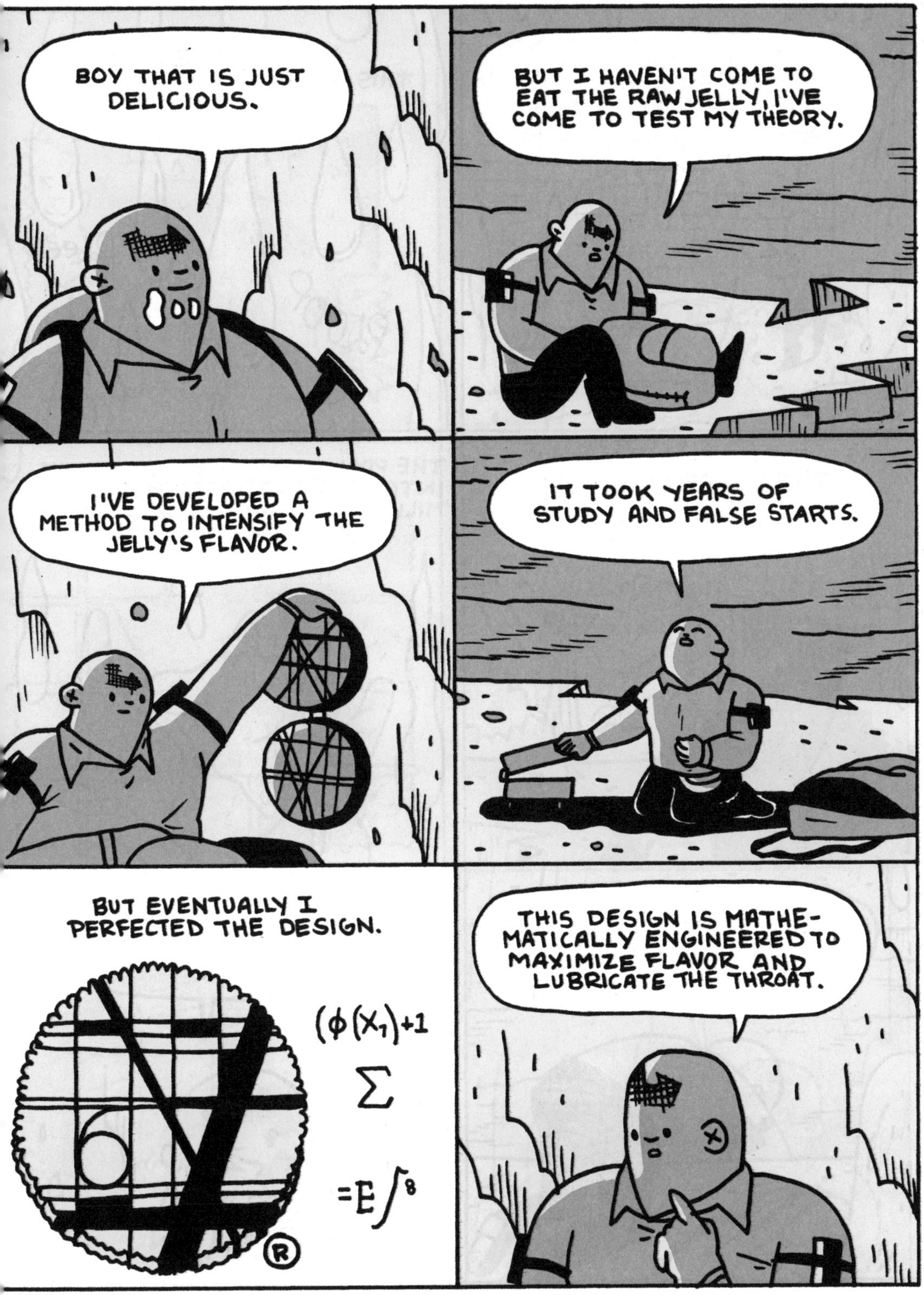
BOY THAT IS JUST DELICIOUS.
BUT I HAVEN'T COME TO EAT THE RAW JELLY, I'VE COME TO TEST MY THEORY.
I'VE DEVELOPED A METHOD TO INTENSIFY THE JELLY'S FLAVOR.
IT TOOK YEARS OF STUDY AND FALSE STARTS.
BUT EVENTUALLY I PERFECTED THE DESIGN.
(φ(X1)+1
Σ
=E∫8
®
THIS DESIGN IS MATHEMATICALLY ENGINEERED TO MAXIMIZE FLAVOR AND LUBRICATE THE THROAT.

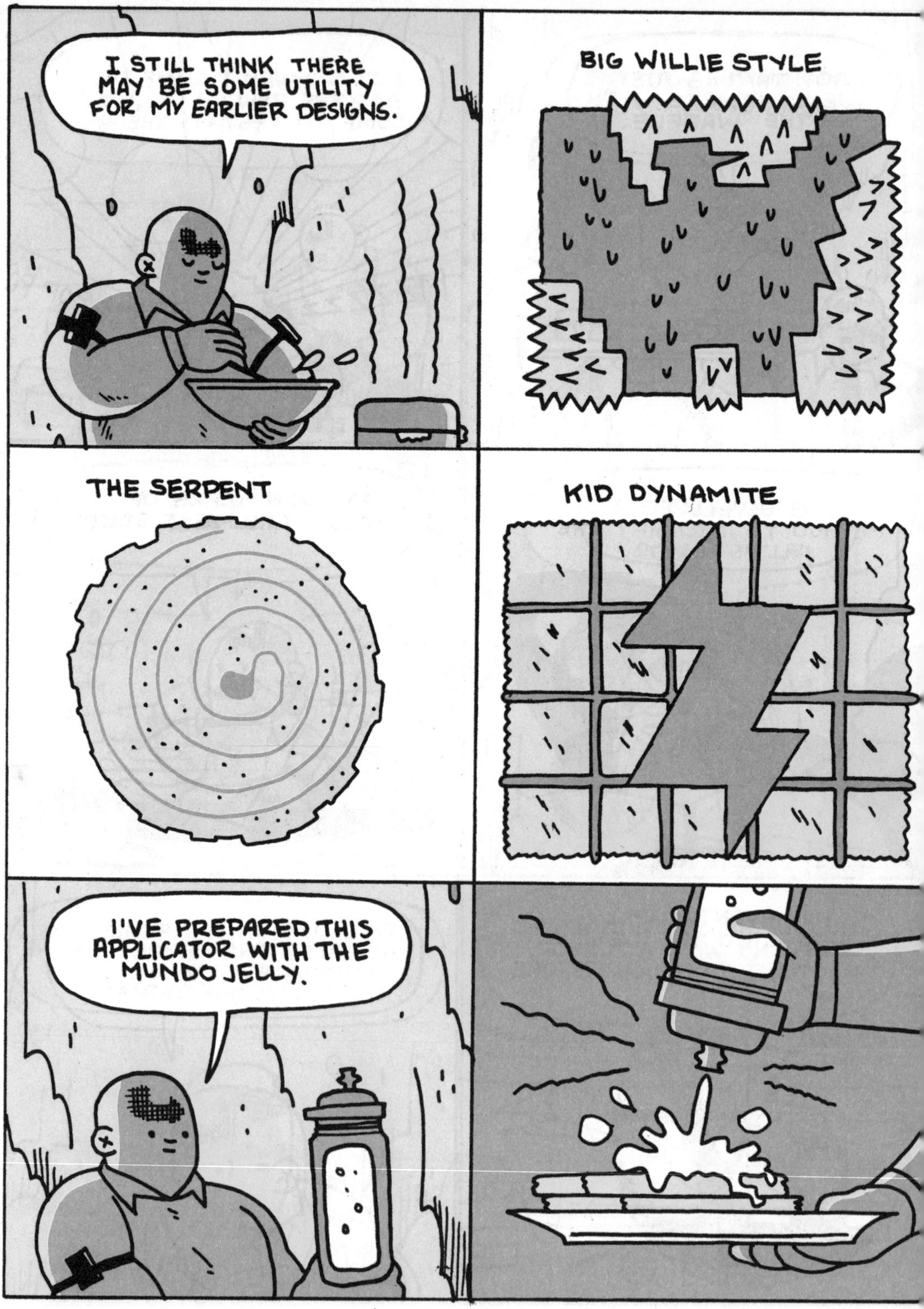
I STILL THINK THERE MAY BE SOME UTILITY FOR MY EARLIER DESIGNS.
BIG WILLIE STYLE
THE SERPENT
KID DYNAMITE
I'VE PREPARED THIS APPLICATOR WITH THE MUNDO JELLY.

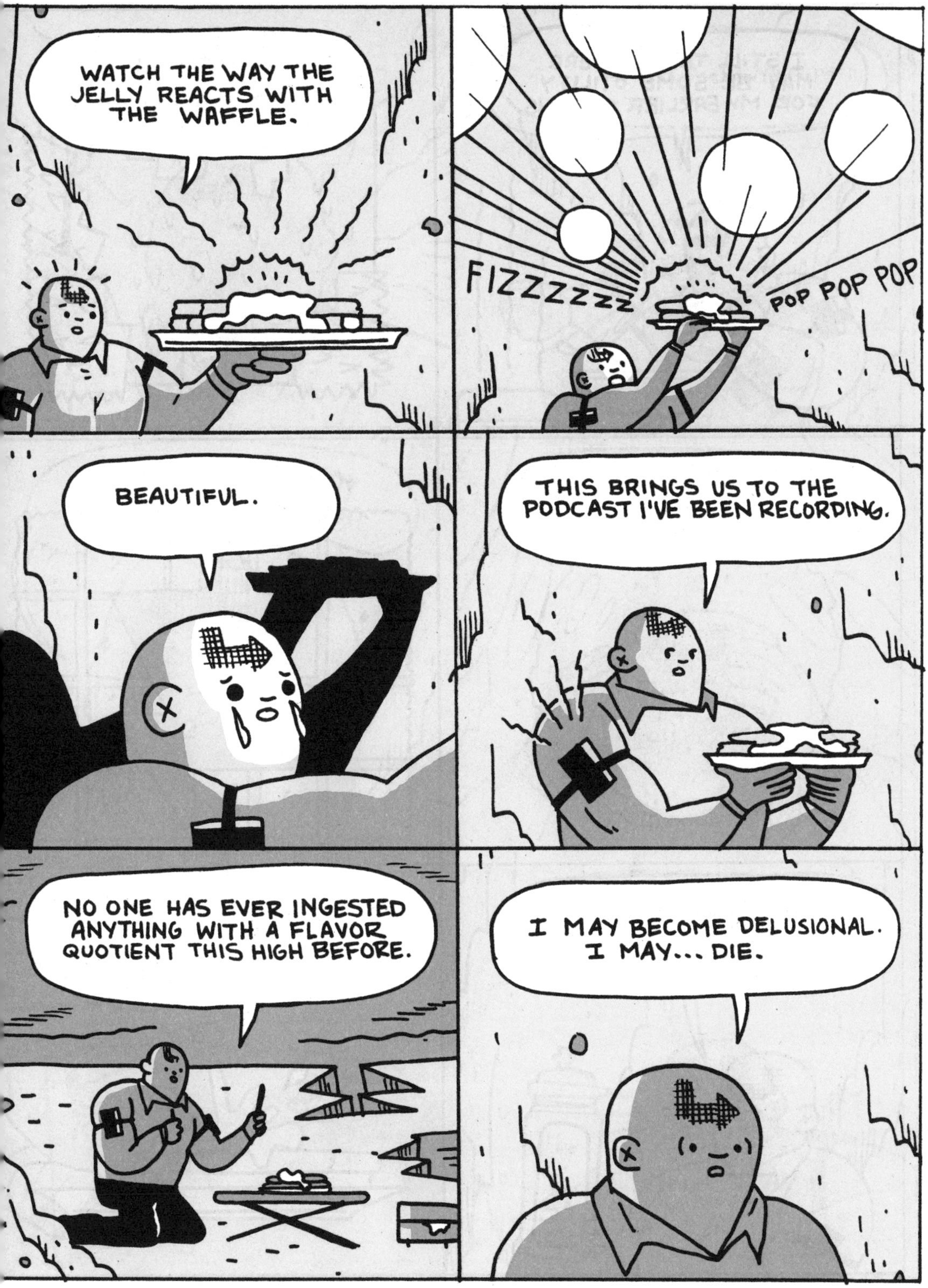
WATCH THE WAY THE JELLY REACTS WITH THE WAFFLE.
FIZZZZZZZ
POP POP POP POP
BEAUTIFUL.
THIS BRINGS US TO THE PODCAST I'VE BEEN RECORDING.
NO ONE HAS EVER INGESTED ANYTHING WITH A FLAVOR QUOTIENT THIS HIGH BEFORE.
I MAY BECOME DELUSIONAL. I MAY... DIE.

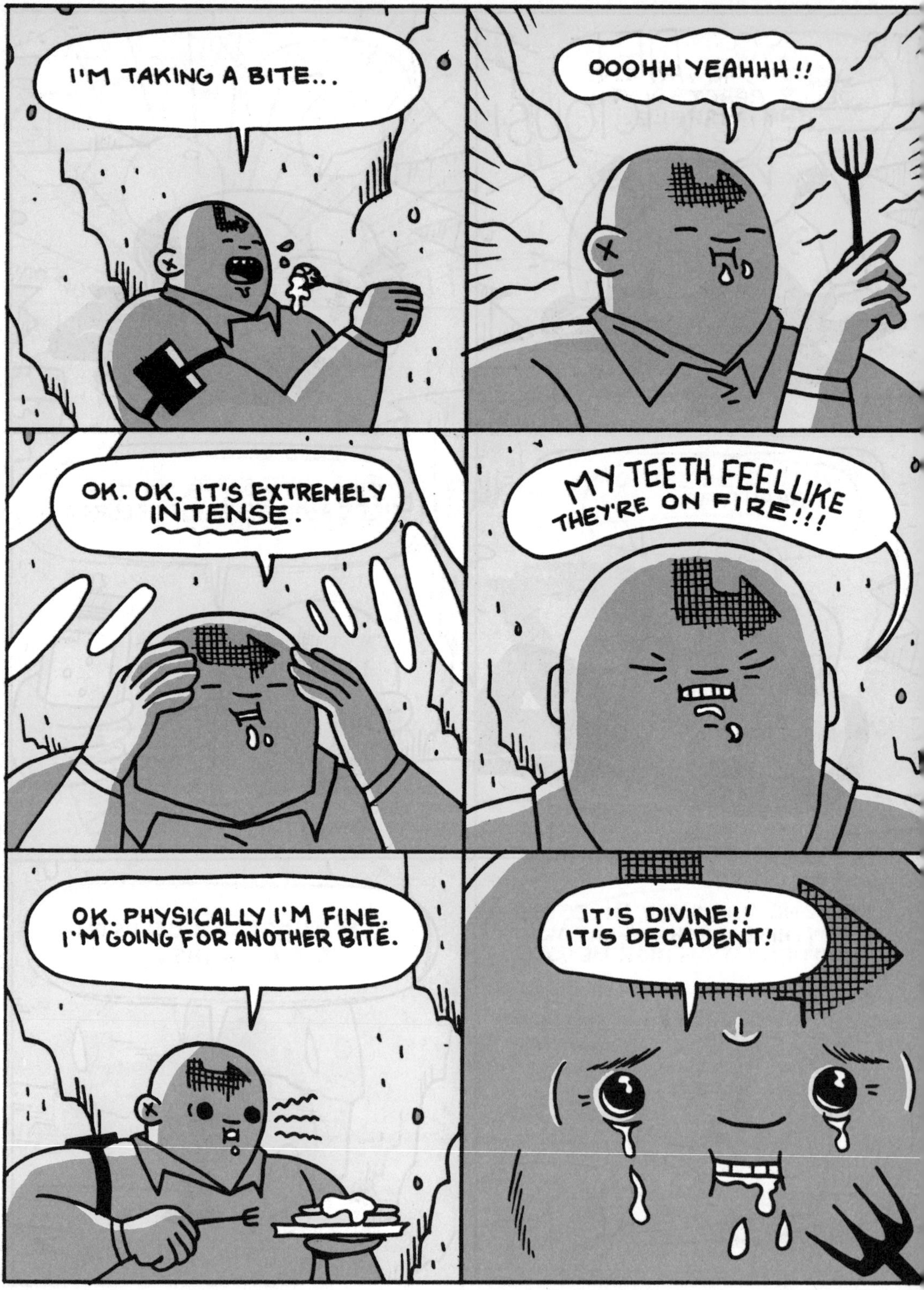
I'M TAKING A BITE...
OOOHH YEAHHH!!
OK. OK. IT'S EXTREMELY INTENSE.
MY TEETH FEEL LIKE THEY'RE ON FIRE!!!
OK. PHYSICALLY I'M FINE. I'M GOING FOR ANOTHER BITE.
IT'S DIVINE!! IT'S DECADENT!

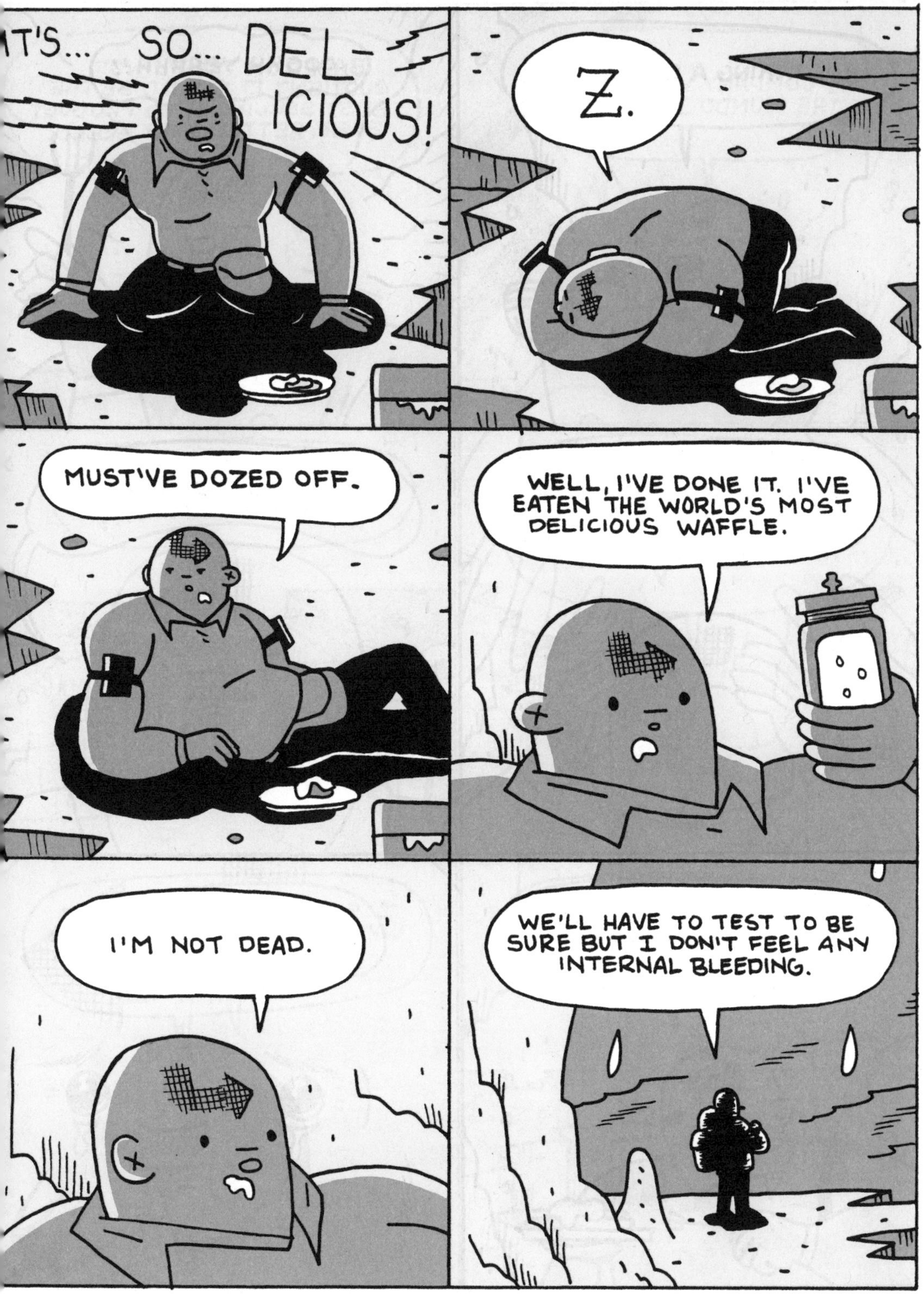
IT'S... SO... DEL-ICIOUS!
Z.
MUST'VE DOZED OFF.
WELL, I'VE DONE IT. I'VE EATEN THE WORLD'S MOST DELICIOUS WAFFLE.
I'M NOT DEAD.
WE'LL HAVE TO TEST TO BE SURE BUT I DON'T FEEL ANY INTERNAL BLEEDING.

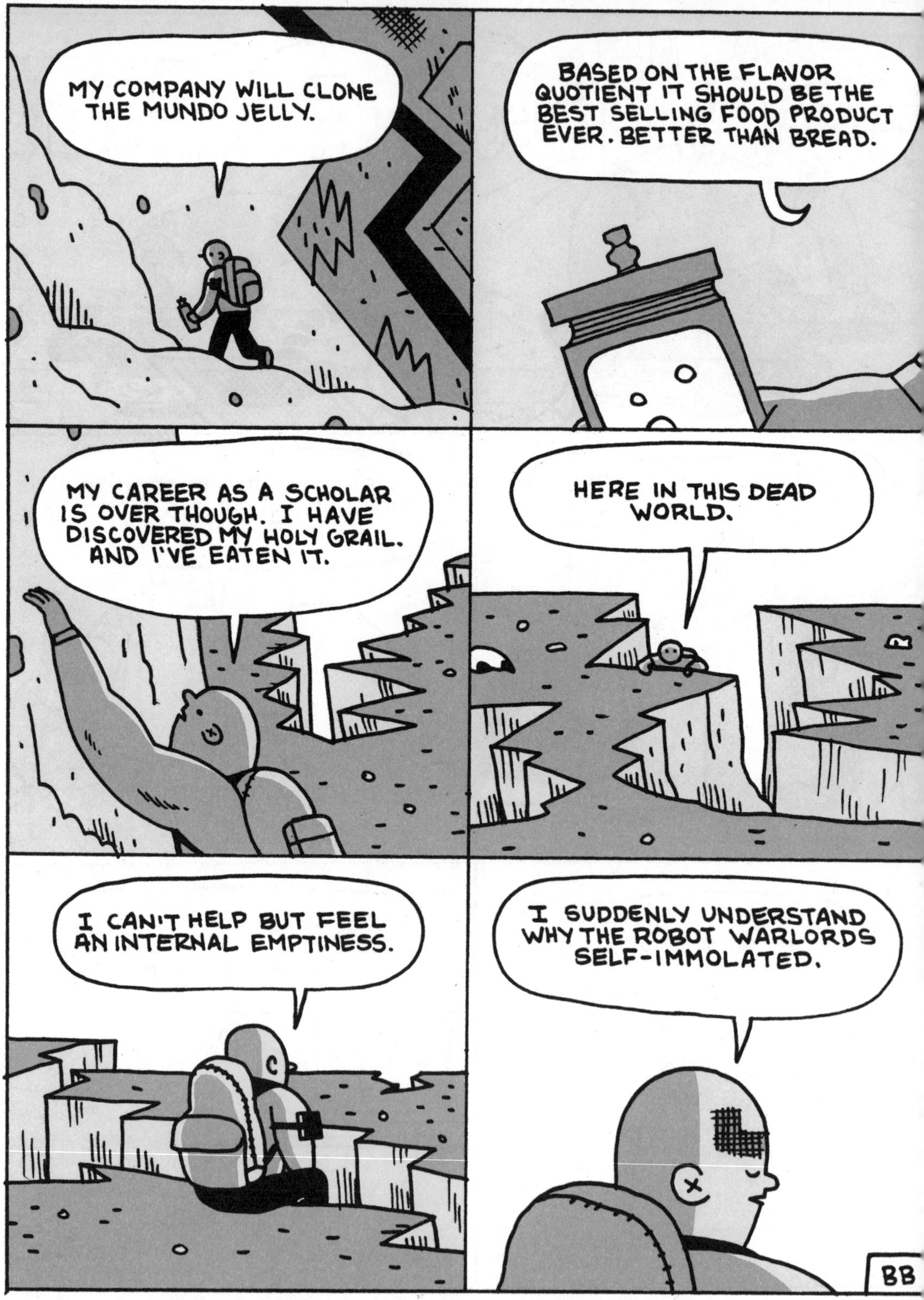
MY COMPANY WILL CLONE THE MUNDO JELLY.
BASED ON THE FLAVOR QUOTIENT IT SHOULD BE THE BEST SELLING FOOD PRODUCT EVER. BETTER THAN BREAD.
MY CAREER AS A SCHOLAR IS OVER THOUGH. I HAVE DISCOVERED MY HOLY GRAIL. AND I'VE EATEN IT.
HERE IN THIS DEAD WORLD.
I CAN'T HELP BUT FEEL AN INTERNAL EMPTINESS.
I SUDDENLY UNDERSTAND WHY THE ROBOT WARLORDS SELF-IMMOLATED.
BB

VOYAGE OF THE GOLDEN RETRIEVER

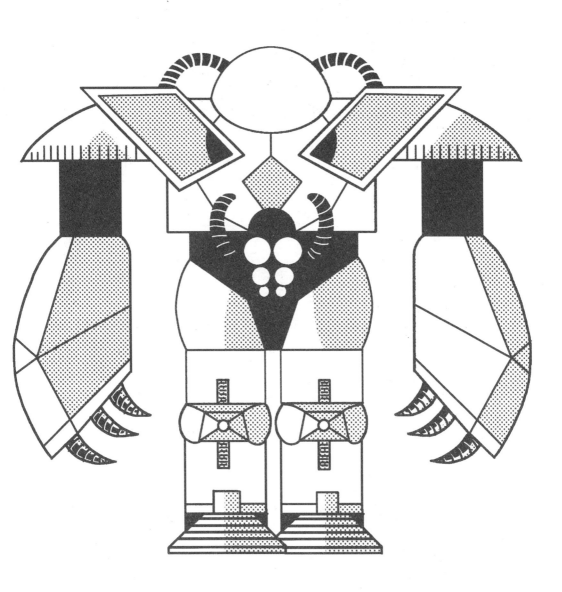

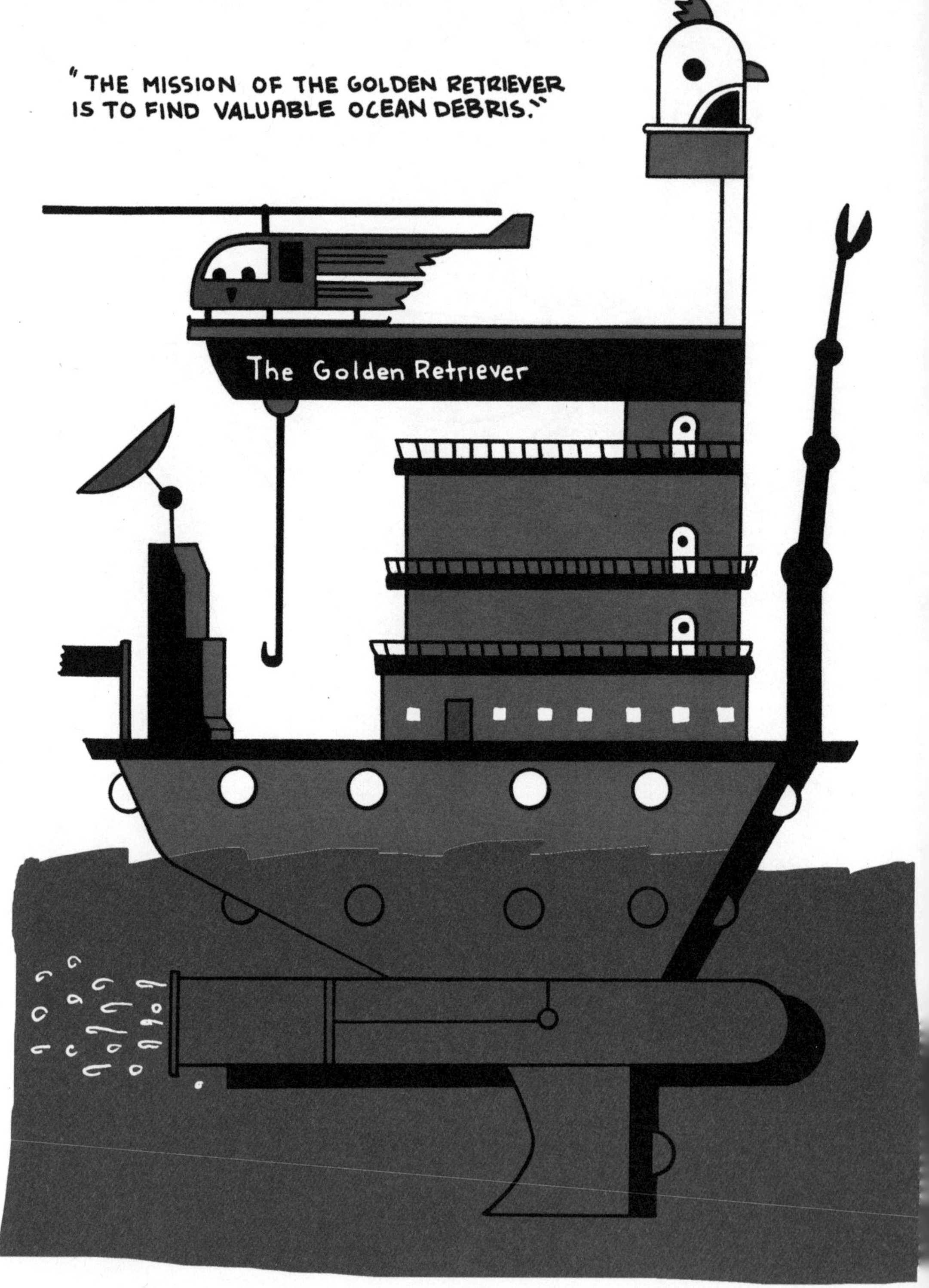
"THE MISSION OF THE GOLDEN RETRIEVER IS TO FIND VALUABLE OCEAN DEBRIS."
The Golden Retriever

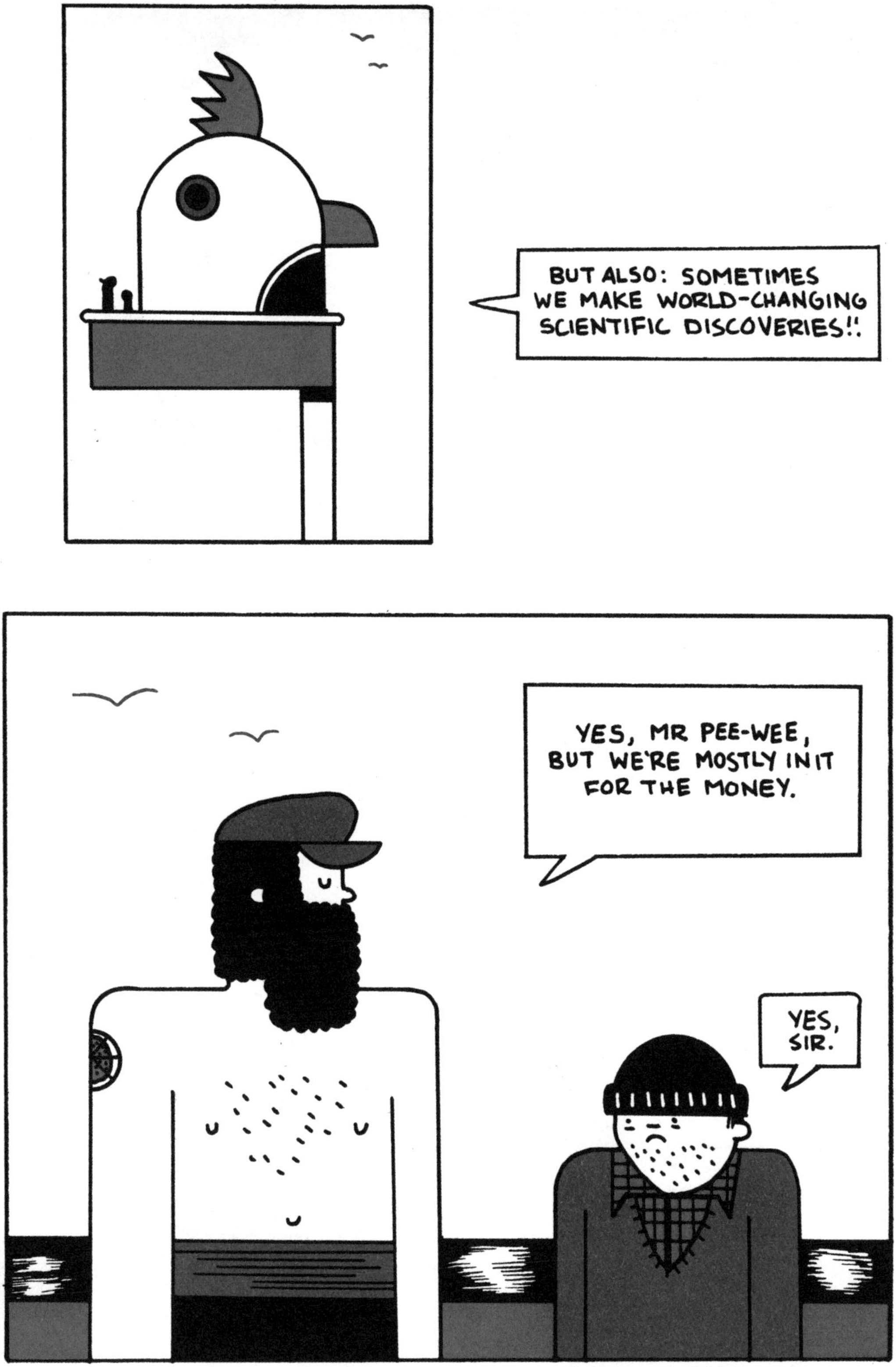
BUT ALSO: SOMETIMES WE MAKE WORLD-CHANGING SCIENTIFIC DISCOVERIES!!
YES, MR PEE-WEE, BUT WE'RE MOSTLY IN IT FOR THE MONEY.
YES, SIR.

*PRONOUNCED "FRON-TEE-YAY"

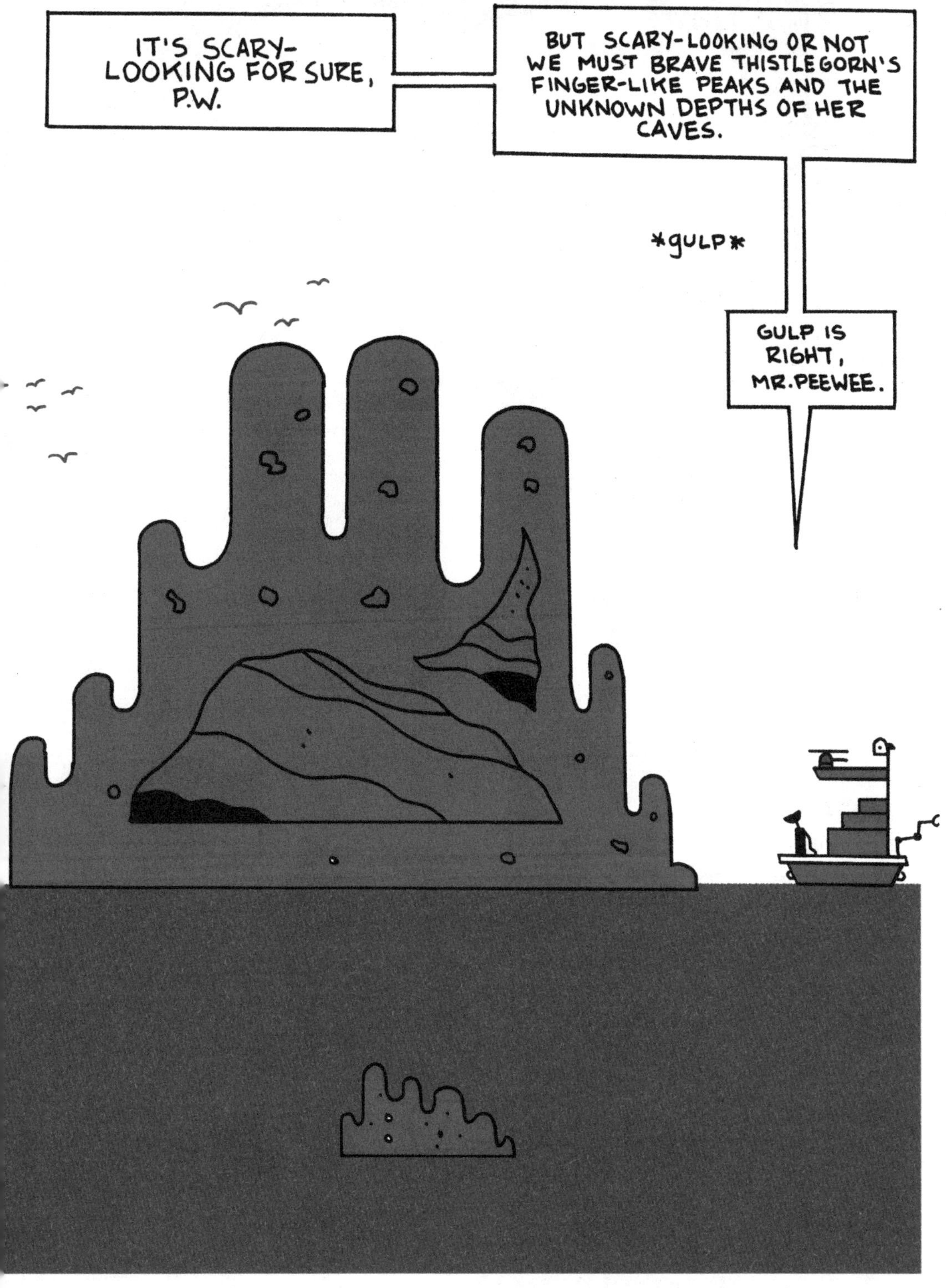
IT'S SCARY-LOOKING FOR SURE, P.W.
BUT SCARY-LOOKING OR NOT WE MUST BRAVE THISTLEGORN'S FINGER-LIKE PEAKS AND THE UNKNOWN DEPTHS OF HER CAVES.
gulp
GULP IS RIGHT, MR.PEEWEE.

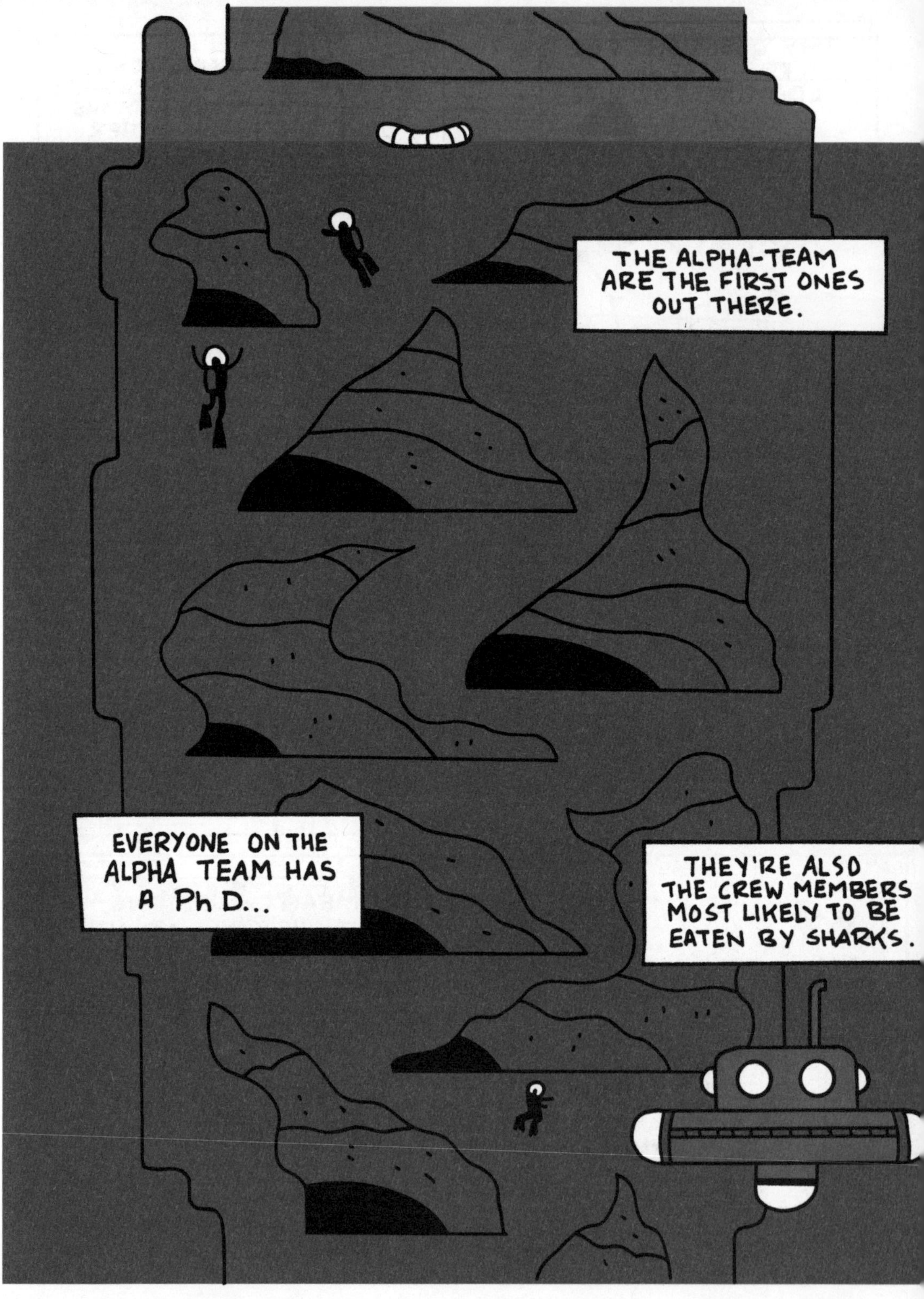
THE ALPHA-TEAM ARE THE FIRST ONES OUT THERE.
EVERYONE ON THE ALPHA TEAM HAS A PhD...
THEY'RE ALSO THE CREW MEMBERS MOST LIKELY TO BE EATEN BY SHARKS.

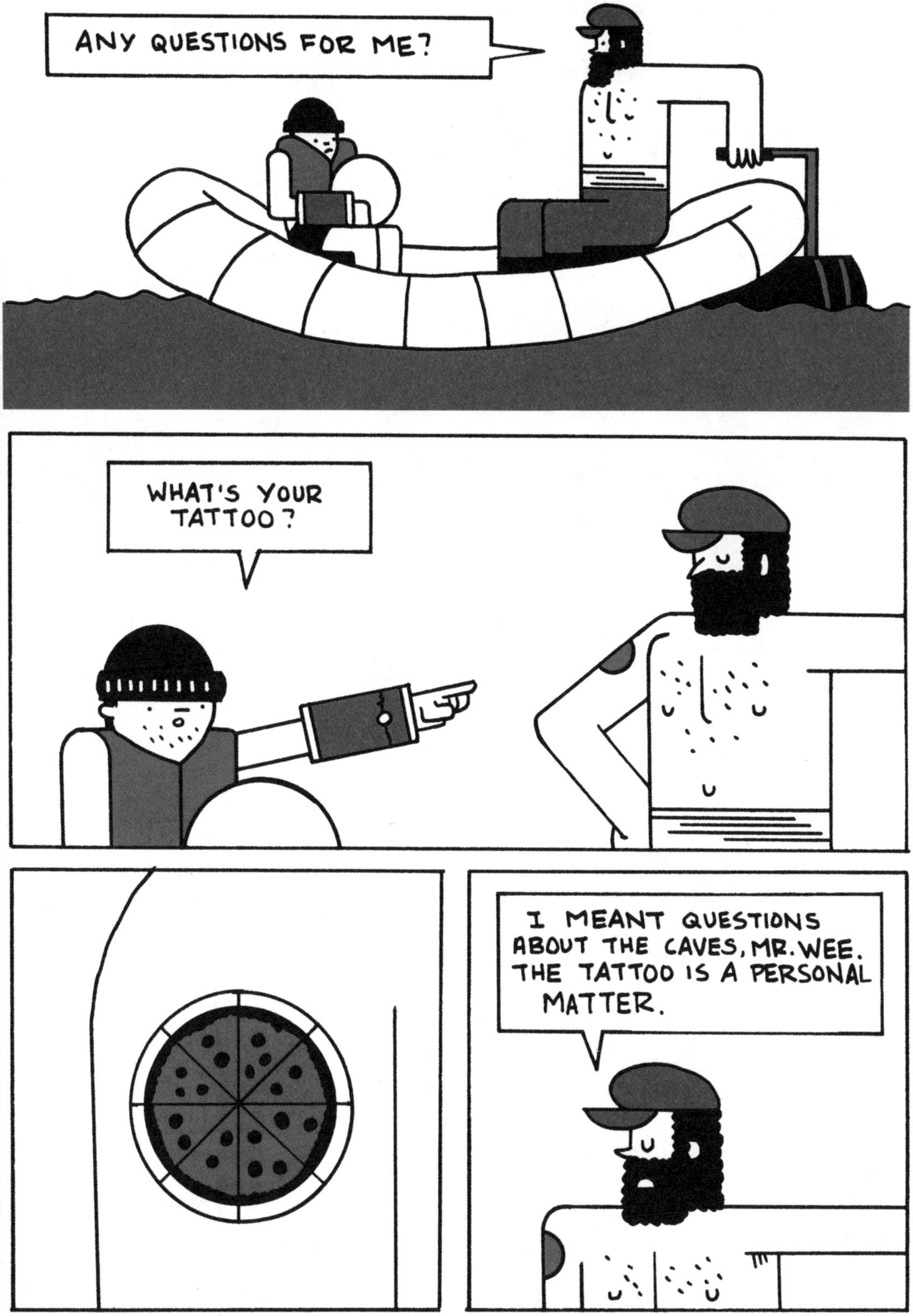
ANY QUESTIONS FOR ME?
WHAT'S YOUR TATTOO?
I MEANT QUESTIONS ABOUT THE CAVES, MR. WEE. THE TATTOO IS A PERSONAL MATTER.

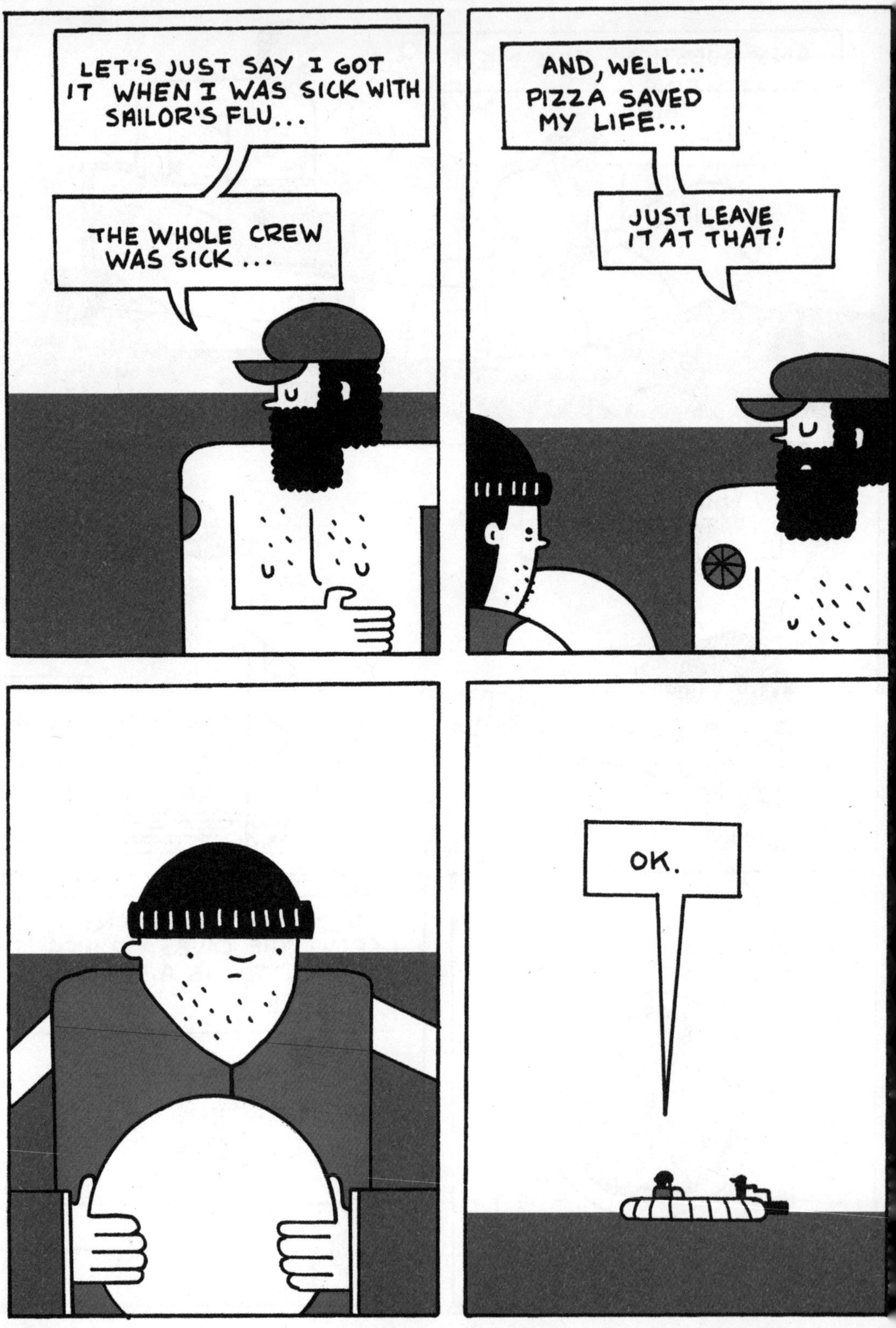
LET'S JUST SAY I GOT IT WHEN I WAS SICK WITH SAILOR'S FLU...
THE WHOLE CREW WAS SICK...
AND, WELL... PIZZA SAVED MY LIFE...
JUST LEAVE IT AT THAT!
OK.

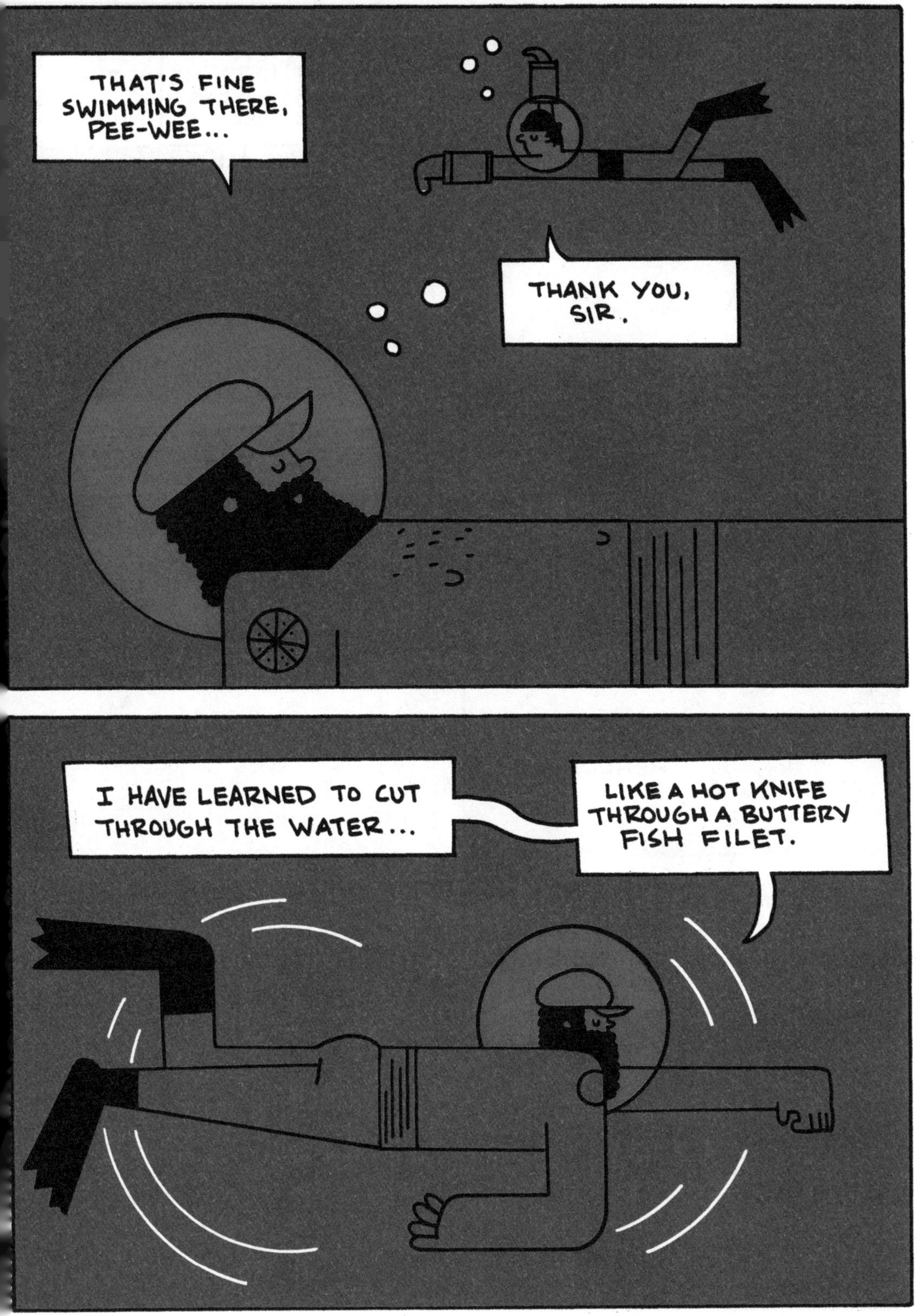
THAT'S FINE SWIMMING THERE, PEE-WEE...
THANK YOU, SIR.
I HAVE LEARNED TO CUT THROUGH THE WATER...
LIKE A HOT KNIFE THROUGH A BUTTERY FISH FILET.

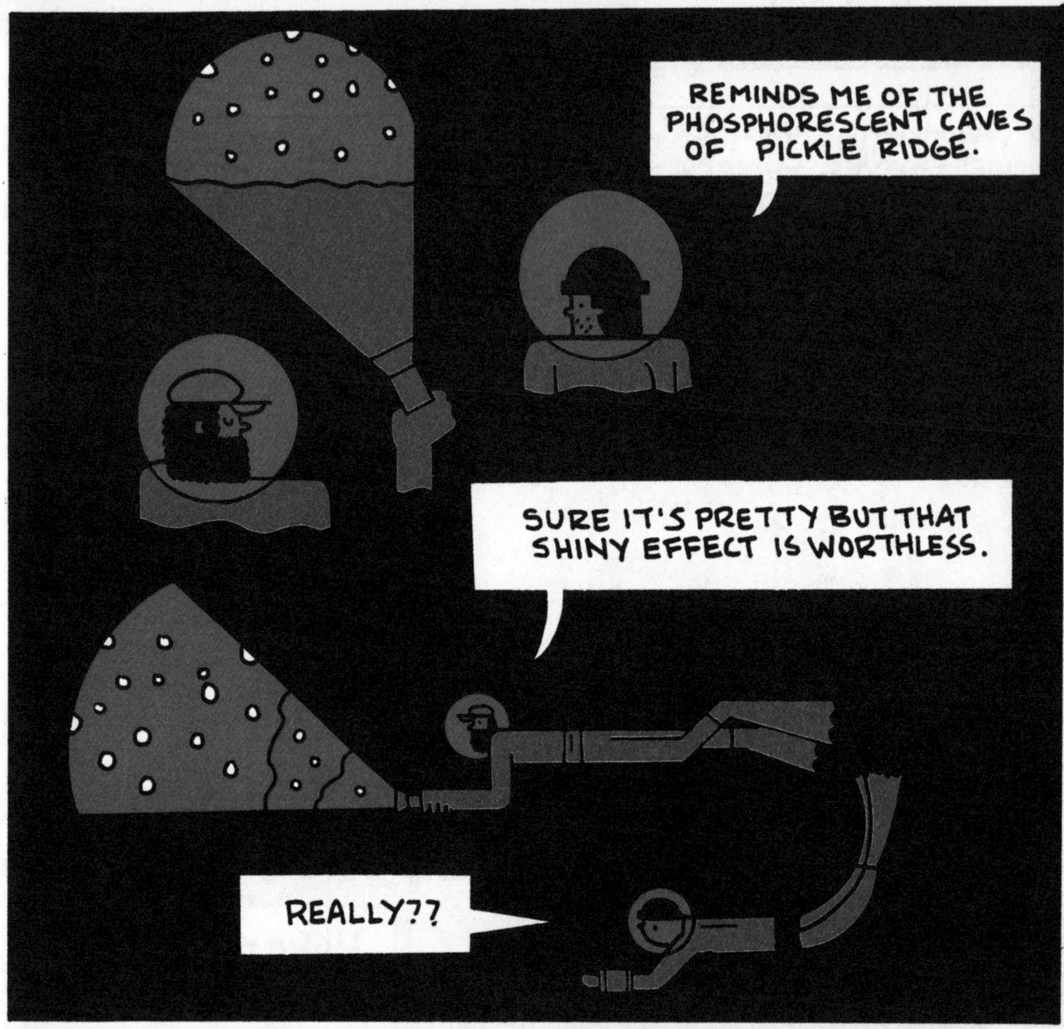
REMINDS ME OF THE PHOSPHORESCENT CAVES OF PICKLE RIDGE.
SURE IT'S PRETTY BUT THAT SHINY EFFECT IS WORTHLESS.
REALLY??

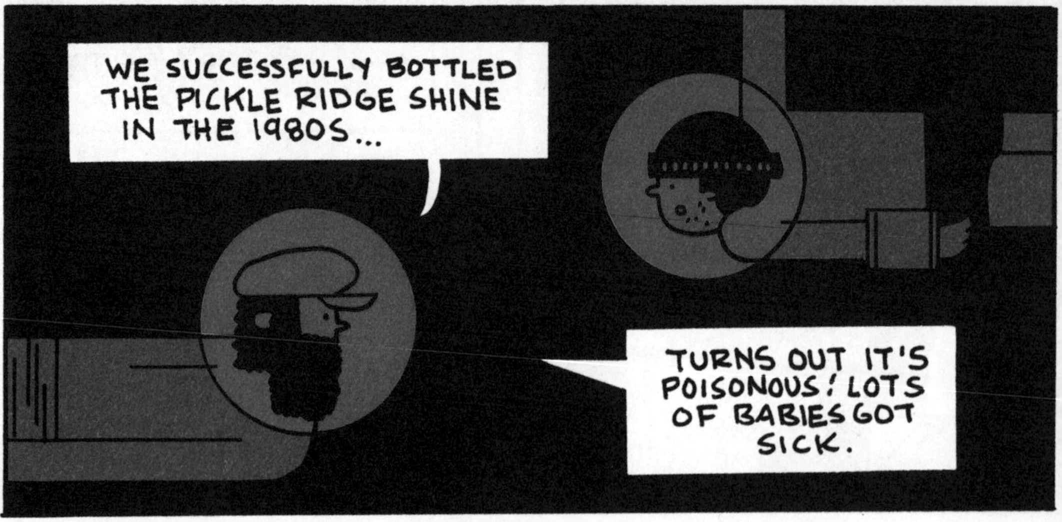
WE SUCCESSFULLY BOTTLED THE PICKLE RIDGE SHINE IN THE 1980S...
TURNS OUT IT'S POISONOUS! LOTS OF BABIES GOT SICK.

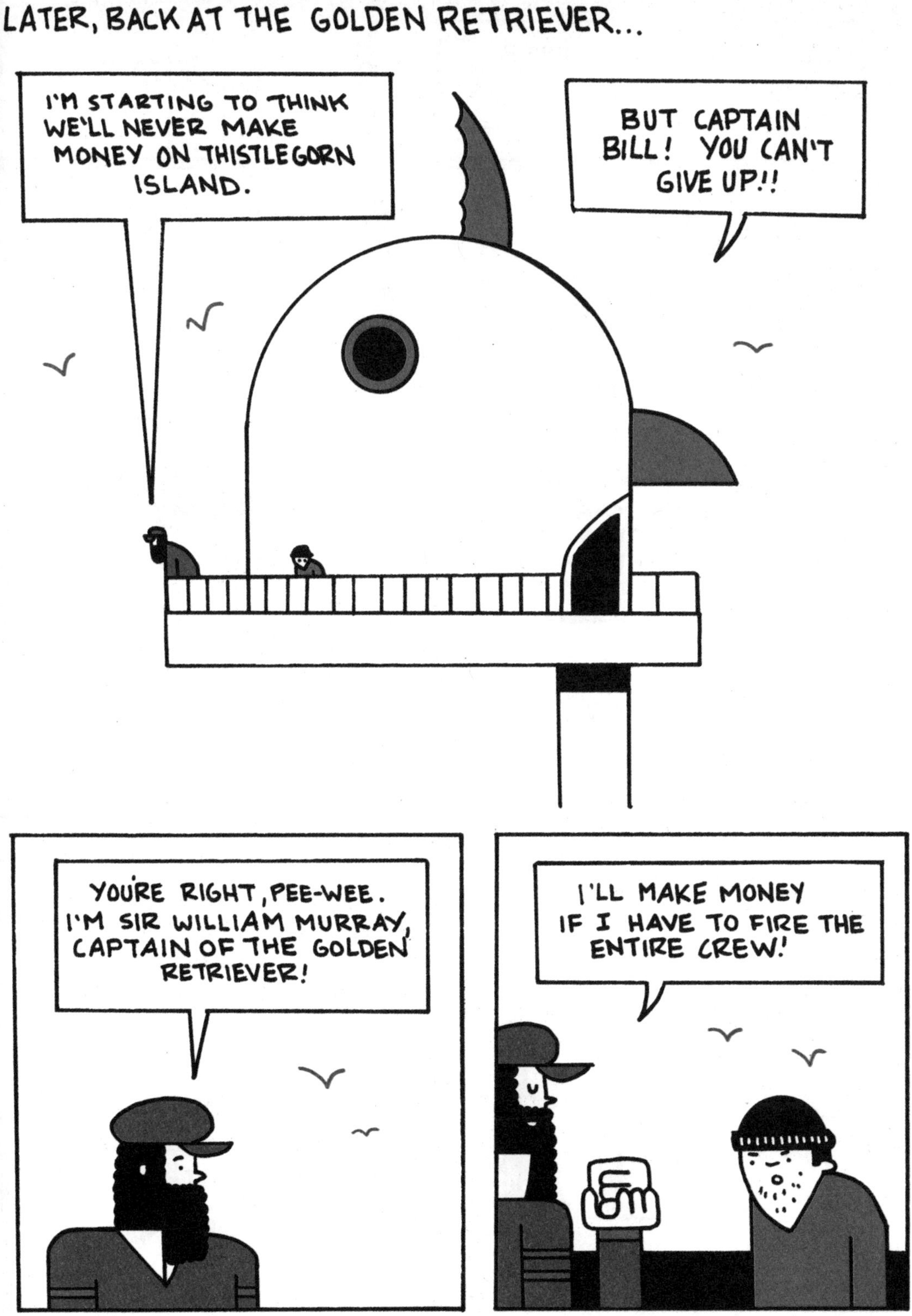
LATER, BACK AT THE GOLDEN RETRIEVER...
I'M STARTING TO THINK WE'LL NEVER MAKE MONEY ON THISTLEGORN ISLAND.
BUT CAPTAIN BILL! YOU CAN'T GIVE UP!!
YOU'RE RIGHT, PEE-WEE. I'M SIR WILLIAM MURRAY, CAPTAIN OF THE GOLDEN RETRIEVER!
I'LL MAKE MONEY IF I HAVE TO FIRE THE ENTIRE CREW!

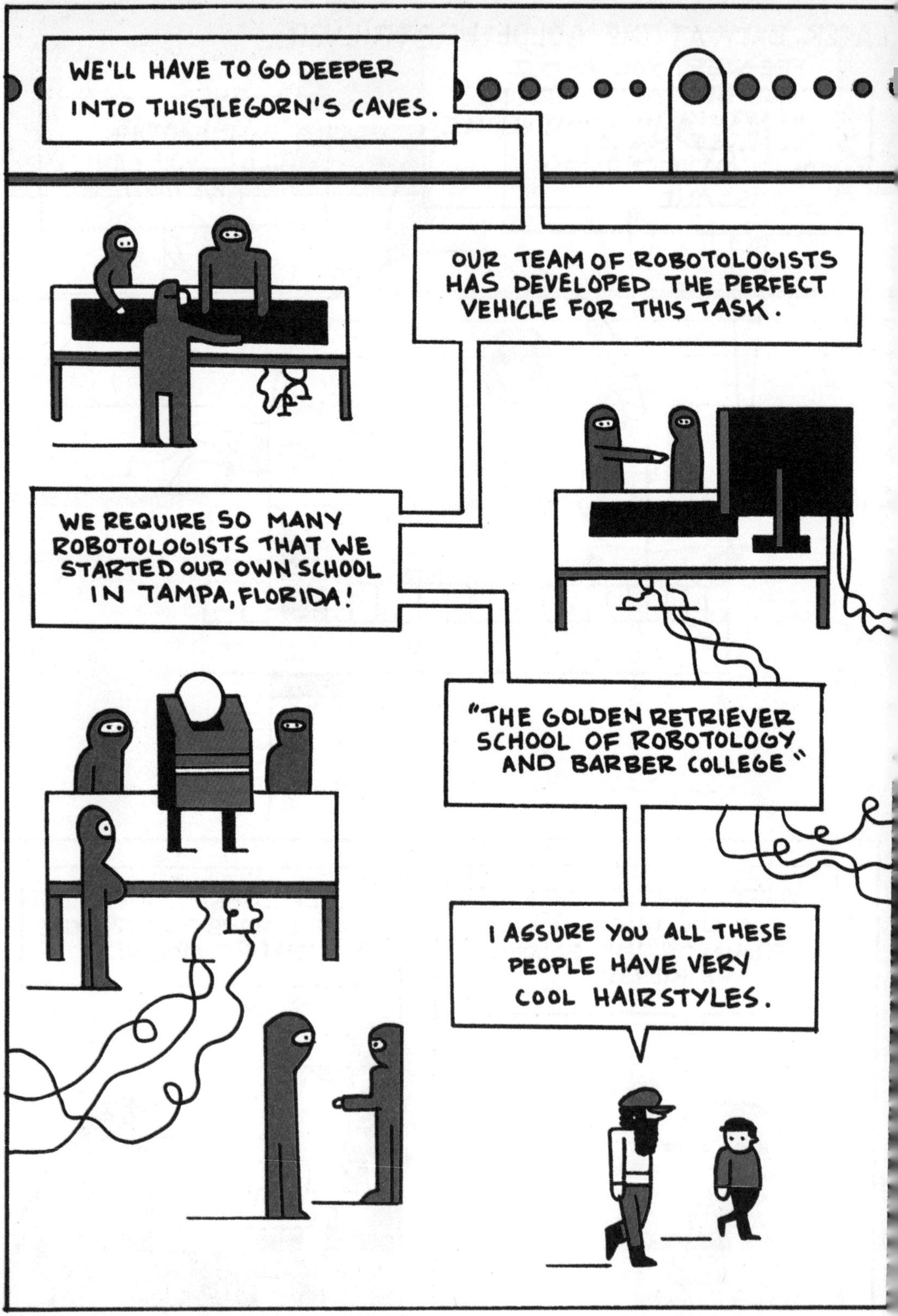
WE'LL HAVE TO GO DEEPER INTO THISTLEGORN'S CAVES.
OUR TEAM OF ROBOTOLOGISTS HAS DEVELOPED THE PERFECT VEHICLE FOR THIS TASK.
WE REQUIRE SO MANY ROBOTOLOGISTS THAT WE STARTED OUR OWN SCHOOL IN TAMPA, FLORIDA!
"THE GOLDEN RETRIEVER SCHOOL OF ROBOTOLOGY AND BARBER COLLEGE"
I ASSURE YOU ALL THESE PEOPLE HAVE VERY COOL HAIRSTYLES.

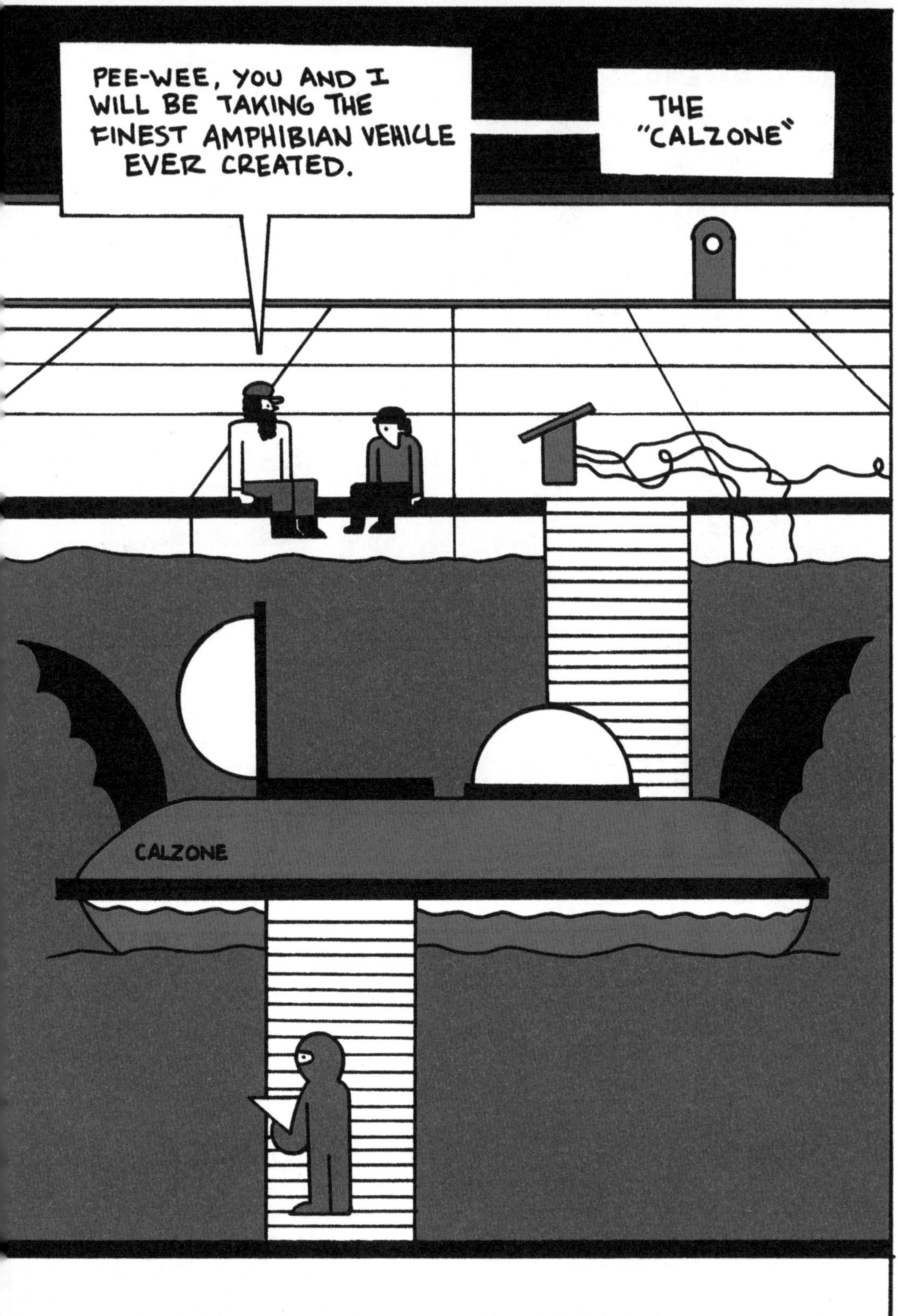
PEE-WEE, YOU AND I WILL BE TAKING THE FINEST AMPHIBIAN VEHICLE EVER CREATED.
THE "CALZONE"
CALZONE

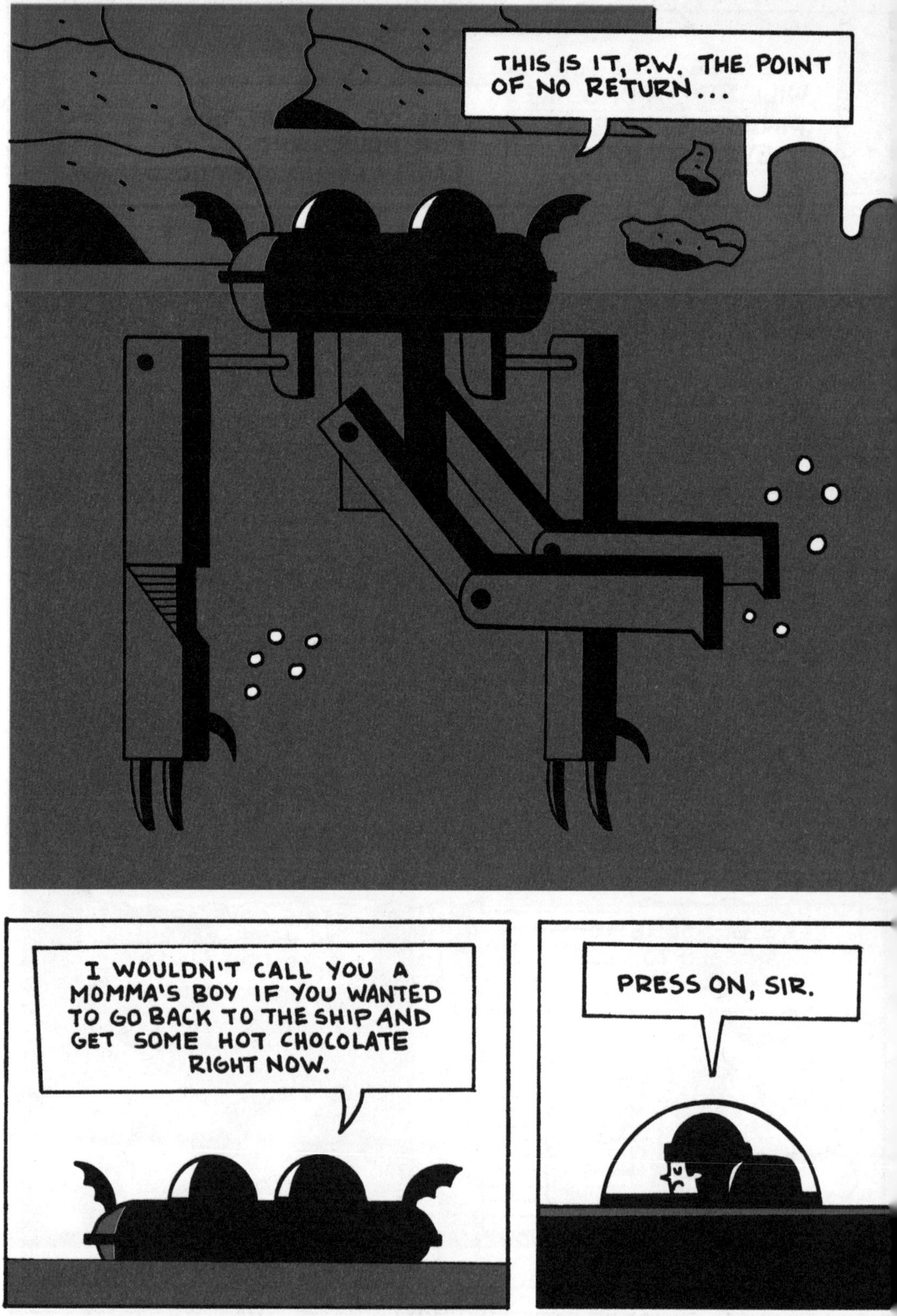
THIS IS IT, P.W. THE POINT OF NO RETURN...
I WOULDN'T CALL YOU A MOMMA'S BOY IF YOU WANTED TO GO BACK TO THE SHIP AND GET SOME HOT CHOCOLATE RIGHT NOW.
PRESS ON, SIR.

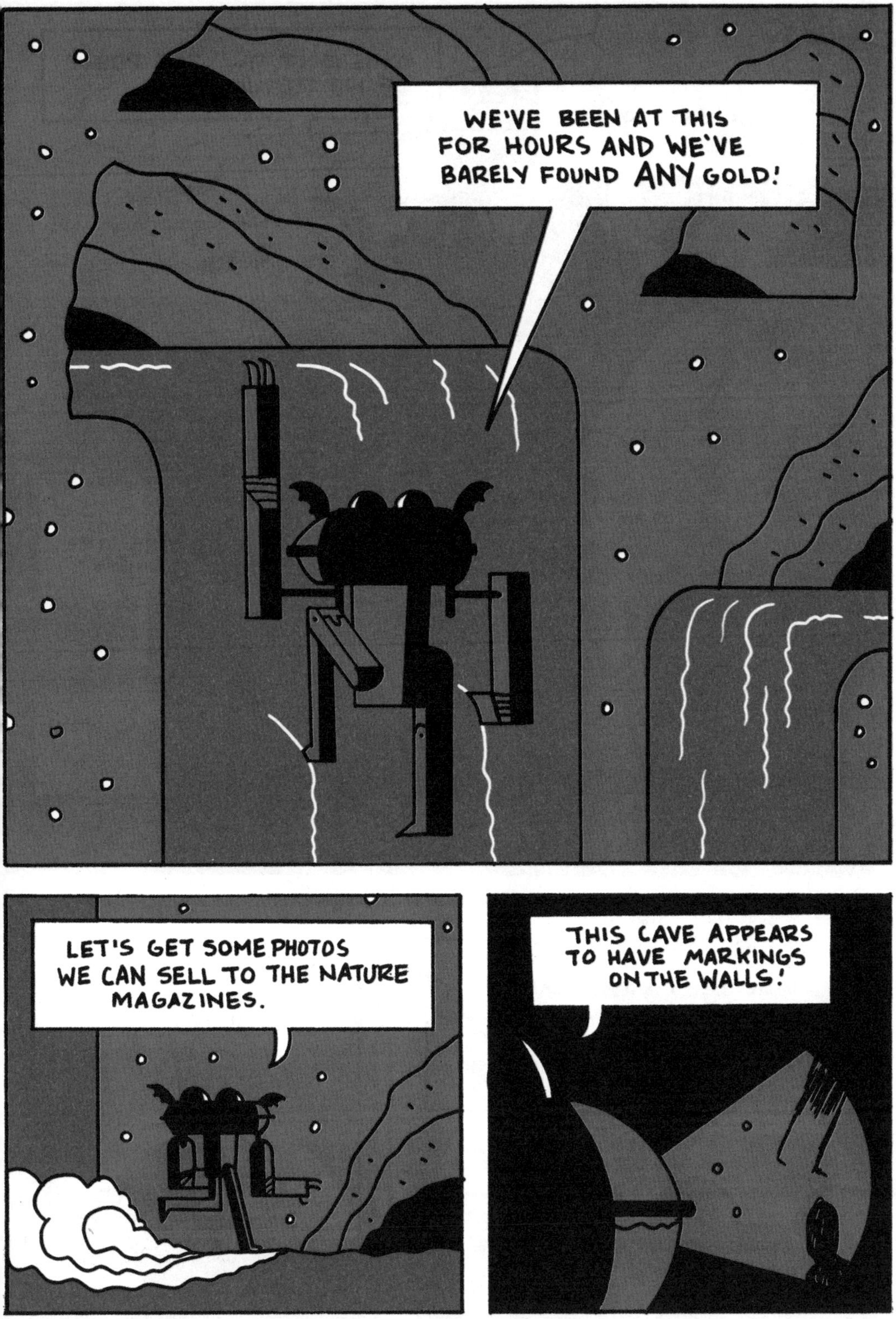
WE'VE BEEN AT THIS FOR HOURS AND WE'VE BARELY FOUND ANY GOLD!
LET'S GET SOME PHOTOS WE CAN SELL TO THE NATURE MAGAZINES.
THIS CAVE APPEARS TO HAVE MARKINGS ON THE WALLS!

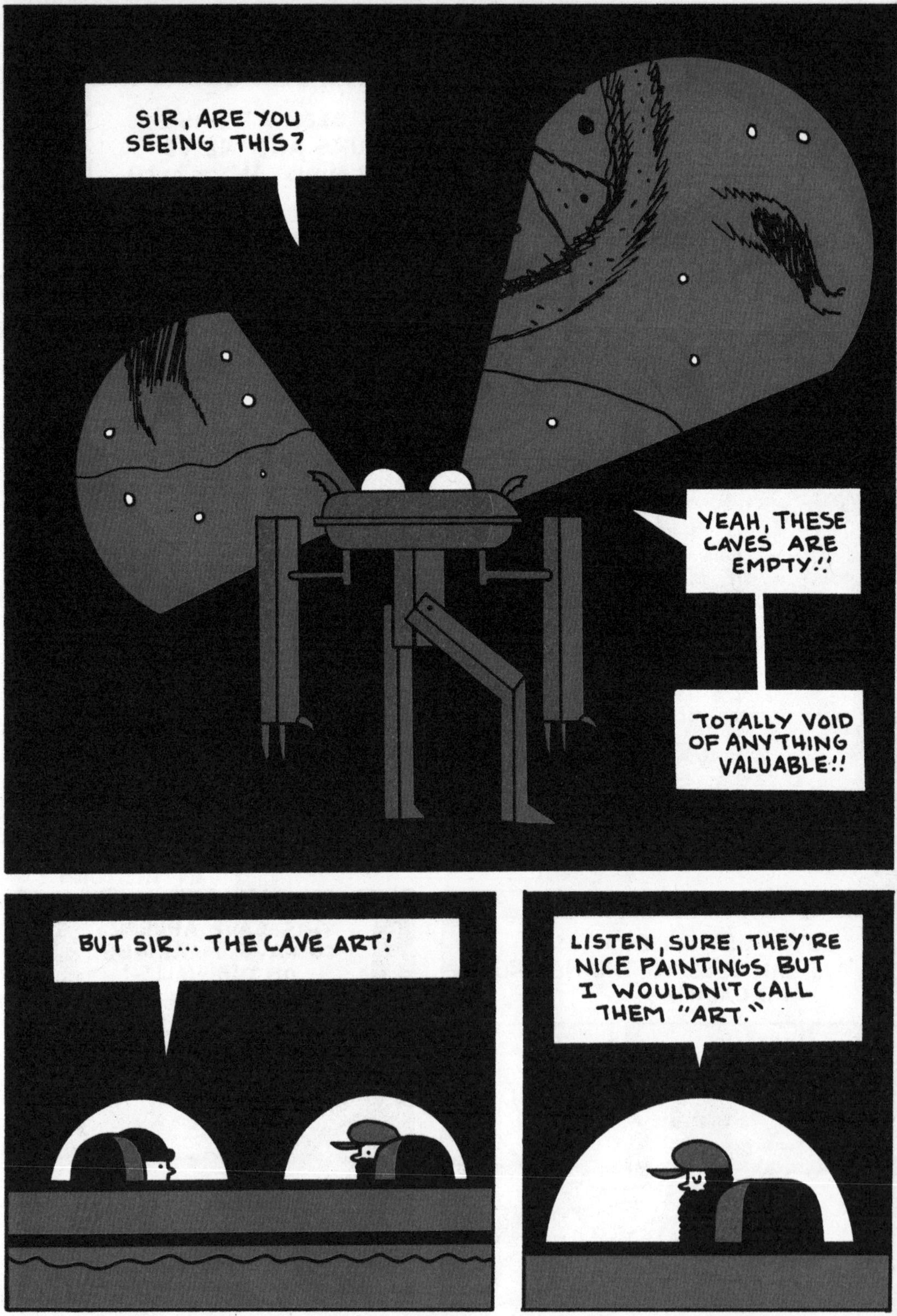
SIR, ARE YOU SEEING THIS?
YEAH, THESE CAVES ARE EMPTY!!
TOTALLY VOID OF ANYTHING VALUABLE!!
BUT SIR... THE CAVE ART!
LISTEN, SURE, THEY'RE NICE PAINTINGS BUT I WOULDN'T CALL THEM "ART."

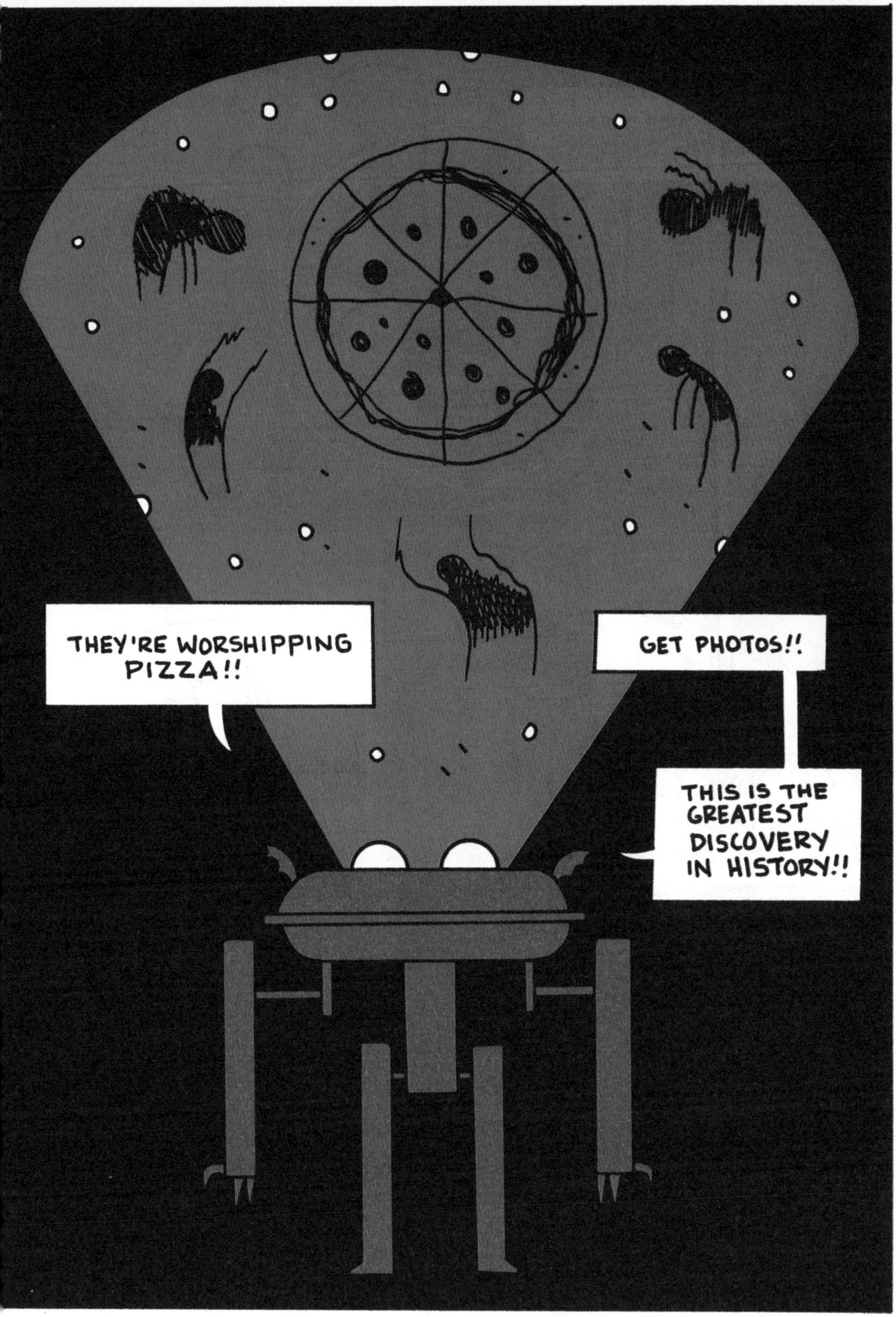
THEY'RE WORSHIPPING PIZZA!!
GET PHOTOS!!
THIS IS THE GREATEST DISCOVERY IN HISTORY!!

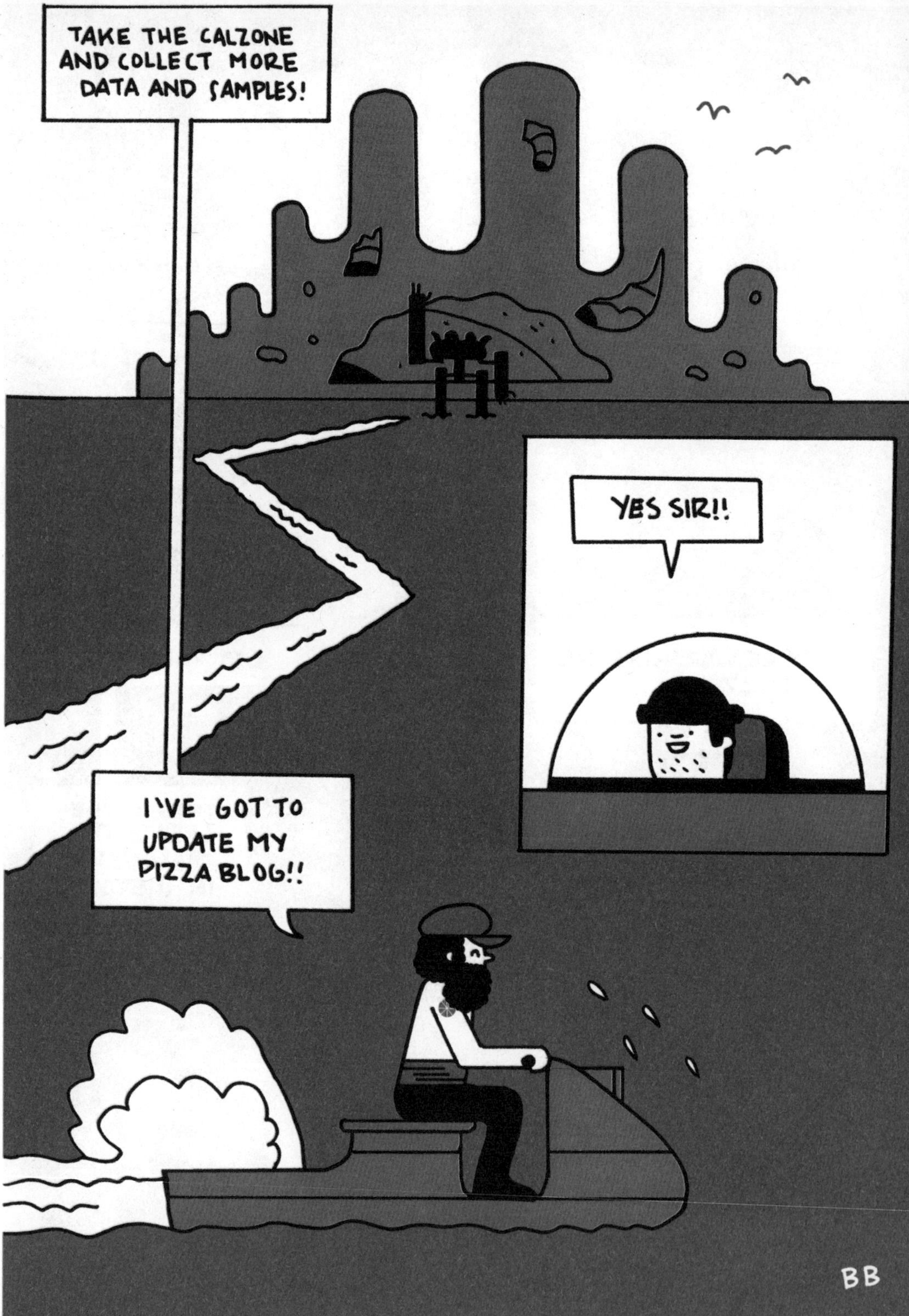
TAKE THE CALZONE AND COLLECT MORE DATA AND SAMPLES!
YES SIR!!
I'VE GOT TO UPDATE MY PIZZA BLOG!!
BB

AN ENTITY OBSERVES ALL THINGS

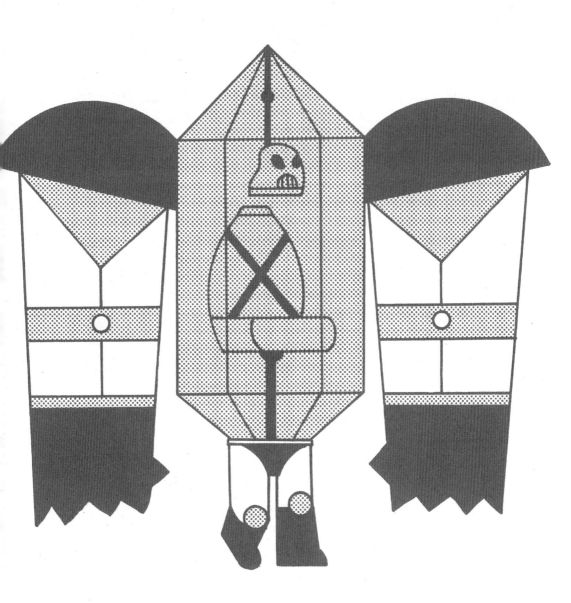

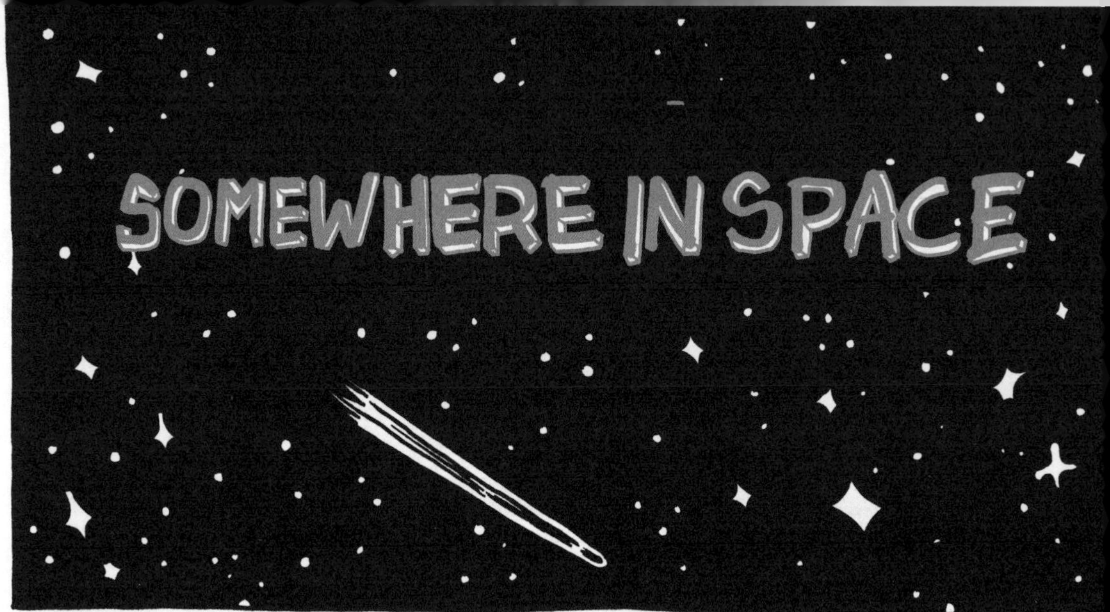
SOMEWHERE IN SPACE

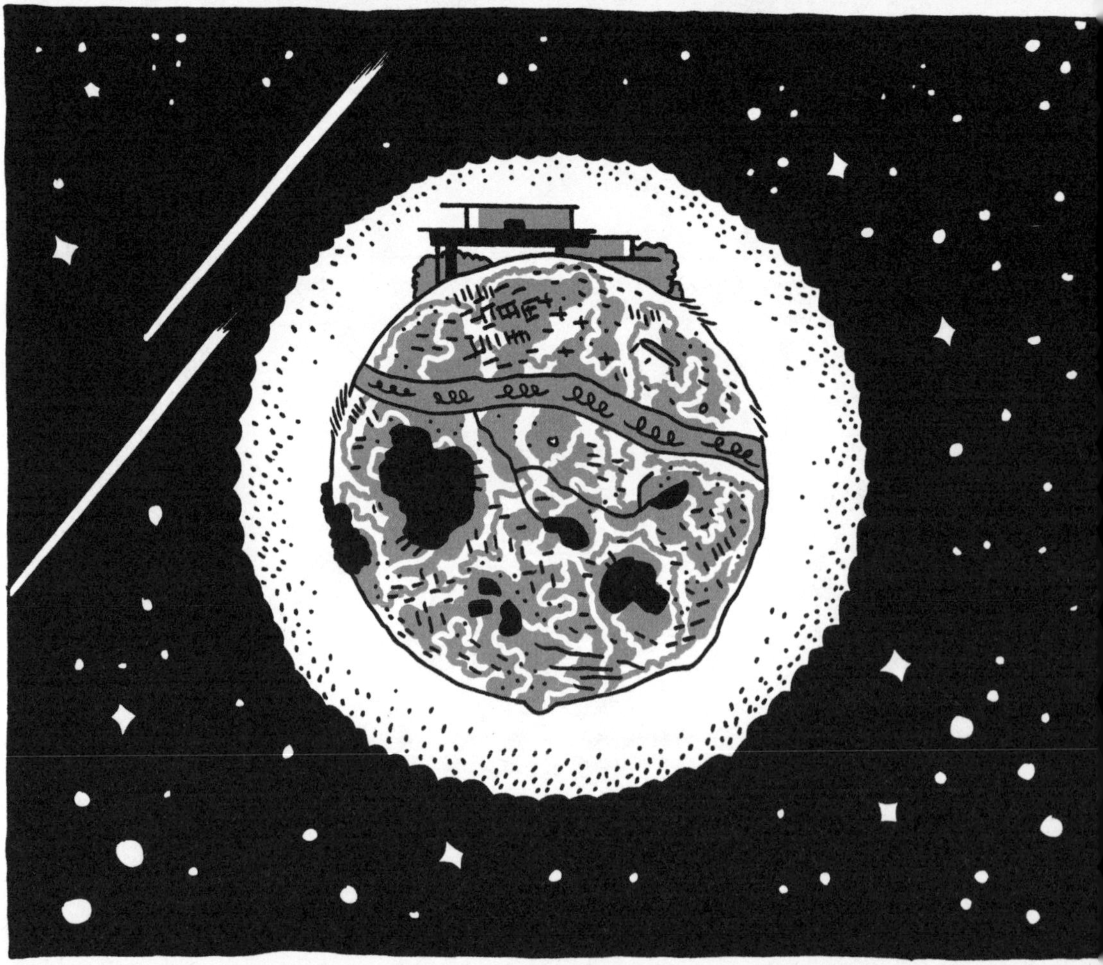

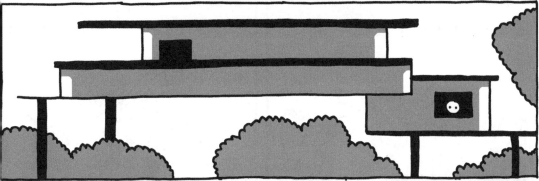

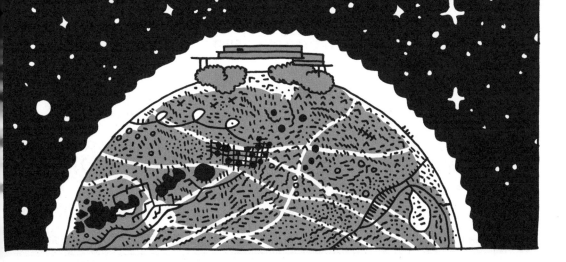

... AN ENTITY OBSERVES ALL THINGS.

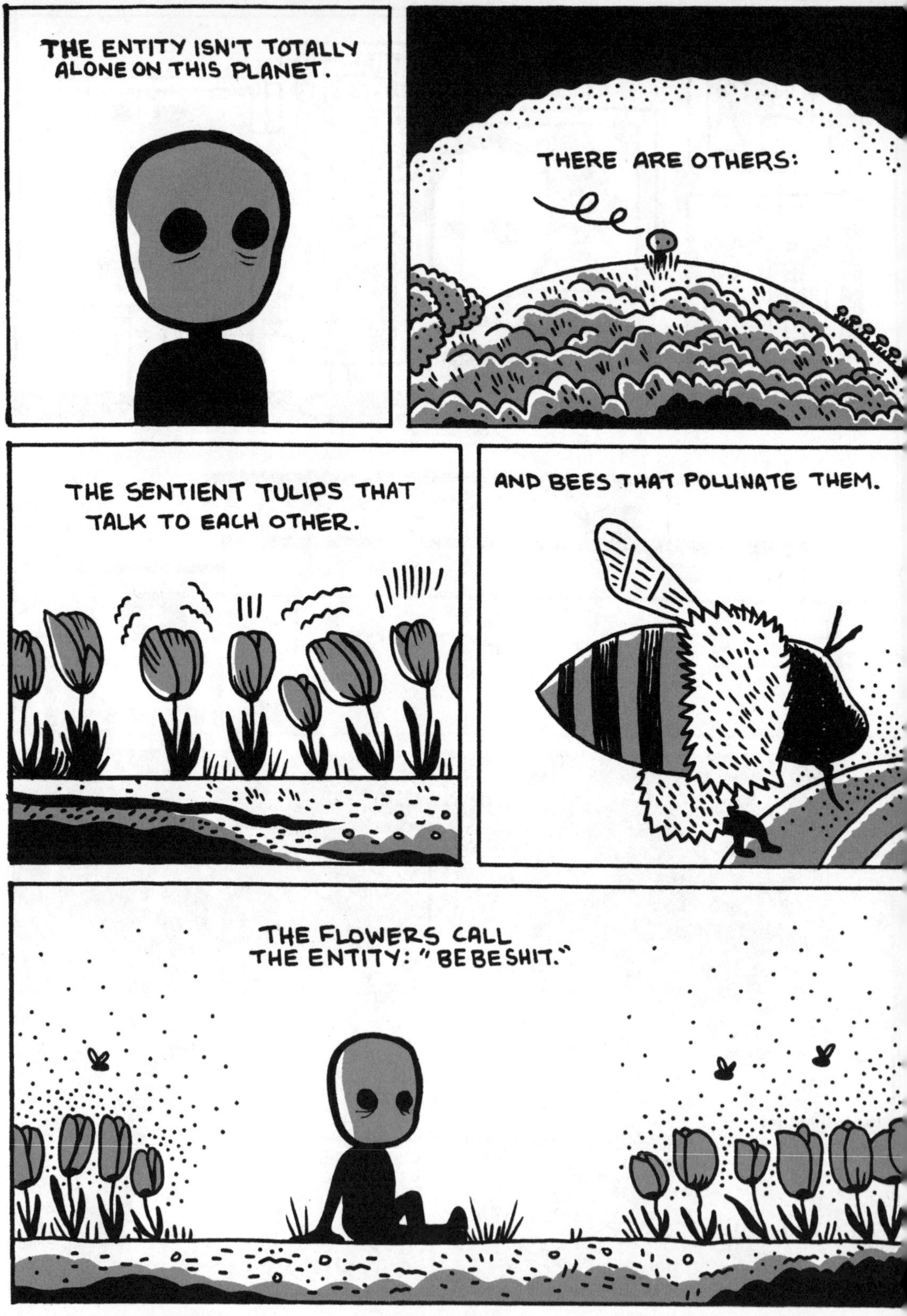
THE ENTITY ISN'T TOTALLY ALONE ON THIS PLANET.
THERE ARE OTHERS:
THE SENTIENT TULIPS THAT TALK TO EACH OTHER.
AND BEES THAT POLLINATE THEM.
THE FLOWERS CALL THE ENTITY: "BEBESHIT."

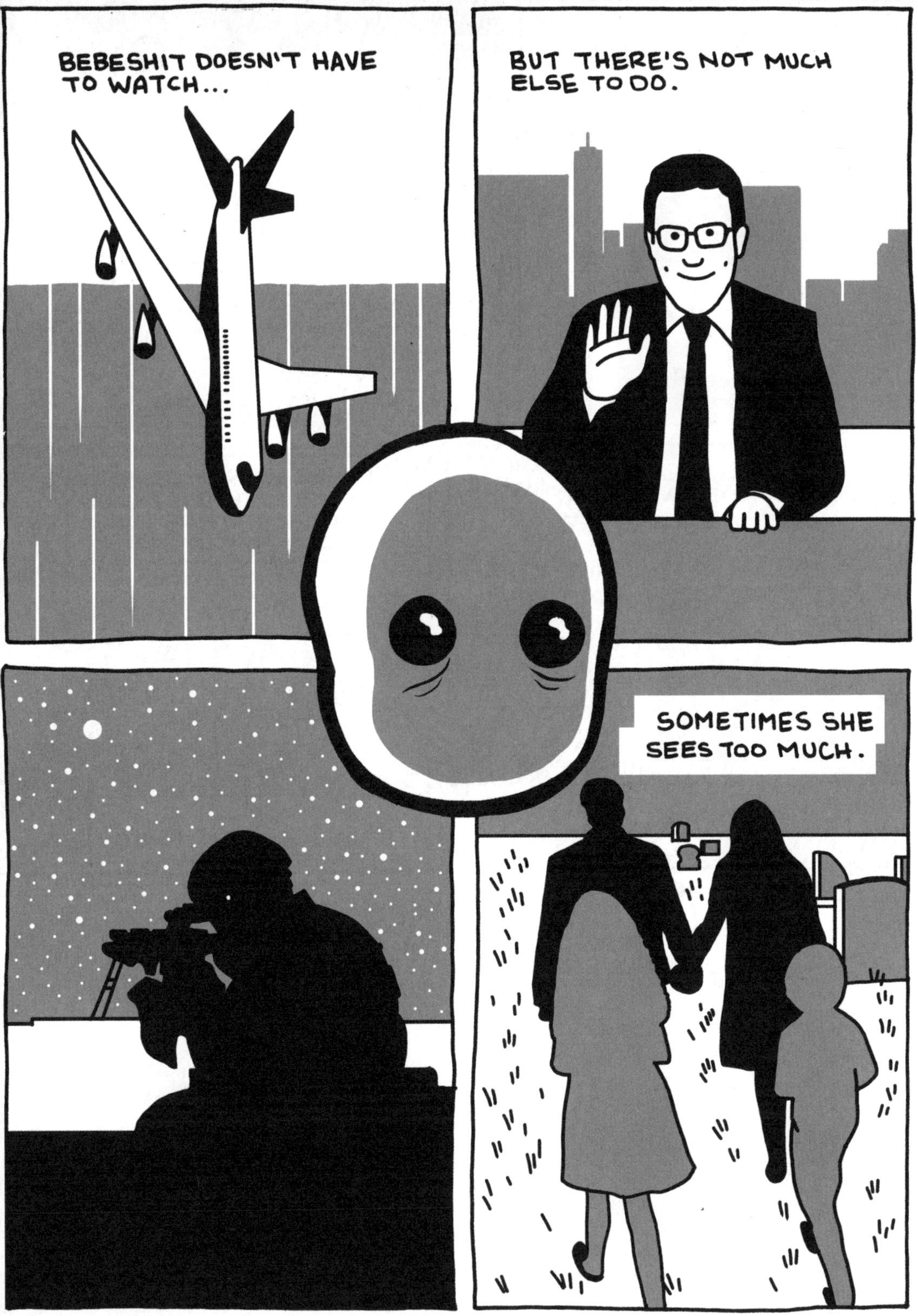
BEBESHIT DOESN'T HAVE TO WATCH...
BUT THERE'S NOT MUCH ELSE TO DO.
SOMETIMES SHE SEES TOO MUCH.

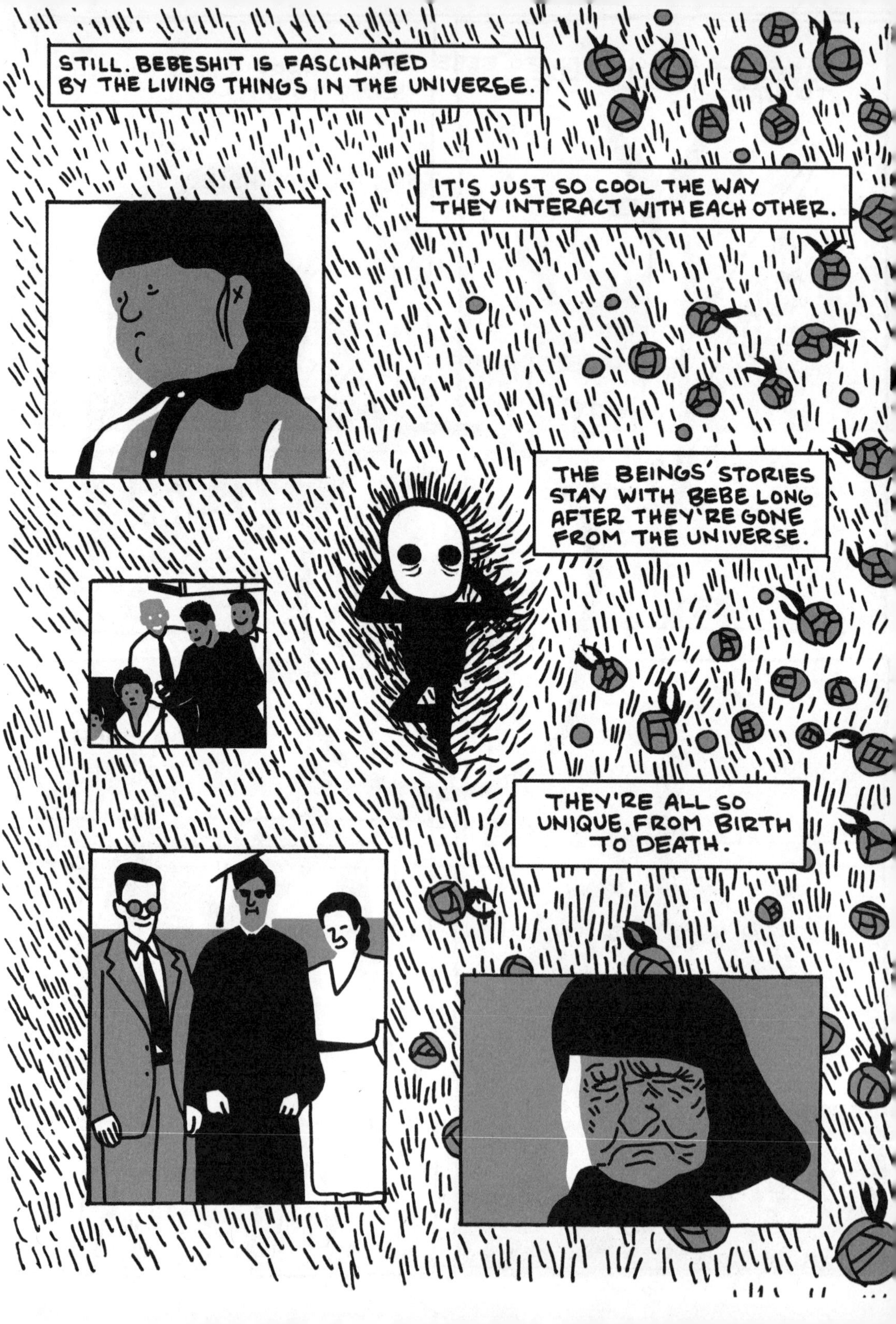
STILL. BEBESHIT IS FASCINATED BY THE LIVING THINGS IN THE UNIVERSE.
IT'S JUST SO COOL THE WAY THEY INTERACT WITH EACH OTHER.
THE BEINGS' STORIES STAY WITH BEBE LONG AFTER THEY'RE GONE FROM THE UNIVERSE.
THEY'RE ALL SO UNIQUE, FROM BIRTH TO DEATH.

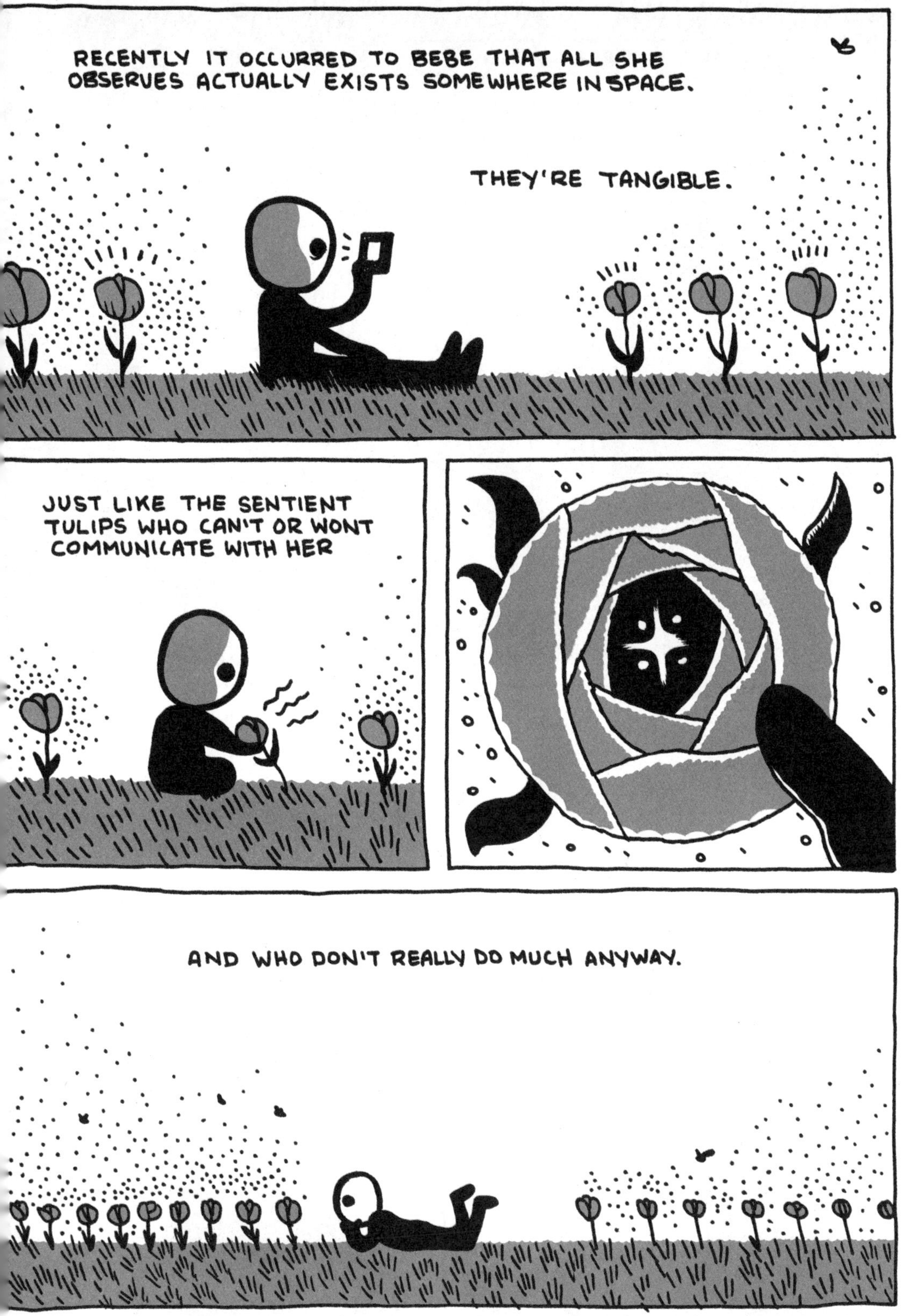
RECENTLY IT OCCURRED TO BEBE THAT ALL SHE OBSERVES ACTUALLY EXISTS SOMEWHERE IN SPACE.
THEY'RE TANGIBLE.
JUST LIKE THE SENTIENT TULIPS WHO CAN'T OR WONT COMMUNICATE WITH HER
AND WHO DON'T REALLY DO MUCH ANYWAY.

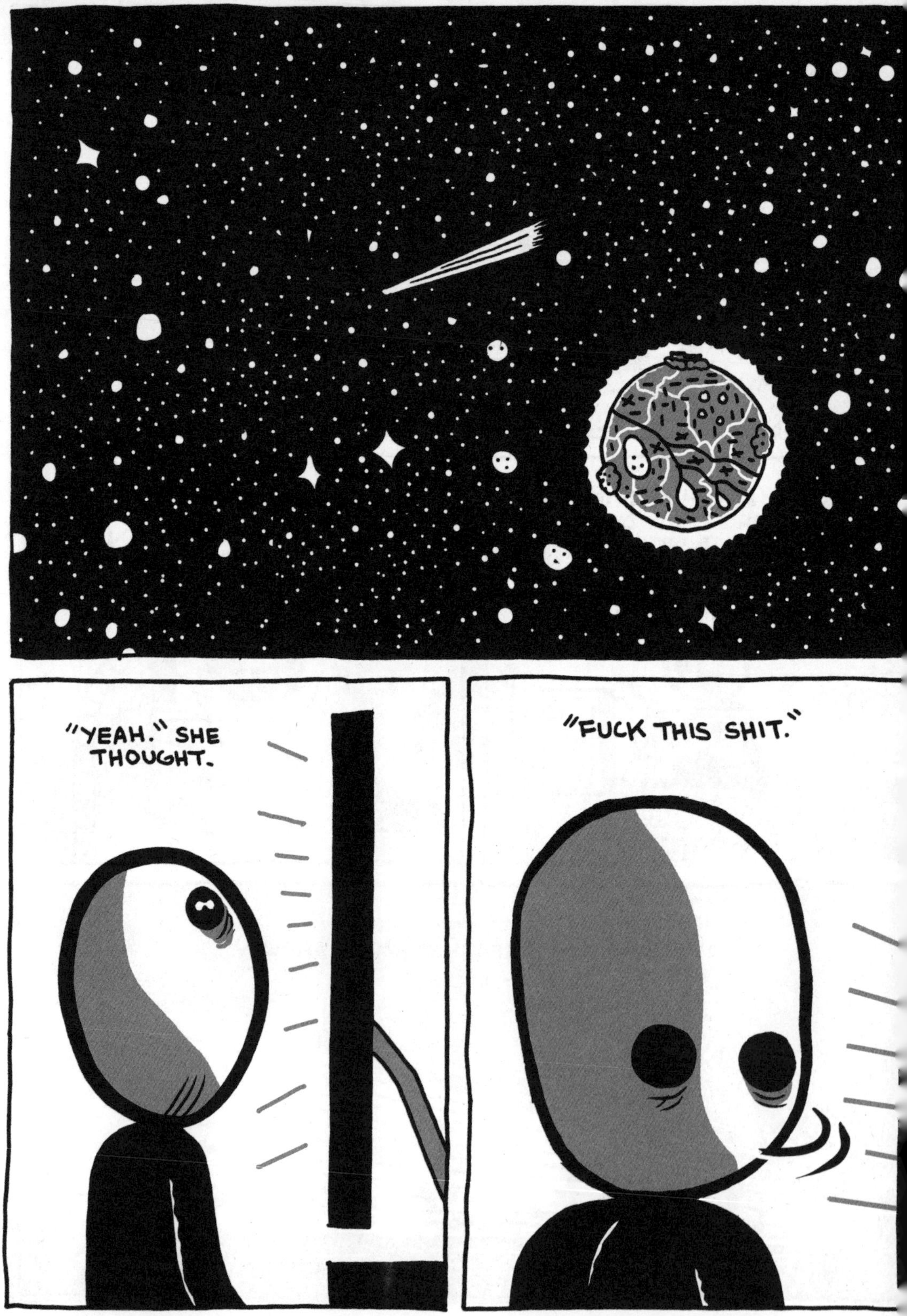
"YEAH." SHE THOUGHT.
"FUCK THIS SHIT."

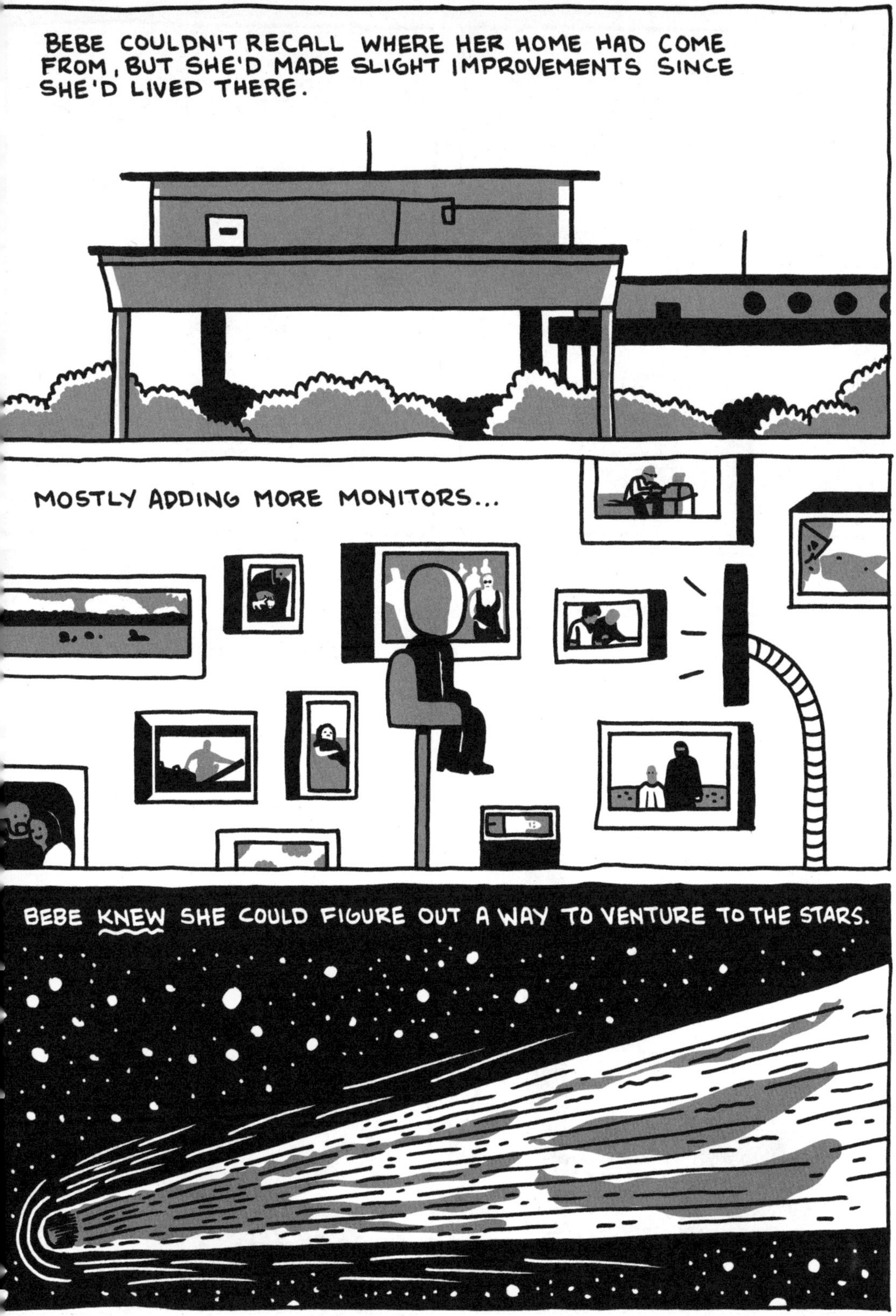
BEBE COULDN'T RECALL WHERE HER HOME HAD COME FROM, BUT SHE'D MADE SLIGHT IMPROVEMENTS SINCE SHE'D LIVED THERE.
MOSTLY ADDING MORE MONITORS...
BEBE KNEW SHE COULD FIGURE OUT A WAY TO VENTURE TO THE STARS.

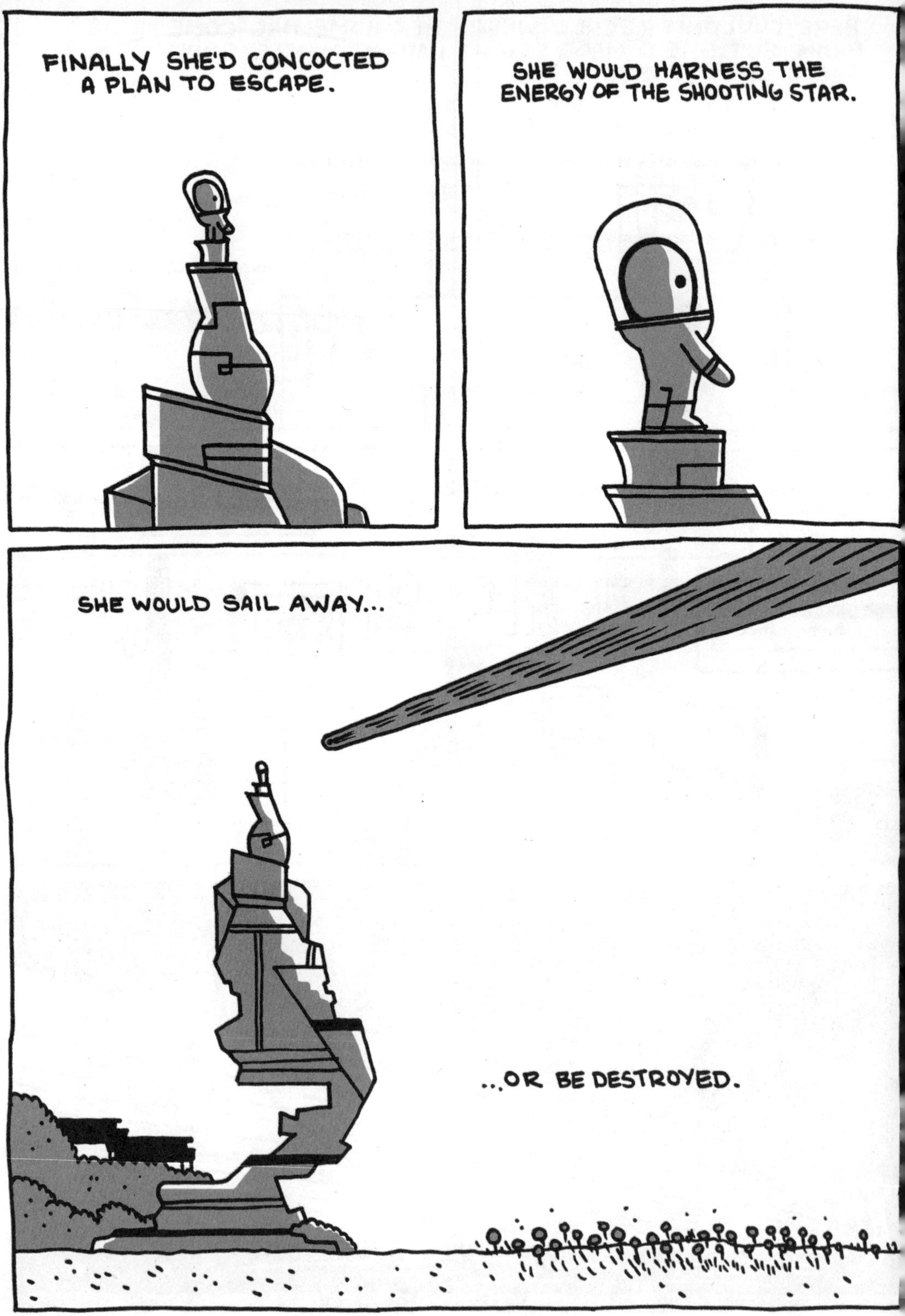
FINALLY SHE'D CONCOCTED A PLAN TO ESCAPE.
SHE WOULD HARNESS THE ENERGY OF THE SHOOTING STAR.
SHE WOULD SAIL AWAY...
...OR BE DESTROYED.

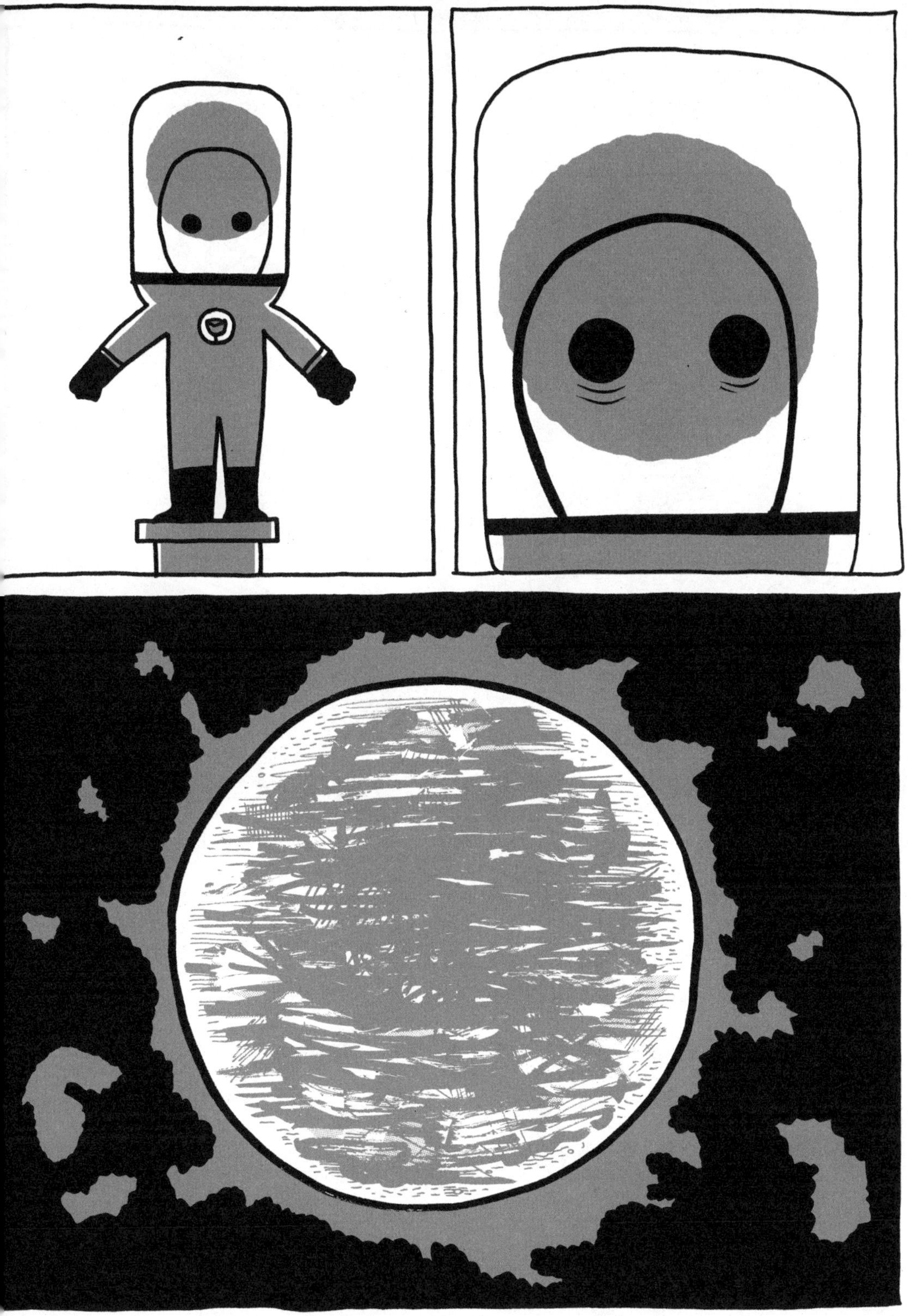

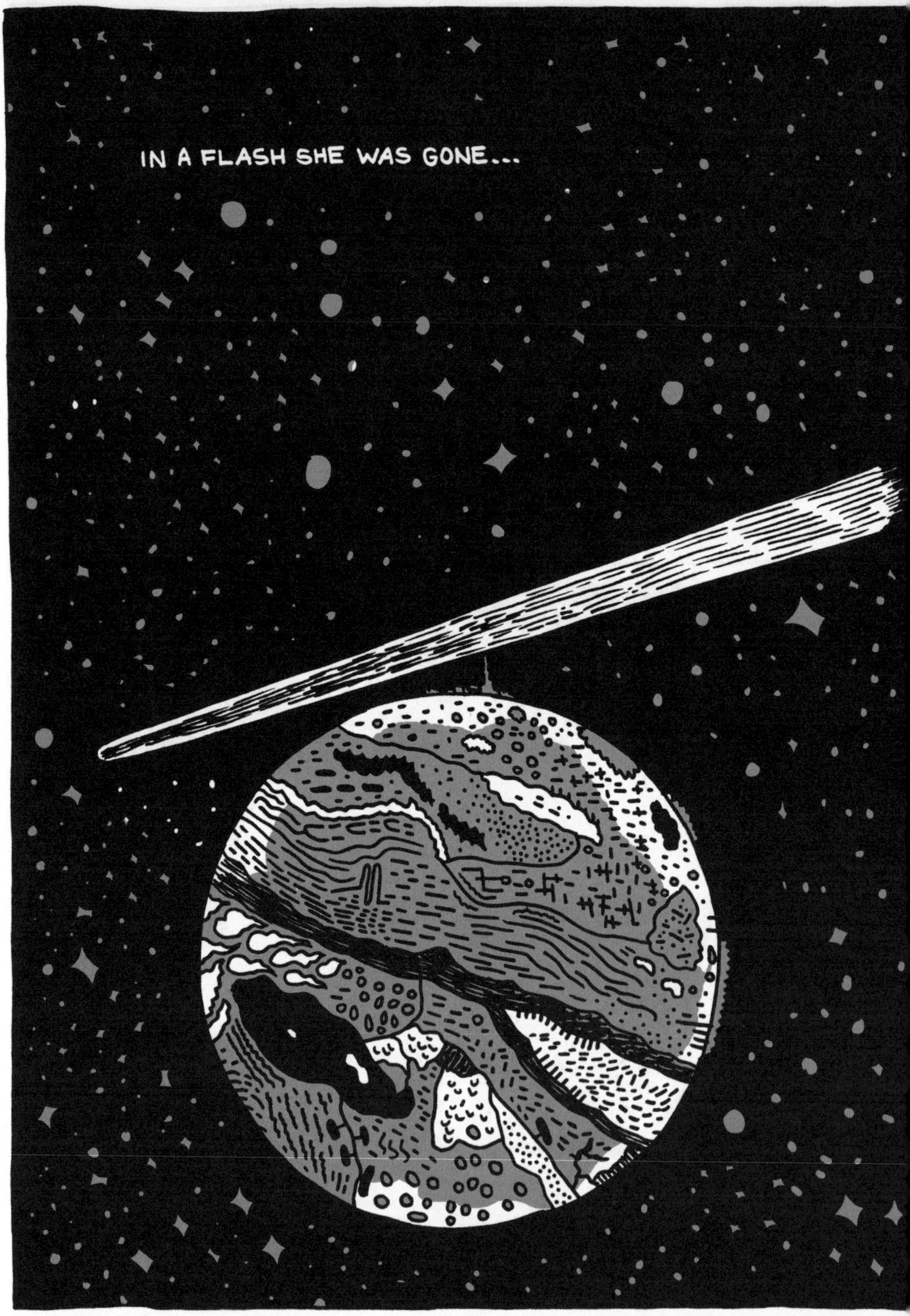
IN A FLASH SHE WAS GONE...

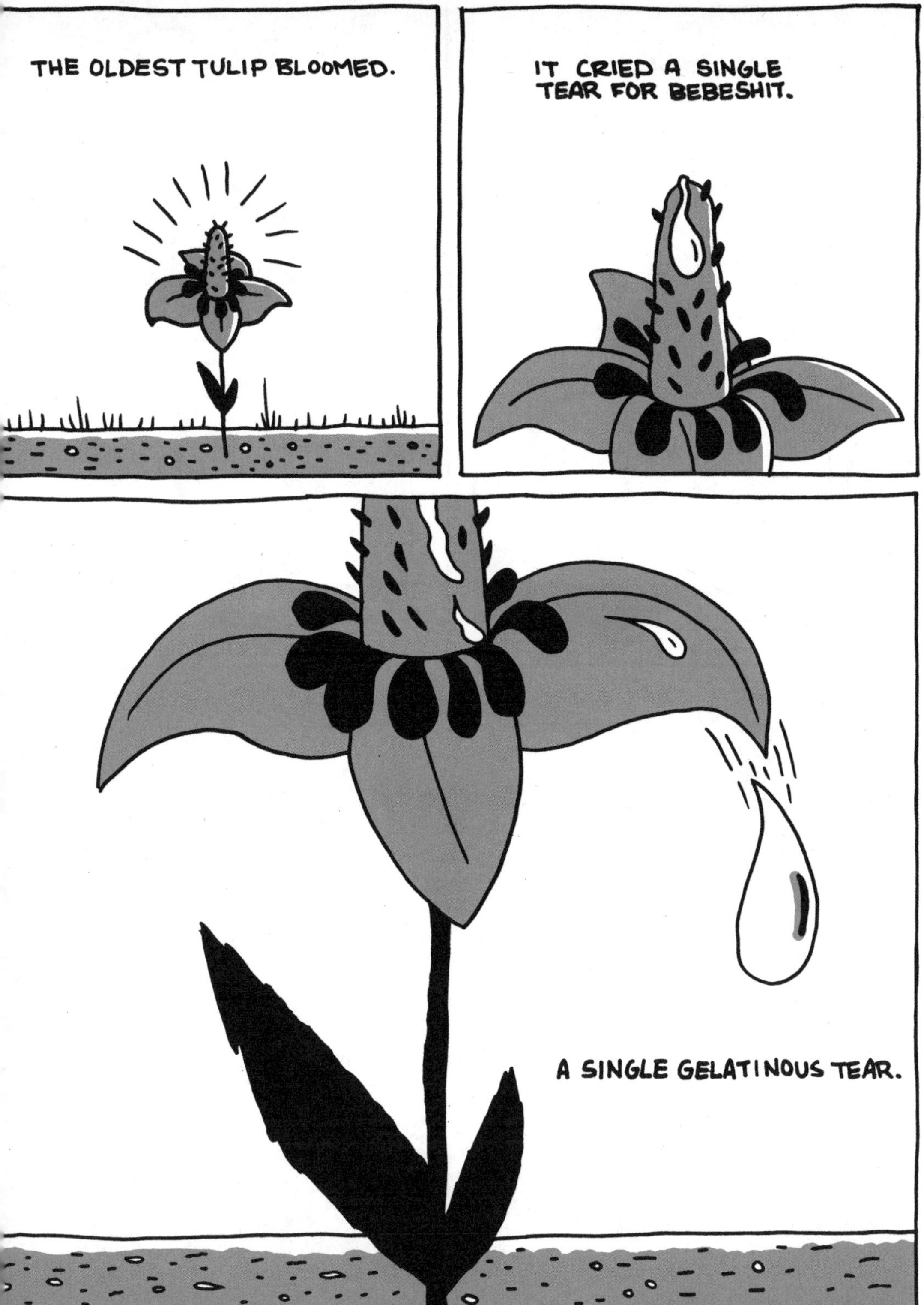
THE OLDEST TULIP BLOOMED.
IT CRIED A SINGLE TEAR FOR BEBESHIT.
A SINGLE GELATINOUS TEAR.

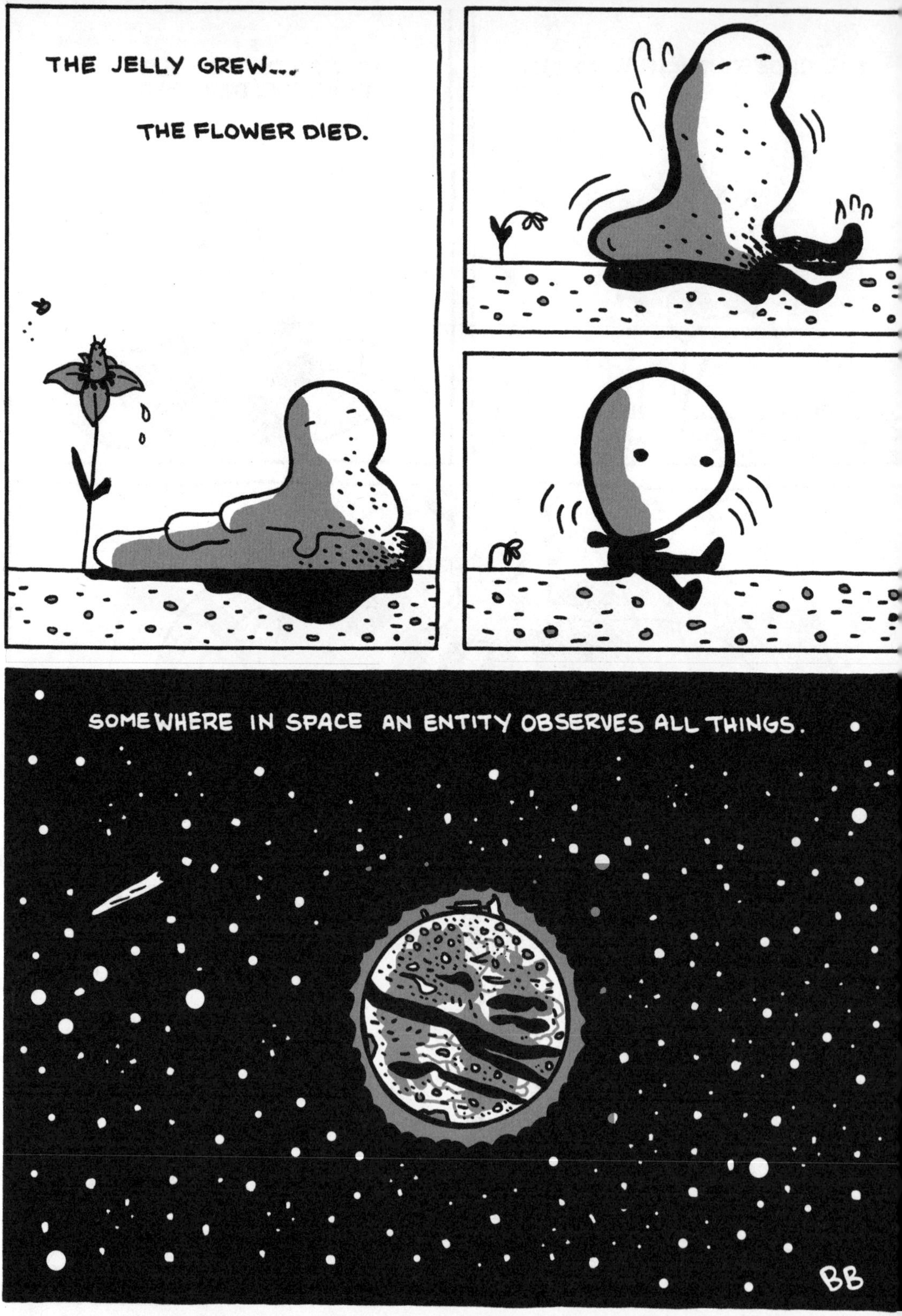
THE JELLY GREW...
THE FLOWER DIED.
SOMEWHERE IN SPACE AN ENTITY OBSERVES ALL THINGS.
BB

TRAVEL

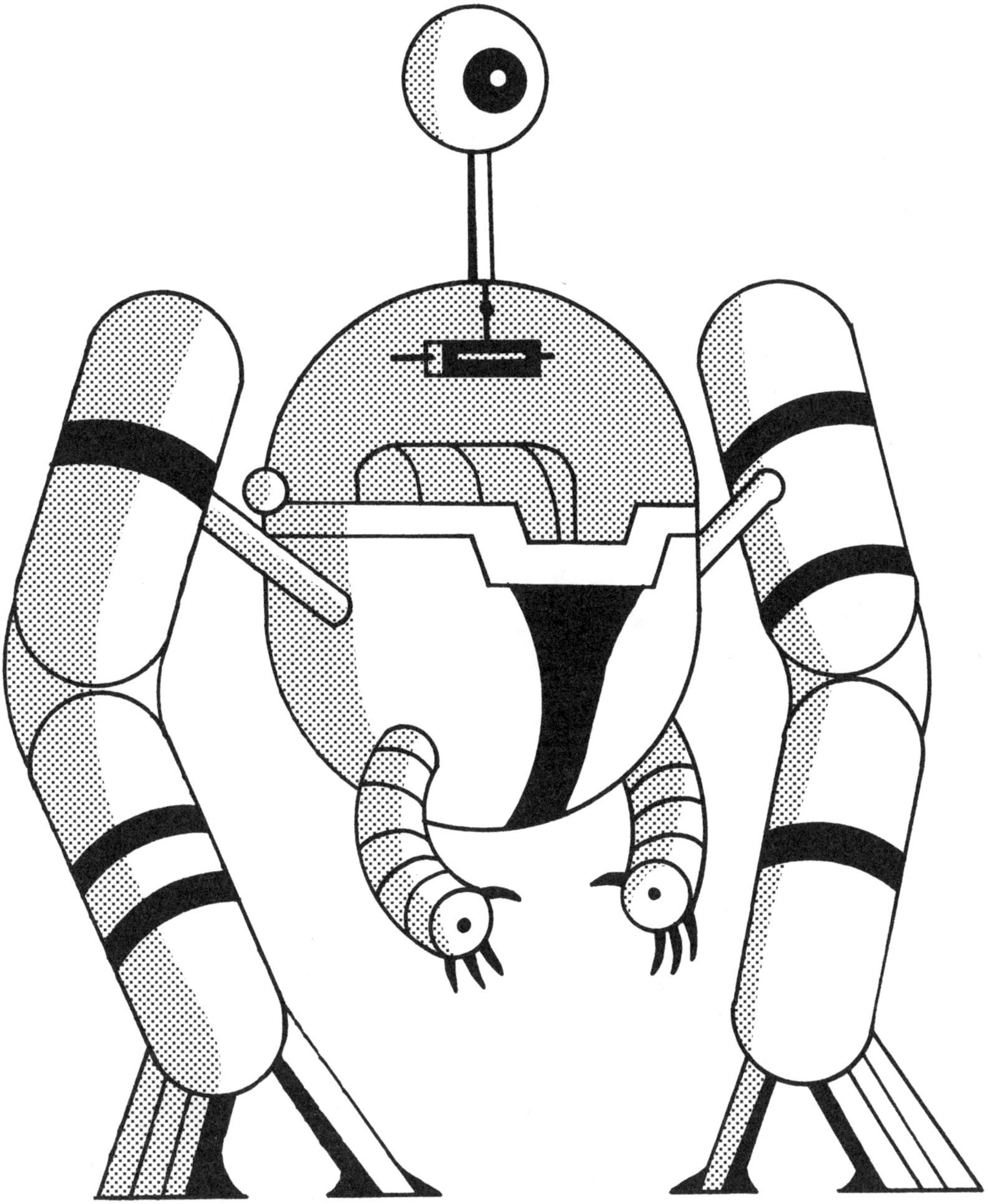

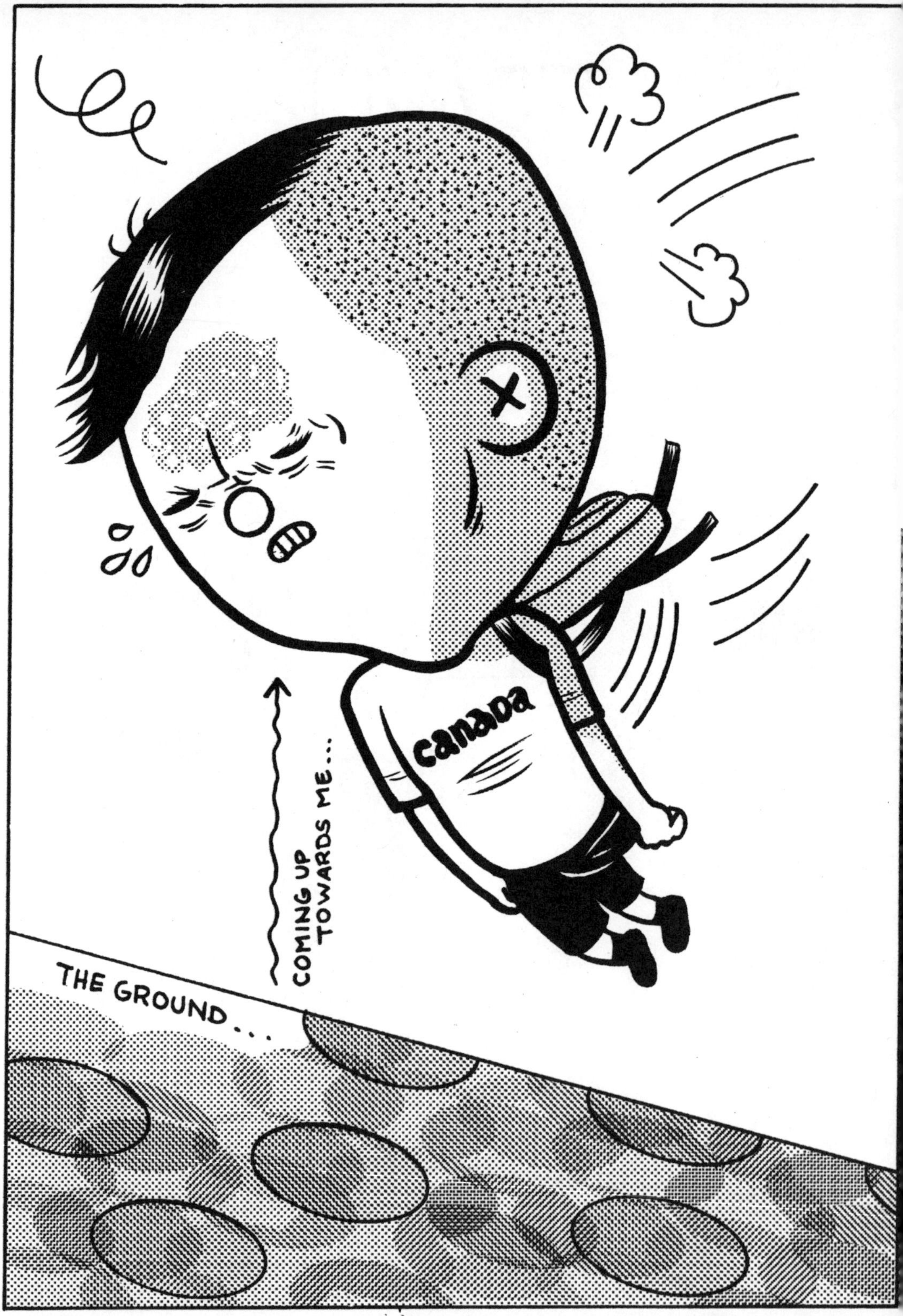
COMING UP TOWARDS ME...
THE GROUND...
canada

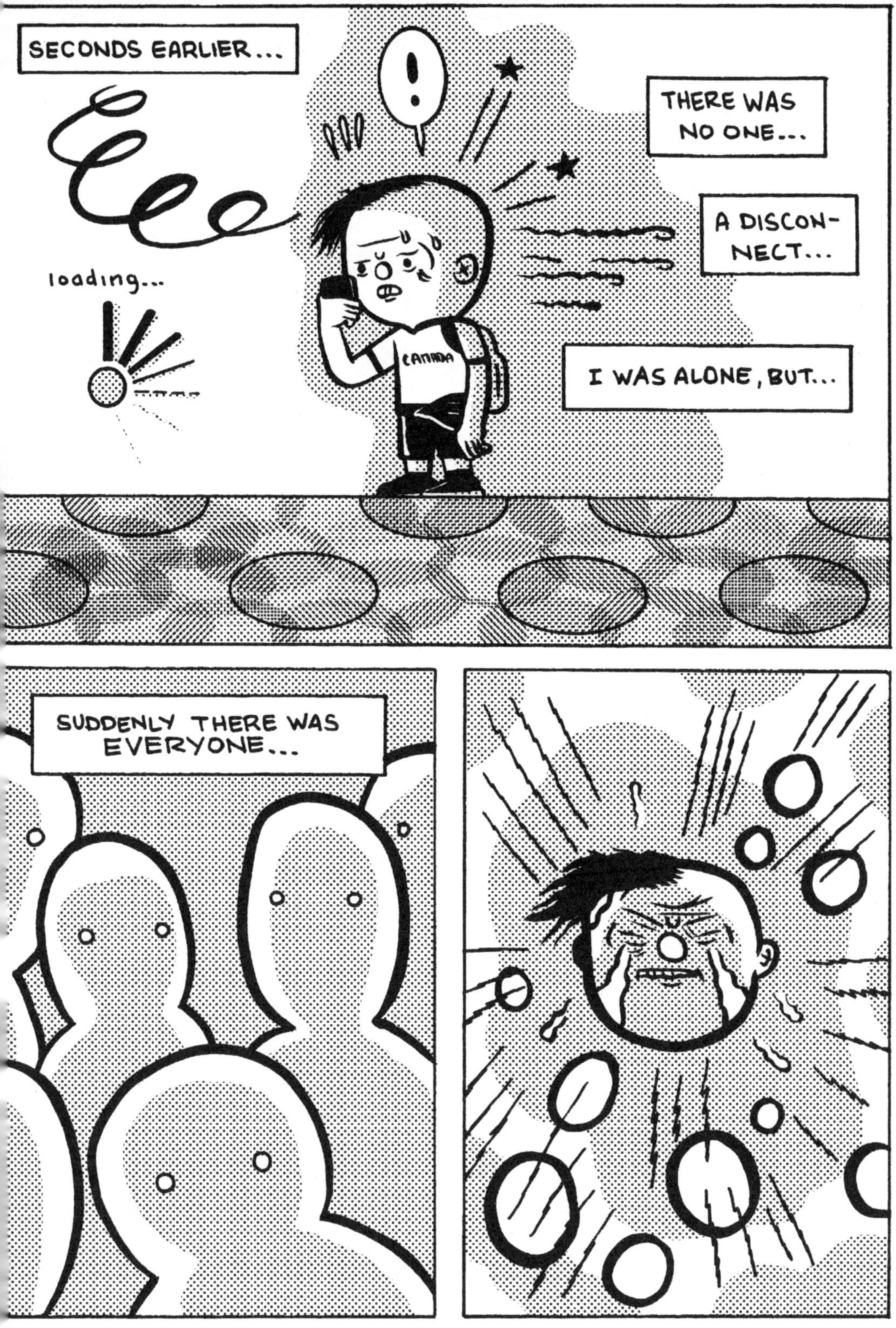
SECONDS EARLIER...
loading...
!
THERE WAS NO ONE...
A DISCON-NECT...
CANADA
I WAS ALONE, BUT...
SUDDENLY THERE WAS EVERYONE...

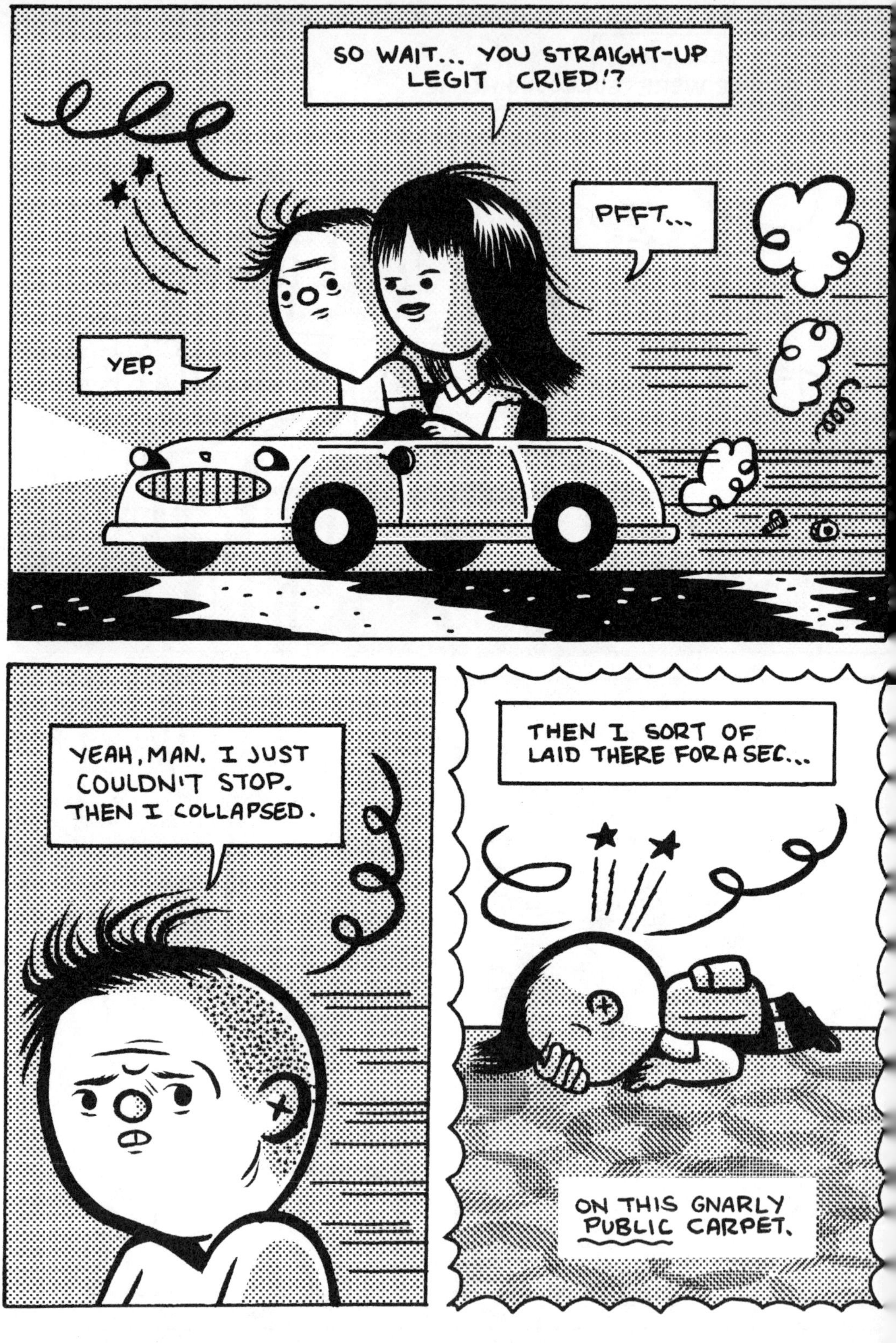
SO WAIT... YOU STRAIGHT-UP LEGIT CRIED!?
PFFT...
YEP.
YEAH, MAN. I JUST COULDN'T STOP. THEN I COLLAPSED.
THEN I SORT OF LAID THERE FOR A SEC...
ON THIS GNARLY PUBLIC CARPET.

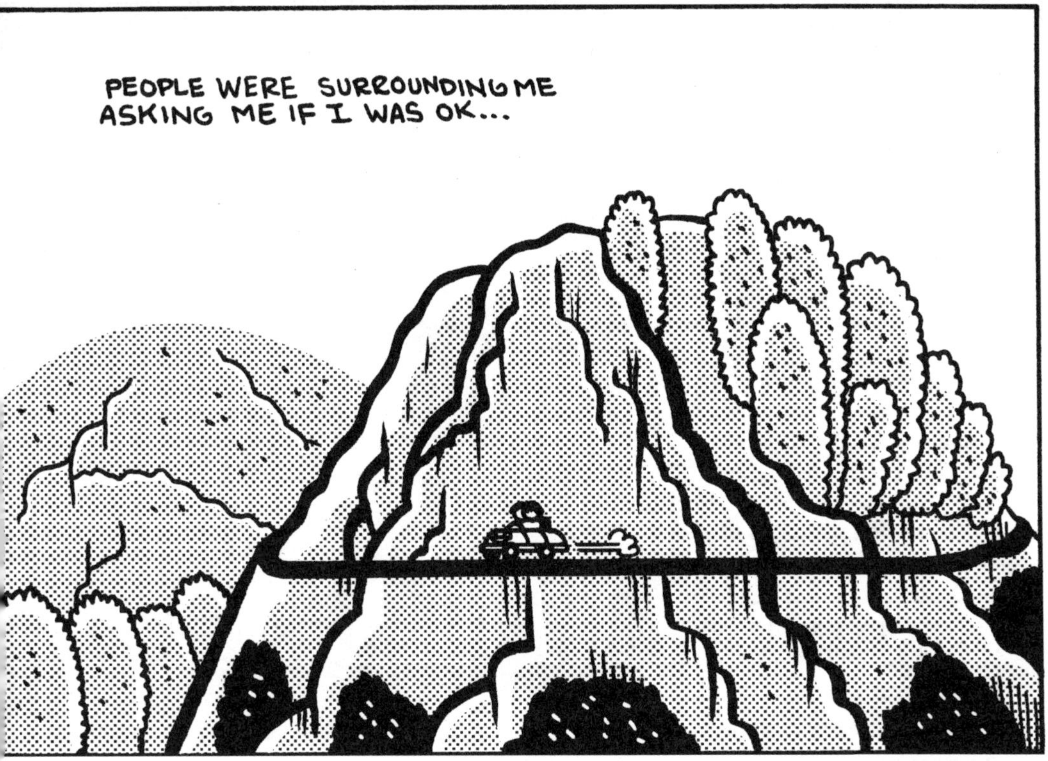
PEOPLE WERE SURROUNDING ME ASKING ME IF I WAS OK...

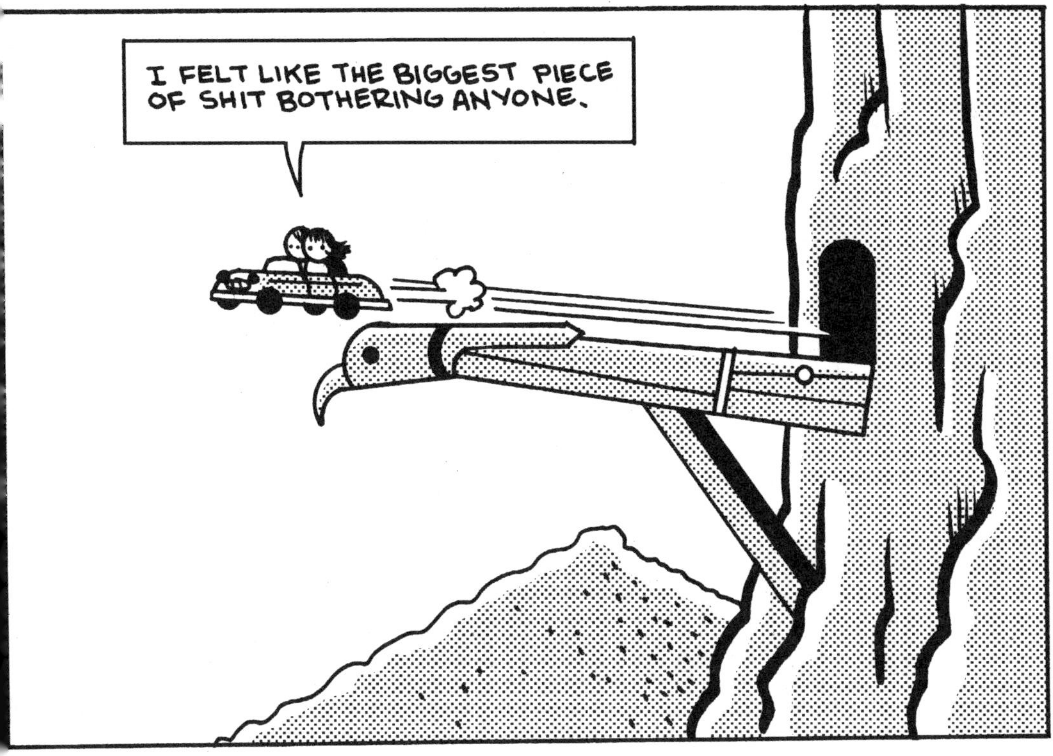
I FELT LIKE THE BIGGEST PIECE OF SHIT BOTHERING ANYONE.

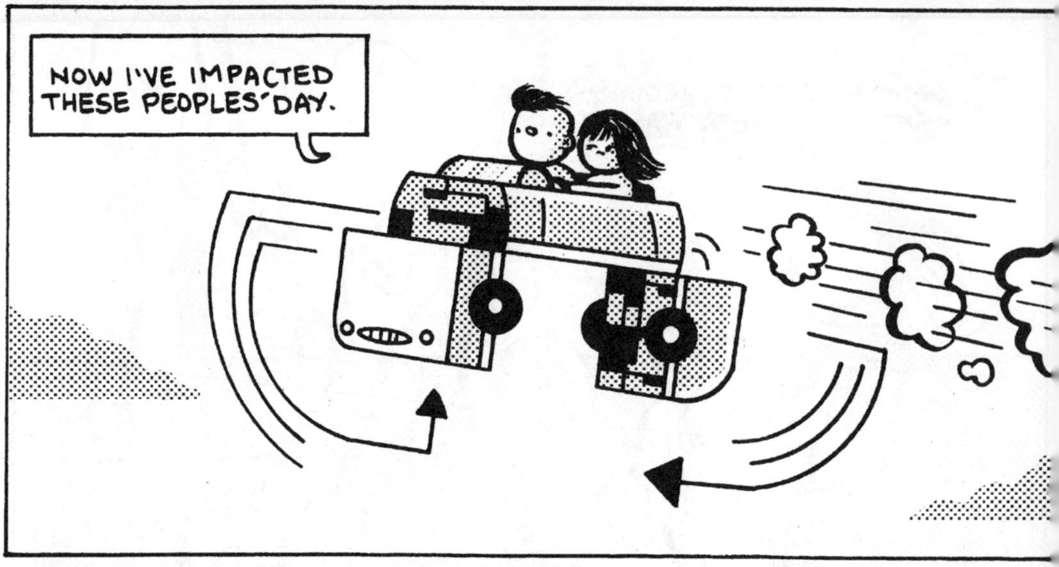
NOW I'VE IMPACTED THESE PEOPLES' DAY.

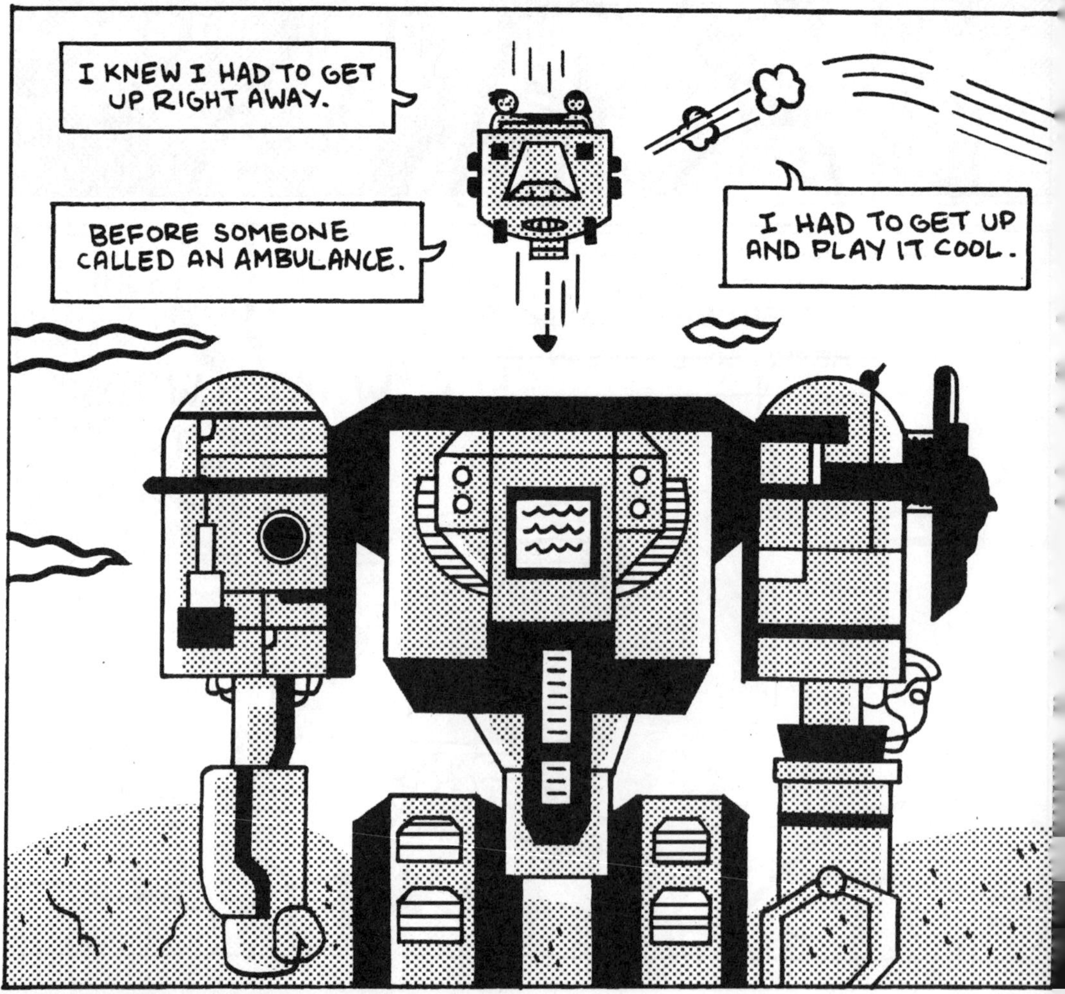
I KNEW I HAD TO GET UP RIGHT AWAY.
BEFORE SOMEONE CALLED AN AMBULANCE.
I HAD TO GET UP AND PLAY IT COOL.

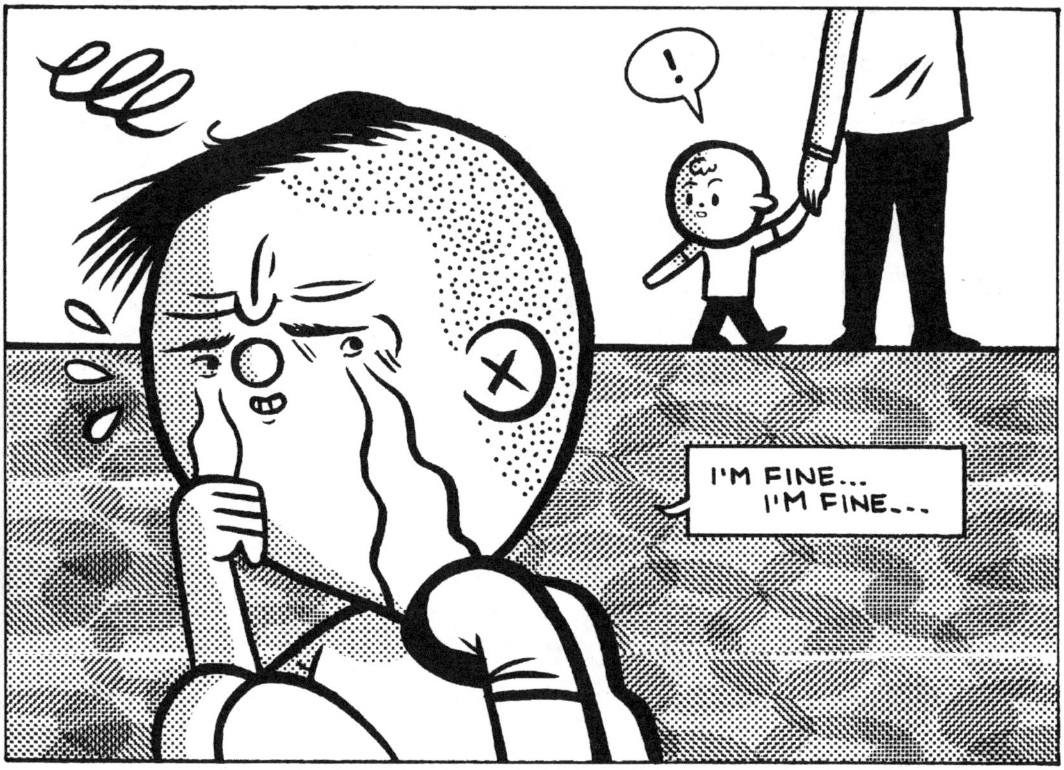
!
I'M FINE...
I'M FINE...

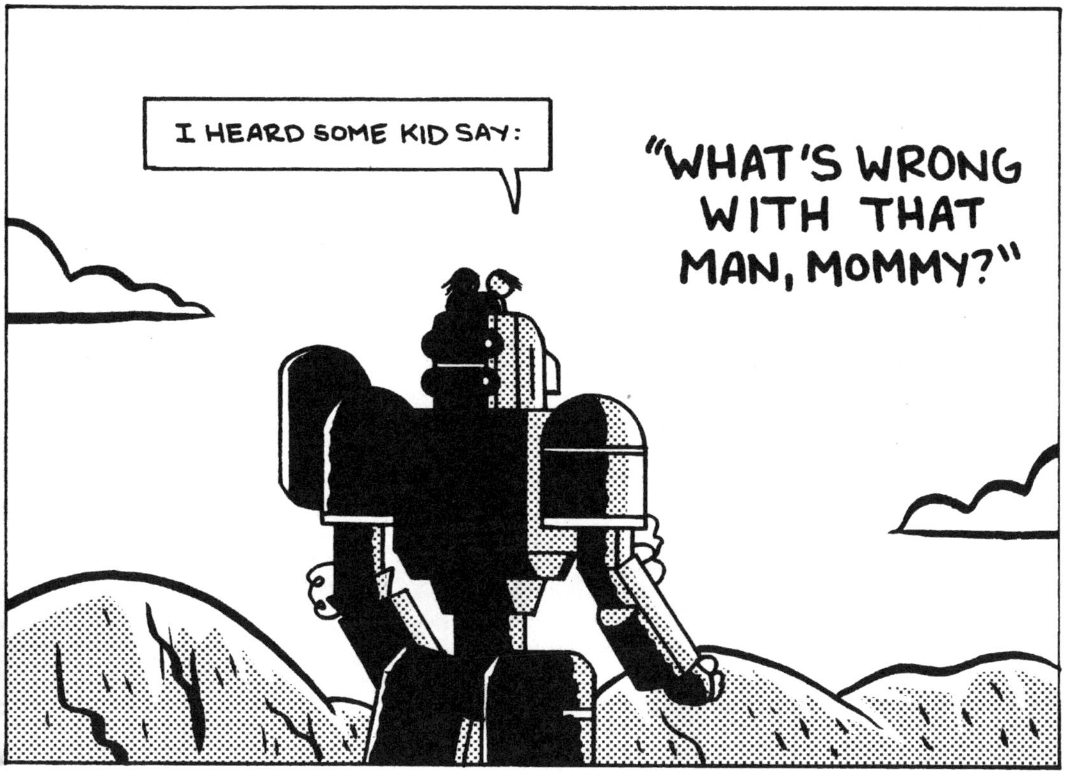
I HEARD SOME KID SAY:
"WHAT'S WRONG WITH THAT MAN, MOMMY?"

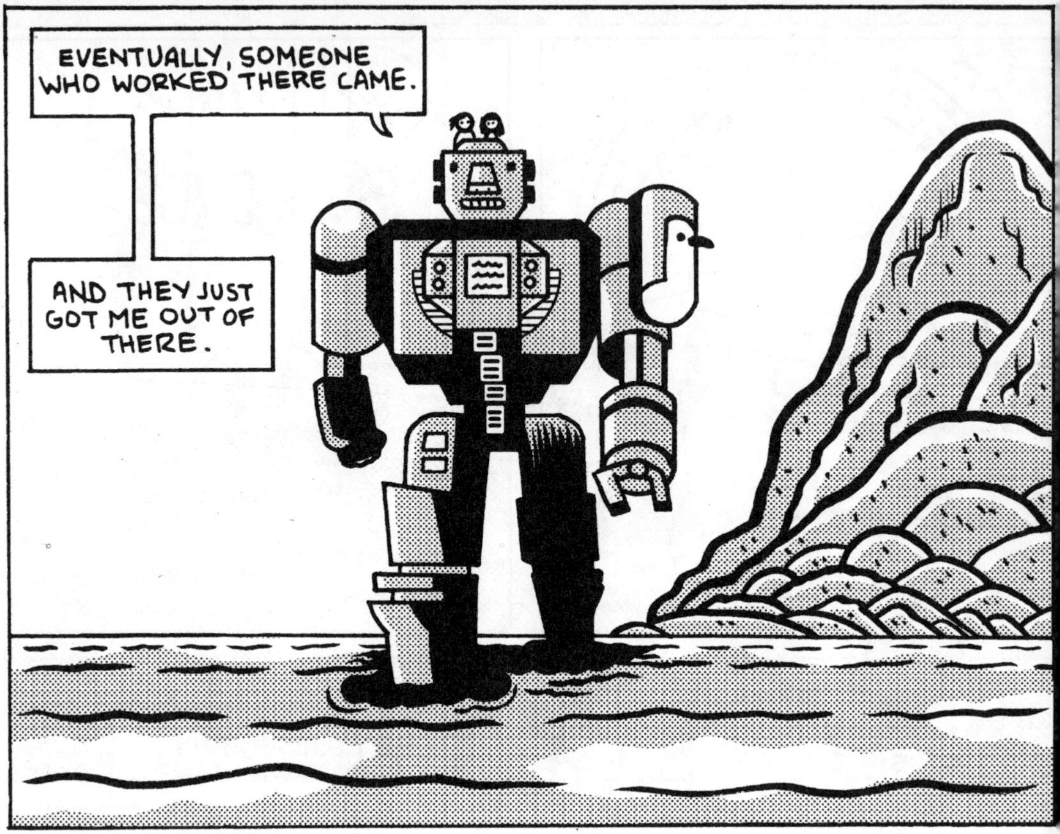
EVENTUALLY, SOMEONE WHO WORKED THERE CAME.
AND THEY JUST GOT ME OUT OF THERE.

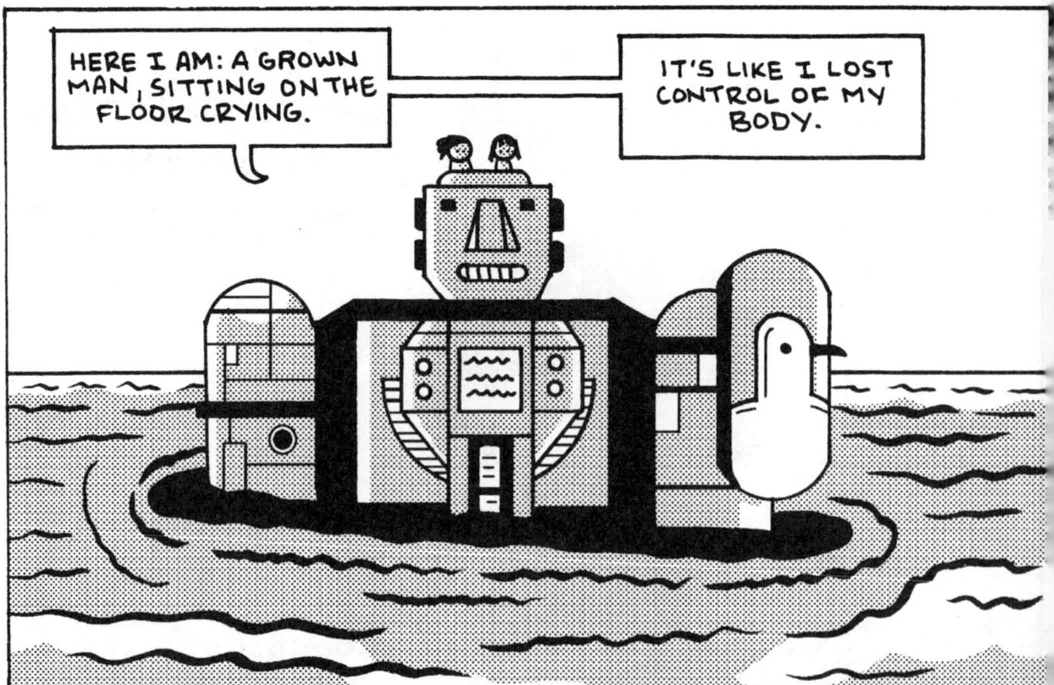
HERE I AM: A GROWN MAN, SITTING ON THE FLOOR CRYING.
IT'S LIKE I LOST CONTROL OF MY BODY.

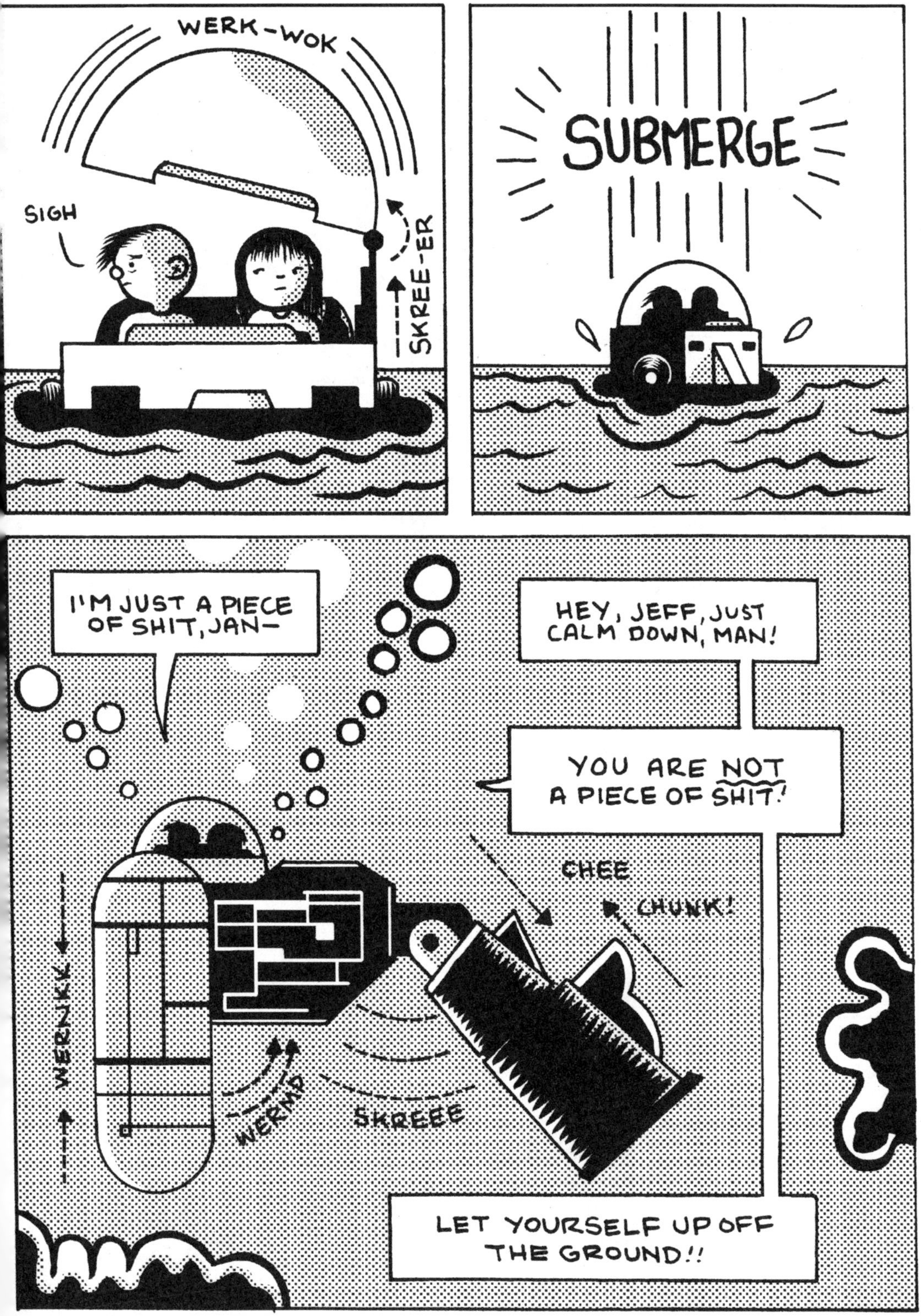
WERK-WOK
SIGH
SKREE-ER
SUBMERGE
I'M JUST A PIECE OF SHIT, JAN—
HEY, JEFF, JUST CALM DOWN, MAN!
YOU ARE NOT A PIECE OF SHIT!
CHEE
CHUNK!
WERNKK
WERMP
SKREEE
LET YOURSELF UP OFF THE GROUND!!

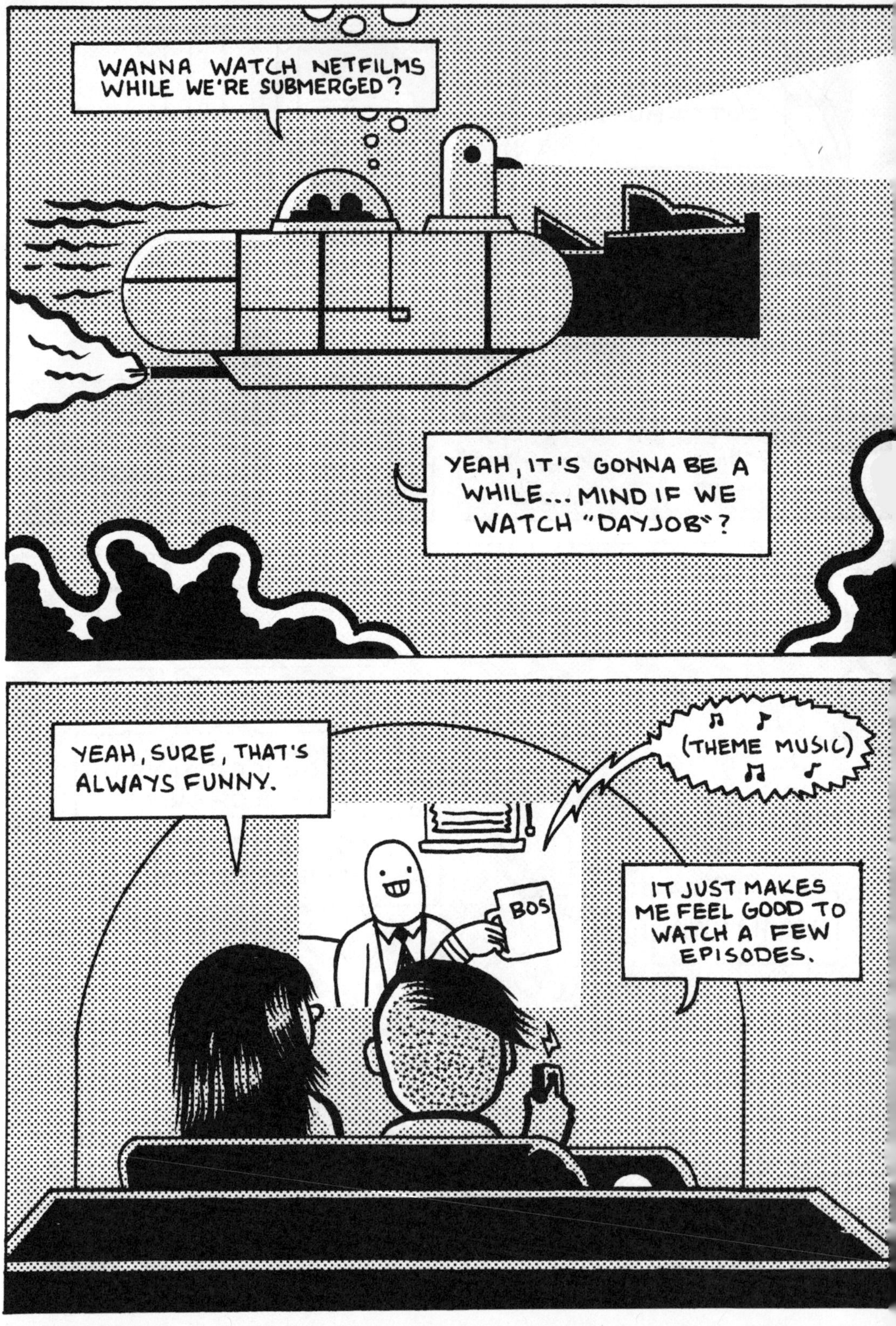
WANNA WATCH NETFILMS WHILE WE'RE SUBMERGED?
YEAH, IT'S GONNA BE A WHILE... MIND IF WE WATCH "DAYJOB"?
YEAH, SURE, THAT'S ALWAYS FUNNY.
(THEME MUSIC)
BOS
IT JUST MAKES ME FEEL GOOD TO WATCH A FEW EPISODES.

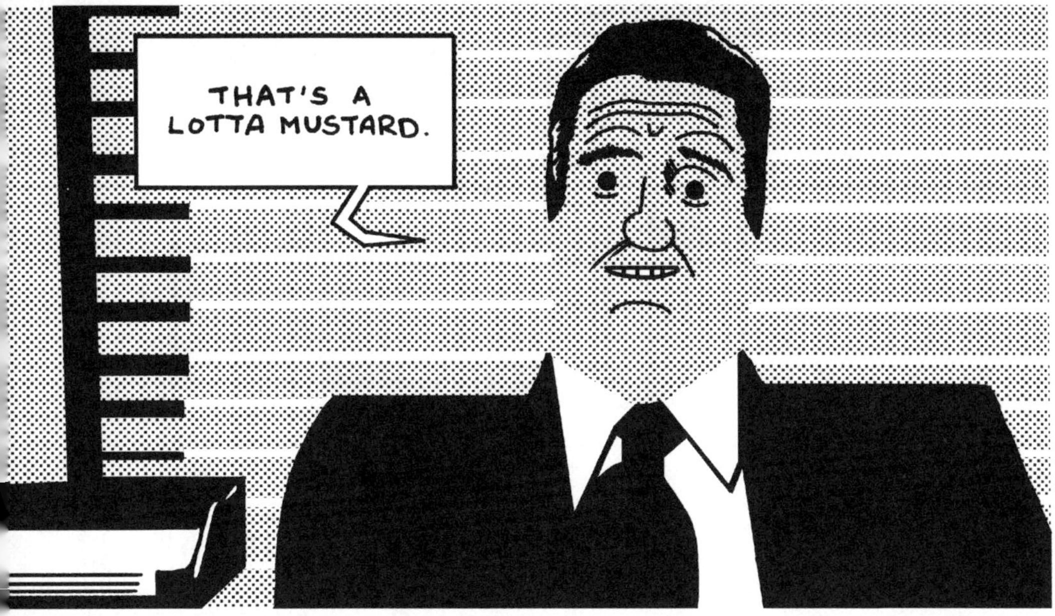
THAT'S A LOTTA MUSTARD.

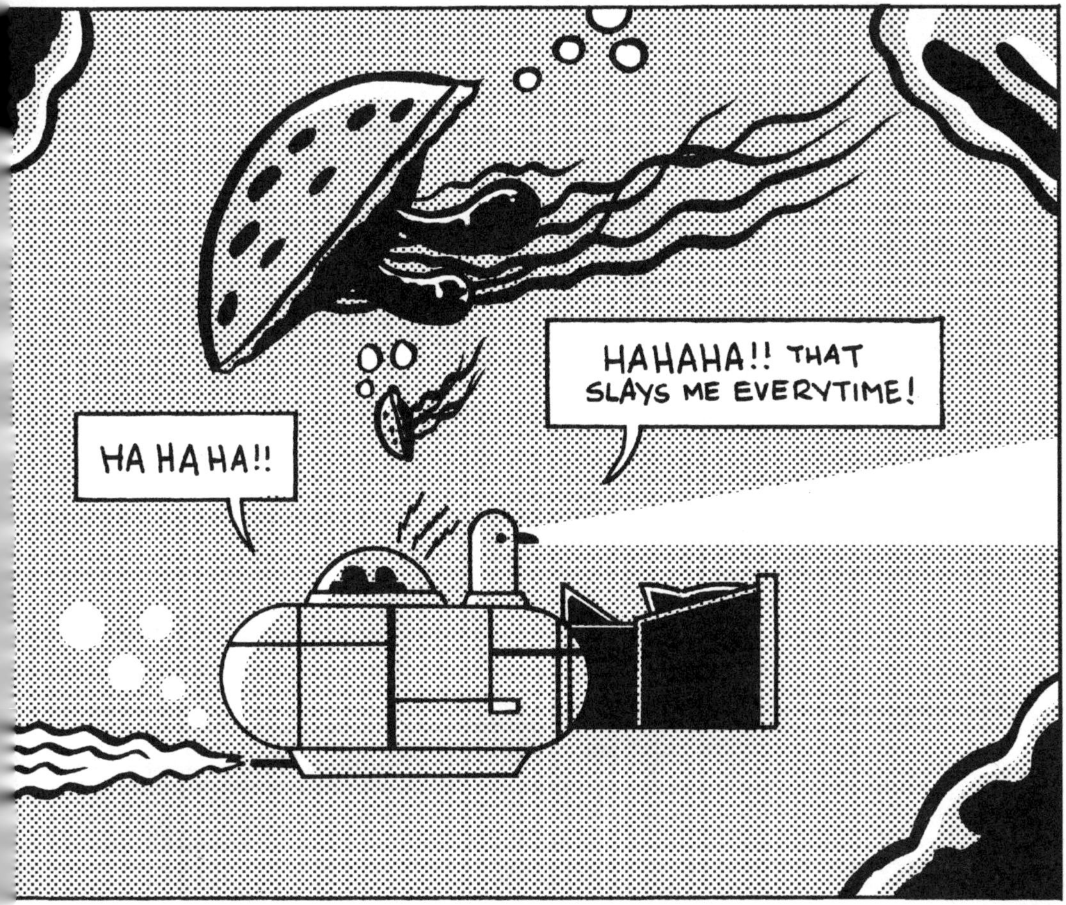
HAHAHA!! THAT SLAYS ME EVERYTIME!
HA HA HA HA!!

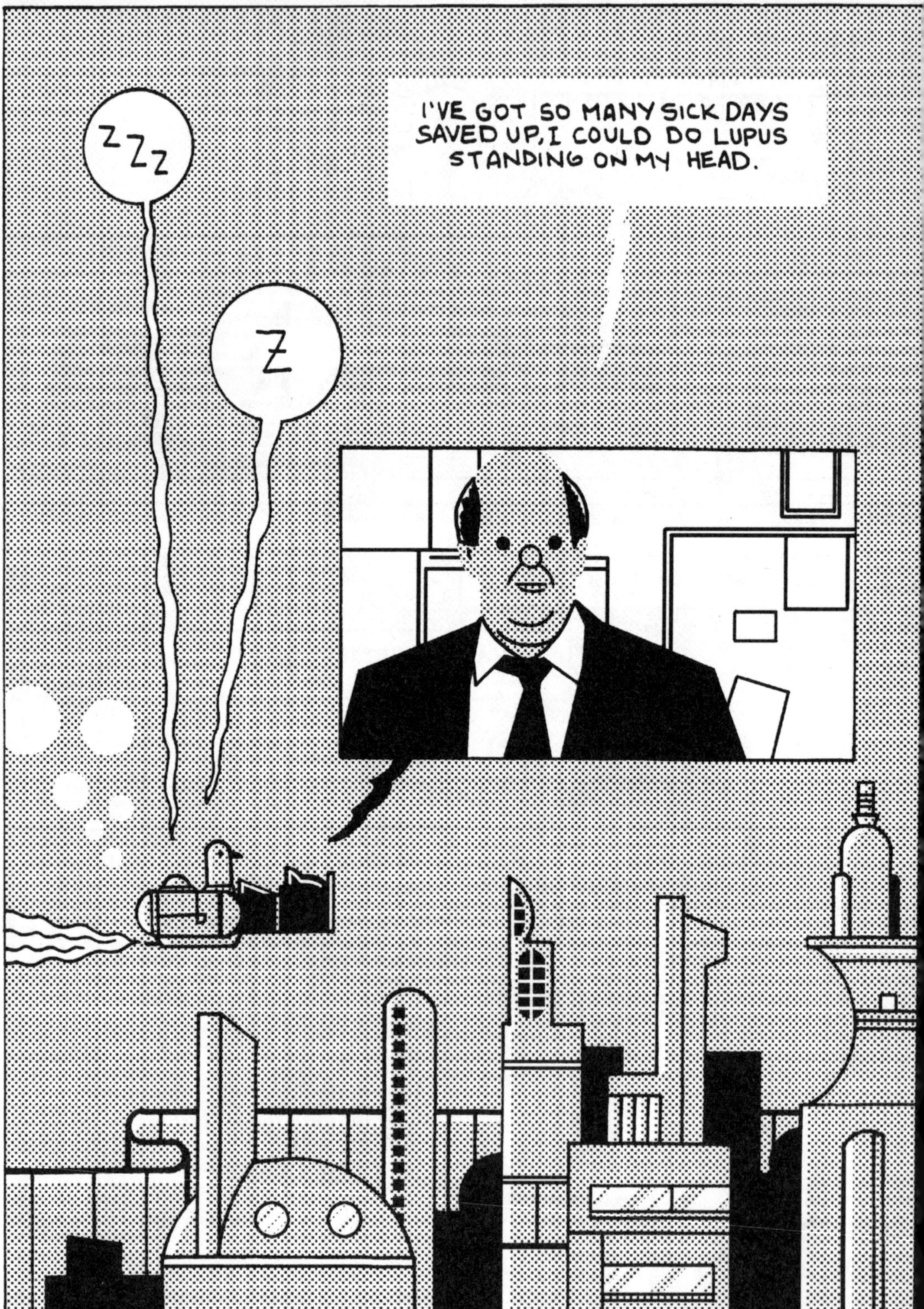
ZZZ
Z
I'VE GOT SO MANY SICK DAYS SAVED UP, I COULD DO LUPUS STANDING ON MY HEAD.

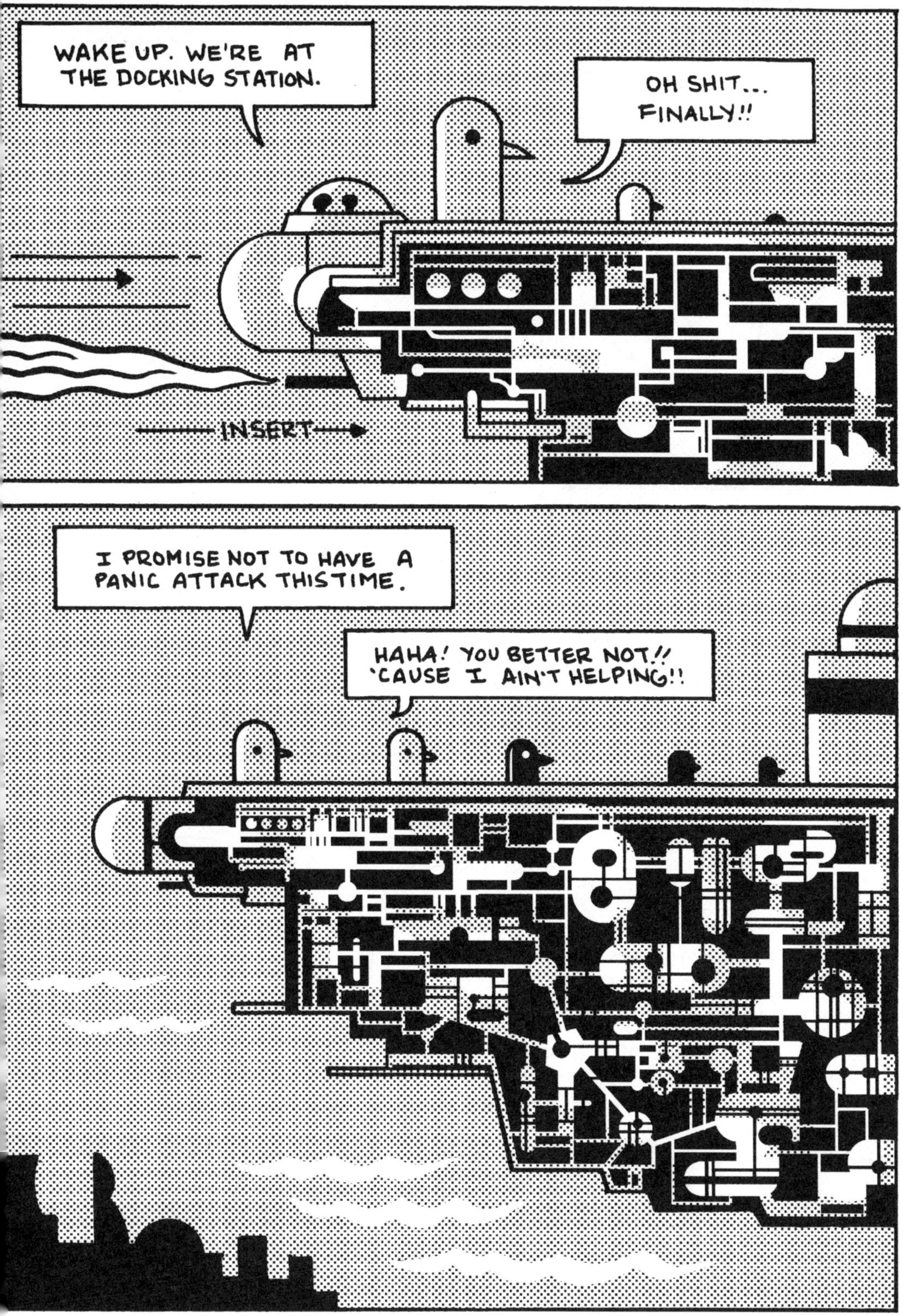
WAKE UP. WE'RE AT THE DOCKING STATION.
OH SHIT... FINALLY!!
INSERT
I PROMISE NOT TO HAVE A PANIC ATTACK THISTIME.
HAHA! YOU BETTER NOT!! 'CAUSE I AIN'T HELPING!!

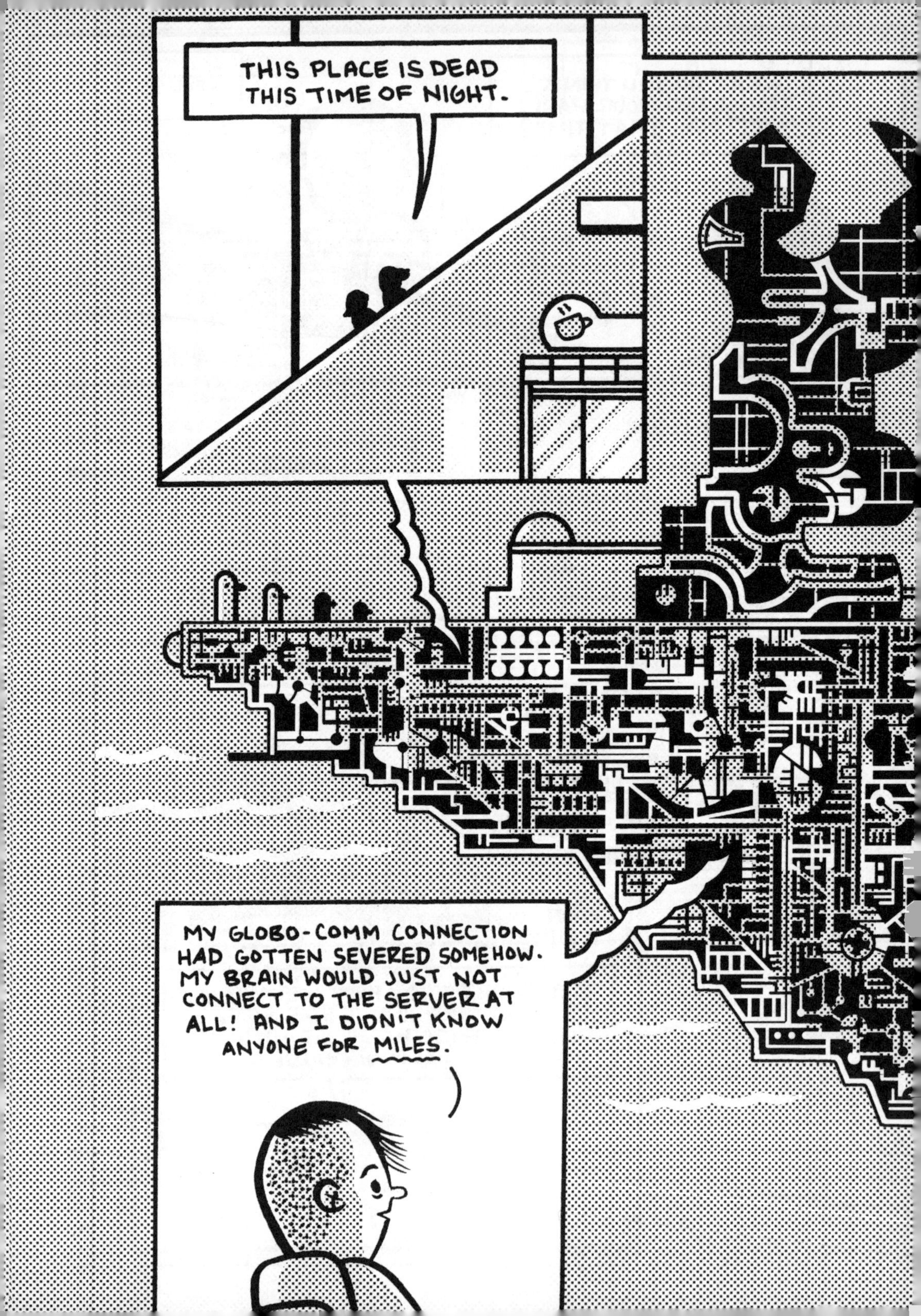
THIS PLACE IS DEAD THIS TIME OF NIGHT.
MY GLOBO-COMM CONNECTION HAD GOTTEN SEVERED SOMEHOW. MY BRAIN WOULD JUST NOT CONNECT TO THE SERVER AT ALL! AND I DIDN'T KNOW ANYONE FOR MILES.

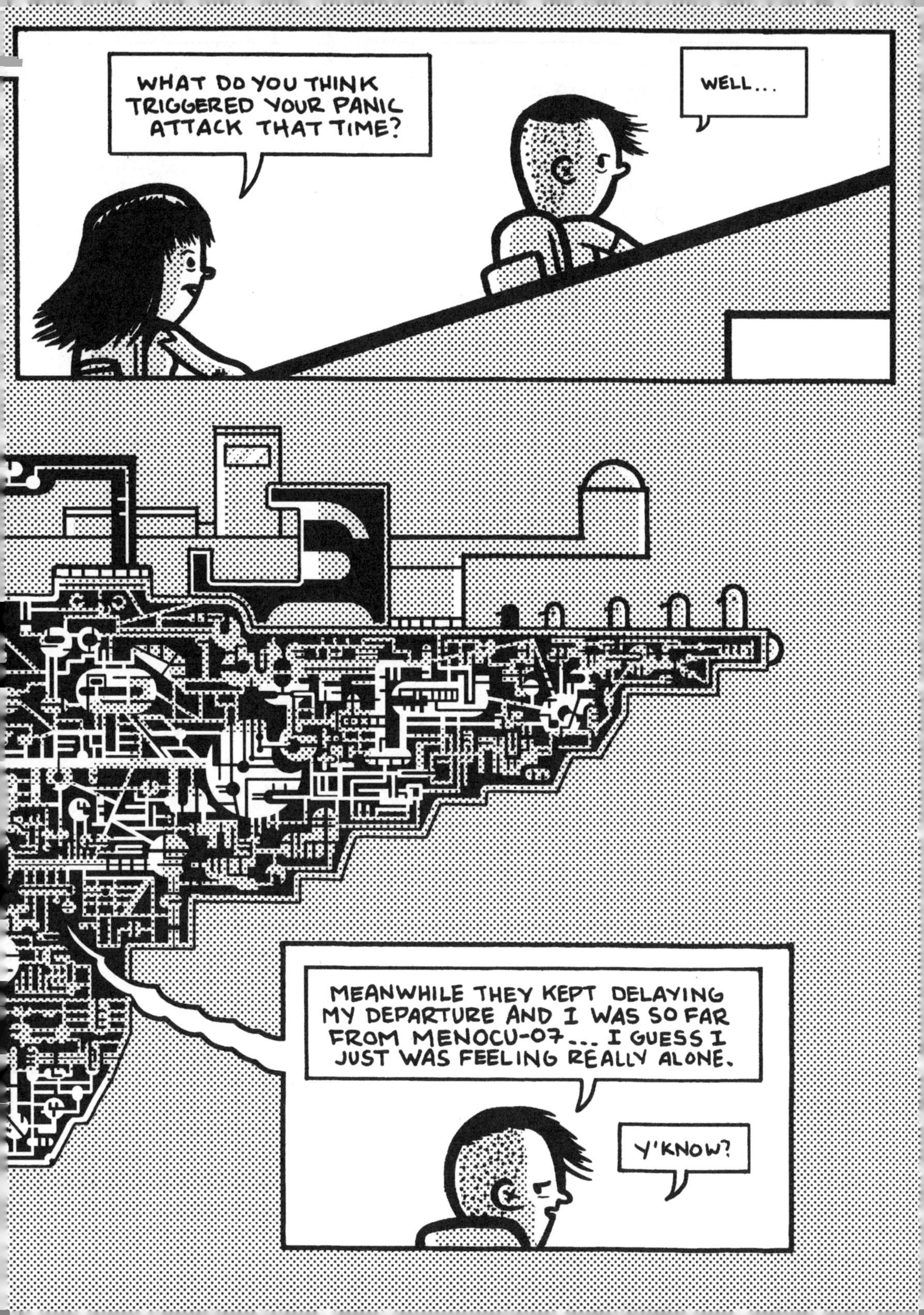
WHAT DO YOU THINK TRIGGERED YOUR PANIC ATTACK THAT TIME?
WELL...
MEANWHILE THEY KEPT DELAYING MY DEPARTURE AND I WAS SO FAR FROM MENOCU-07... I GUESS I JUST WAS FEELING REALLY ALONE.
Y'KNOW?

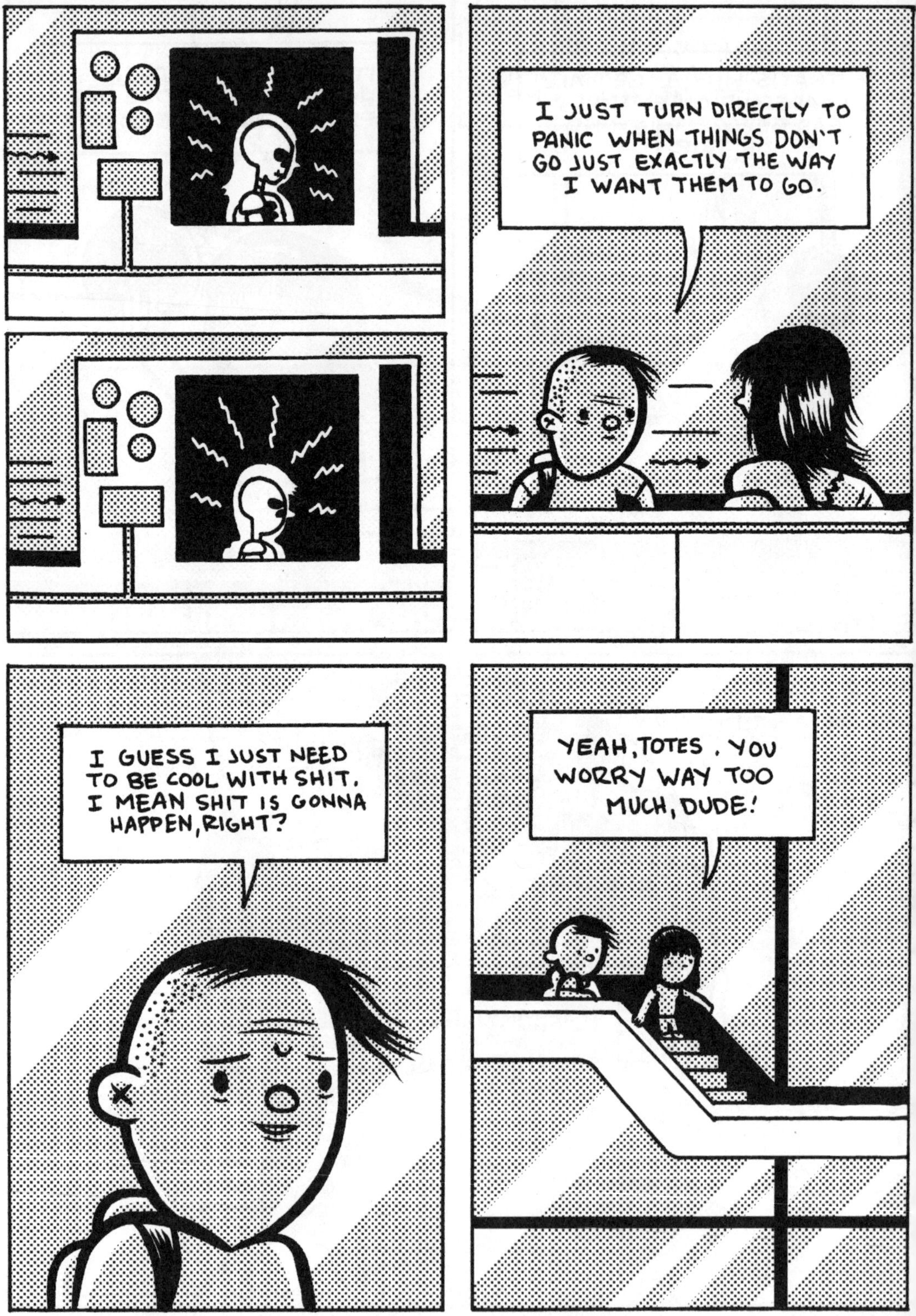
I JUST TURN DIRECTLY TO PANIC WHEN THINGS DON'T GO JUST EXACTLY THE WAY I WANT THEM TO GO.
I GUESS I JUST NEED TO BE COOL WITH SHIT. I MEAN SHIT IS GONNA HAPPEN, RIGHT?
YEAH, TOTES. YOU WORRY WAY TOO MUCH, DUDE!

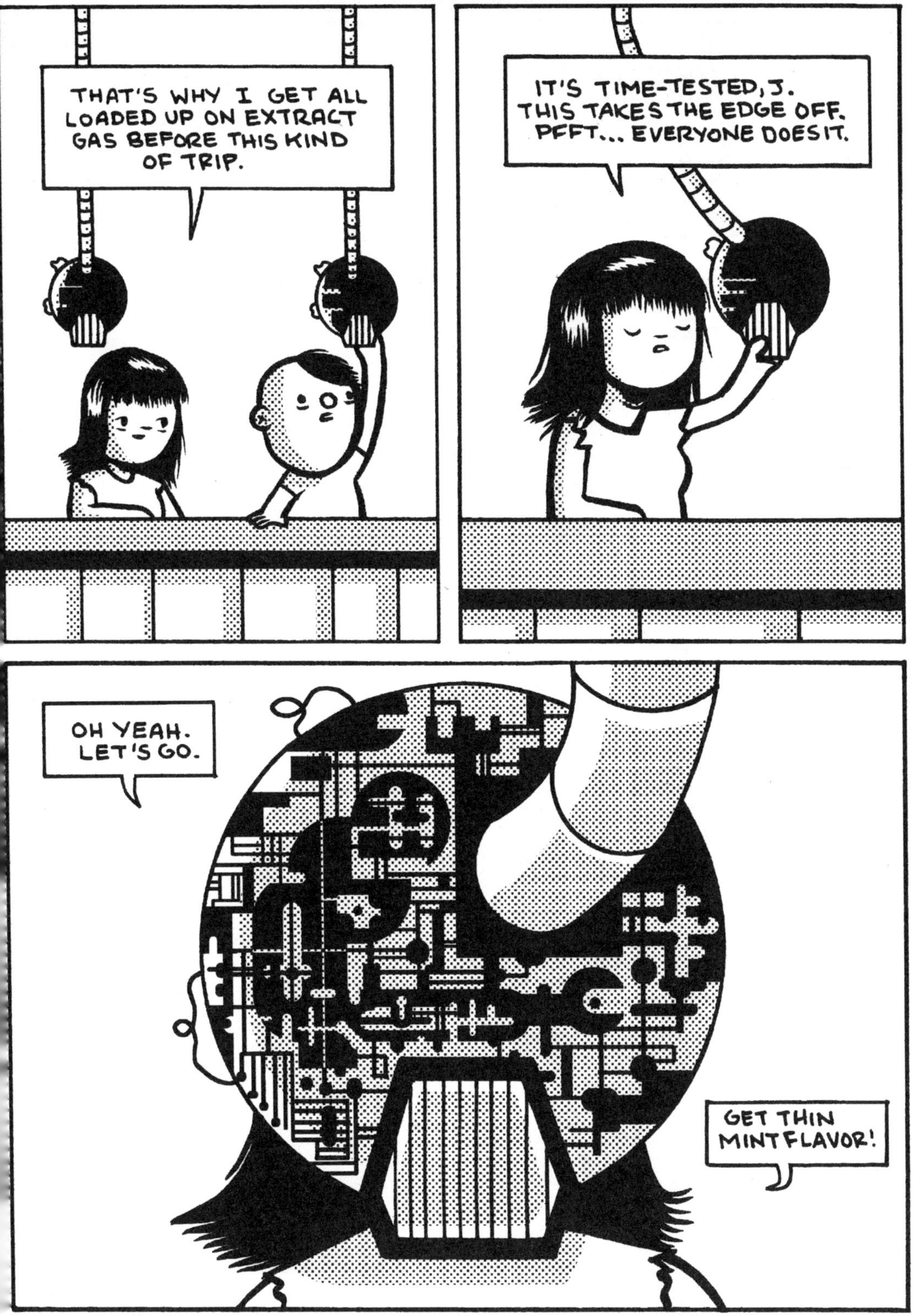
THAT'S WHY I GET ALL LOADED UP ON EXTRACT GAS BEFORE THIS KIND OF TRIP.
IT'S TIME-TESTED, J. THIS TAKES THE EDGE OFF. PFFT... EVERYONE DOES IT.
OH YEAH. LET'S GO.
GET THIN MINT FLAVOR!

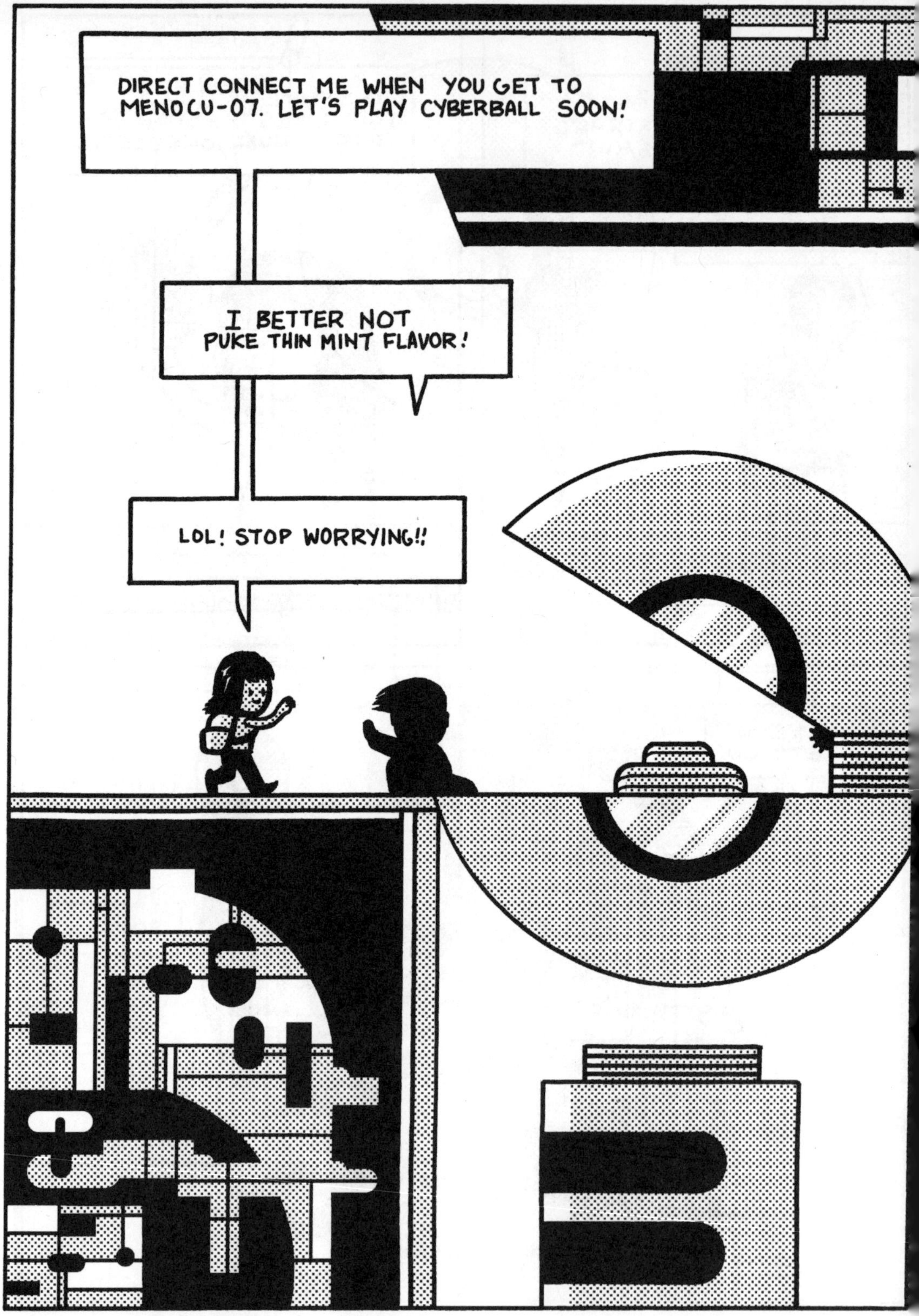
DIRECT CONNECT ME WHEN YOU GET TO MENOCU-07. LET'S PLAY CYBERBALL SOON!
I BETTER NOT PUKE THIN MINT FLAVOR!
LOL! STOP WORRYING!!

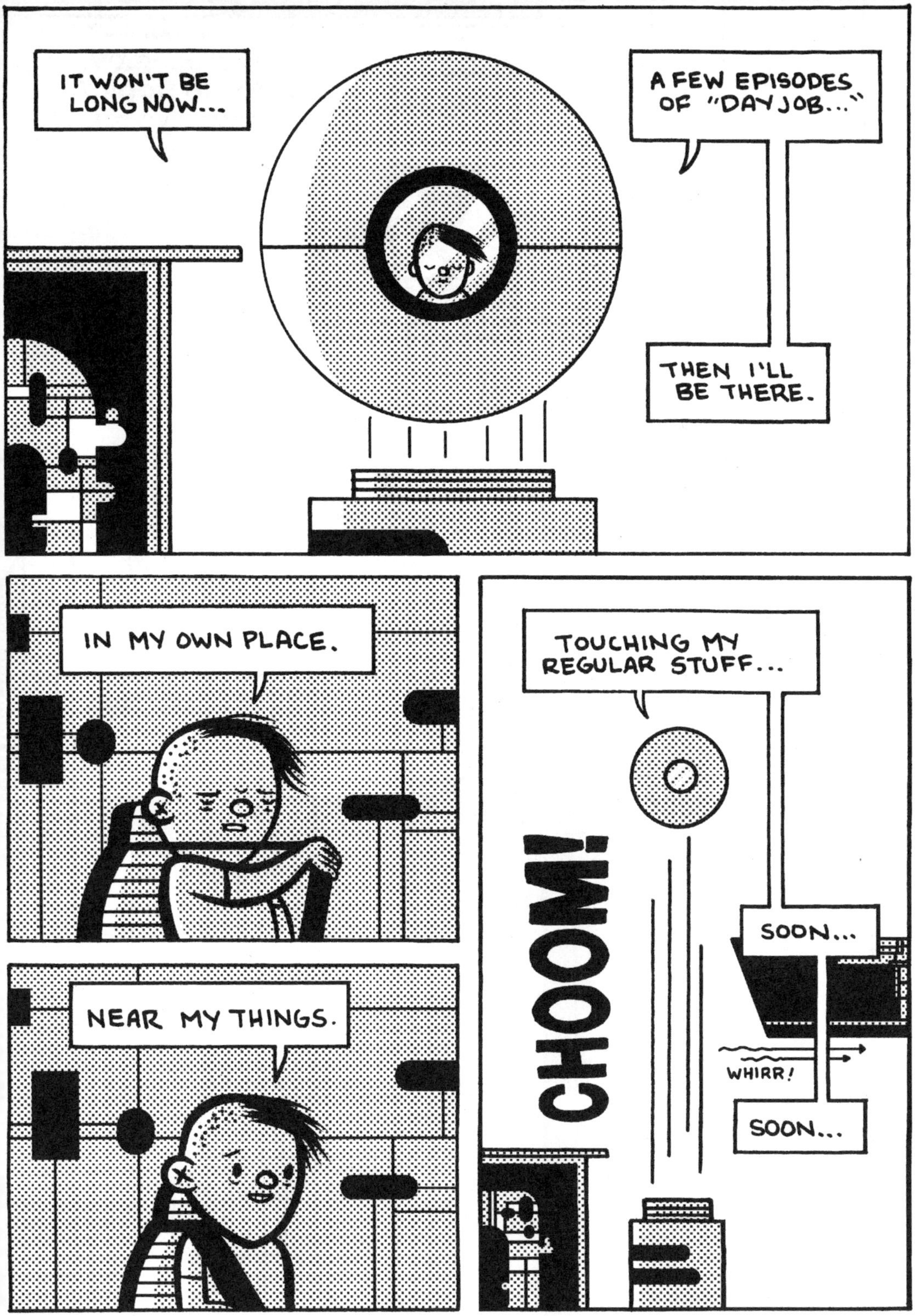
IT WON'T BE LONG NOW...
A FEW EPISODES OF "DAY JOB..."
THEN I'LL BE THERE.
IN MY OWN PLACE.
NEAR MY THINGS.
TOUCHING MY REGULAR STUFF...
CHOOM!
SOON...
WHIRR!
SOON...

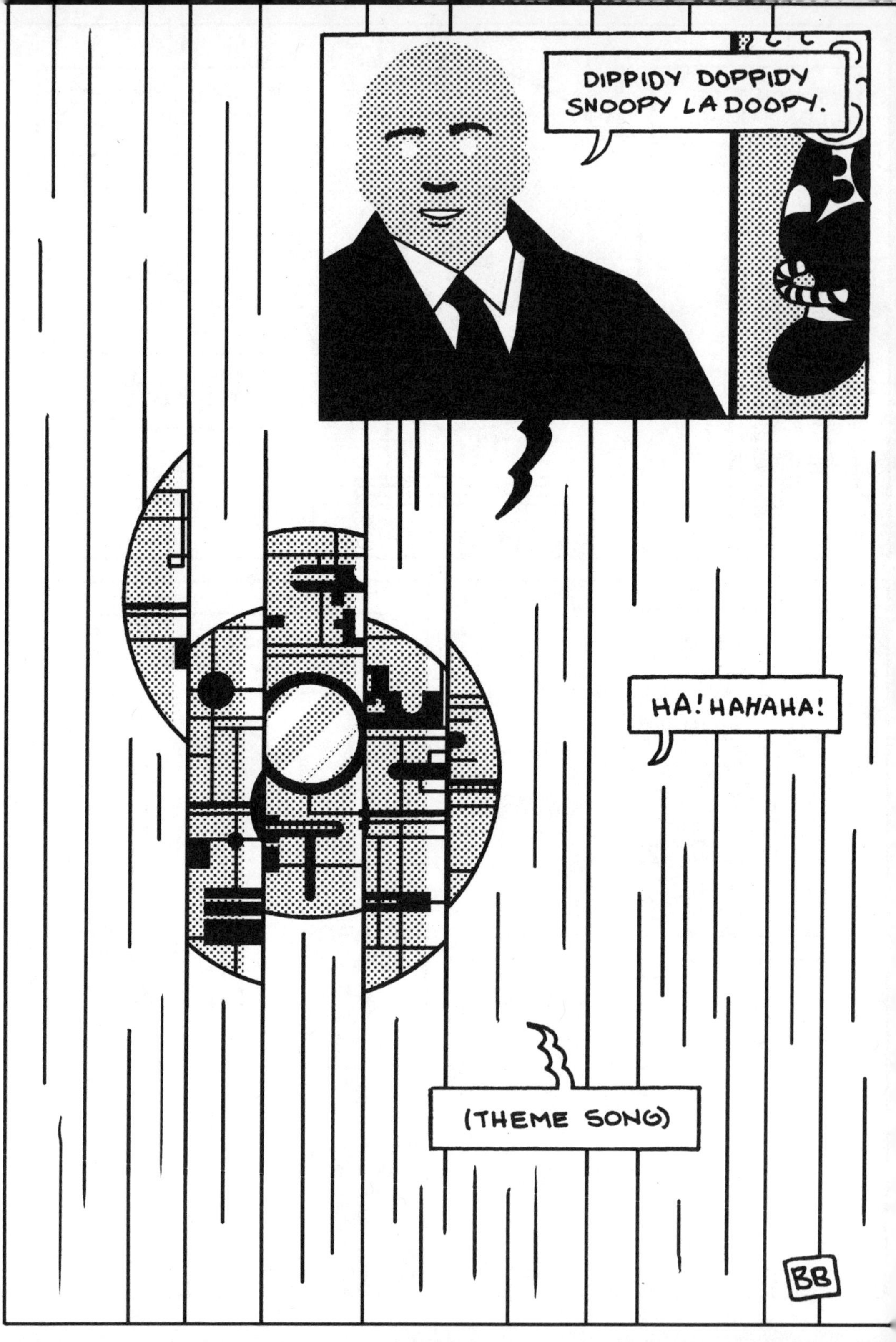
DIPPIDY DOPPIDY SNOOPY LA DOOPY.
HA! HAHAHA!
(THEME SONG)
BB

NEW PHYSICS

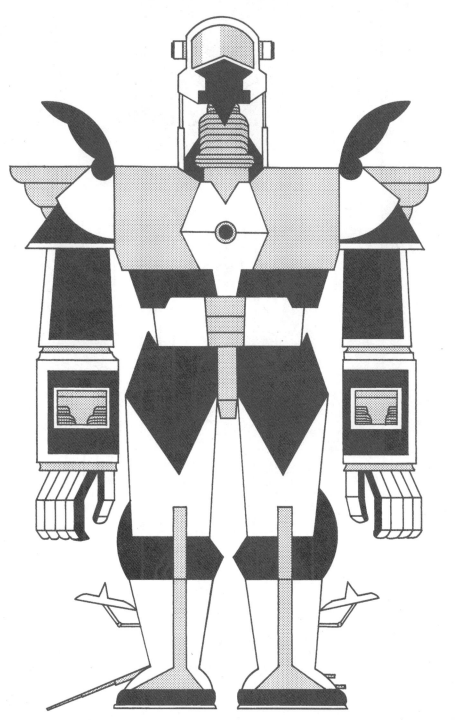

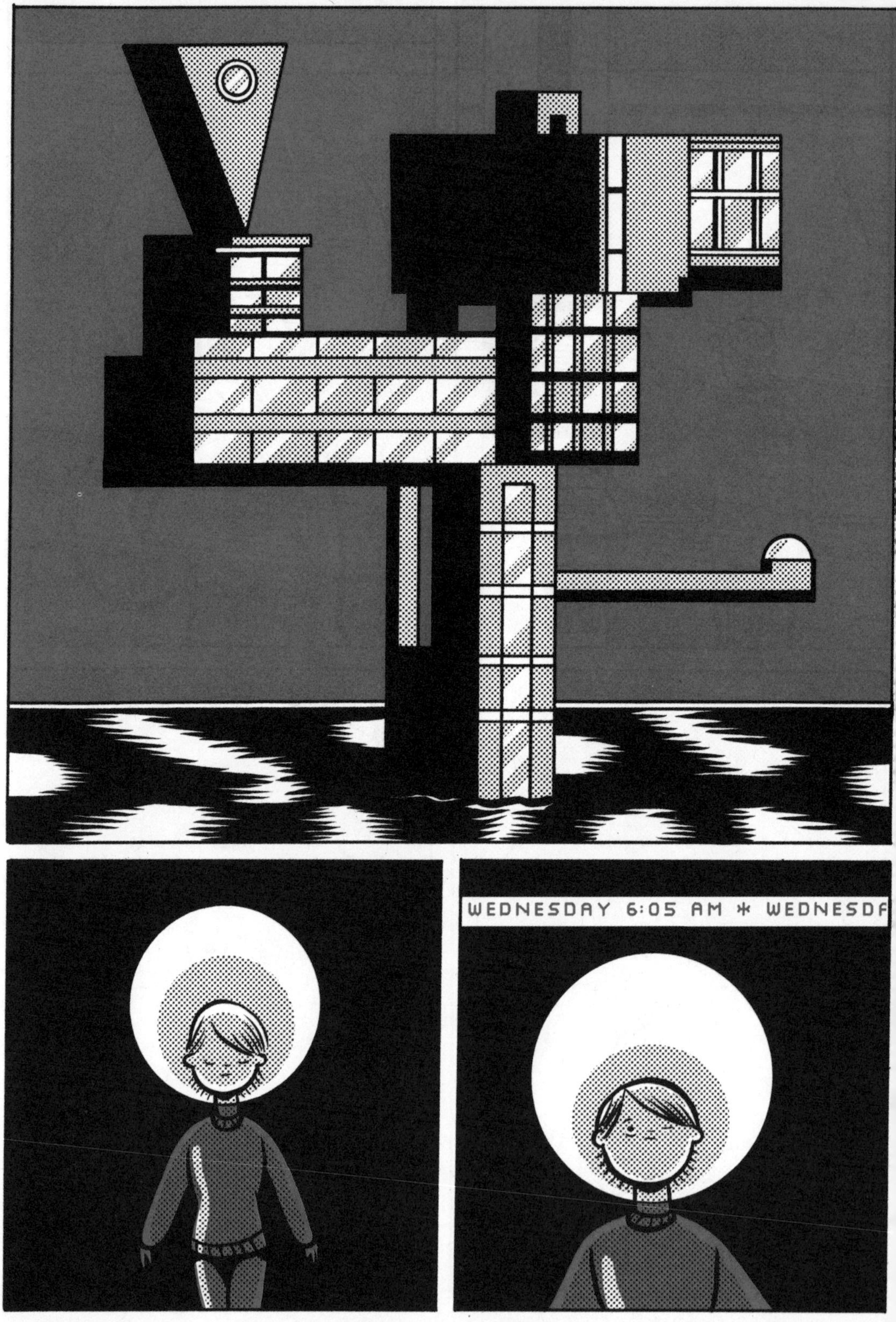
WEDNESDAY 6:05 AM * WEDNESDA

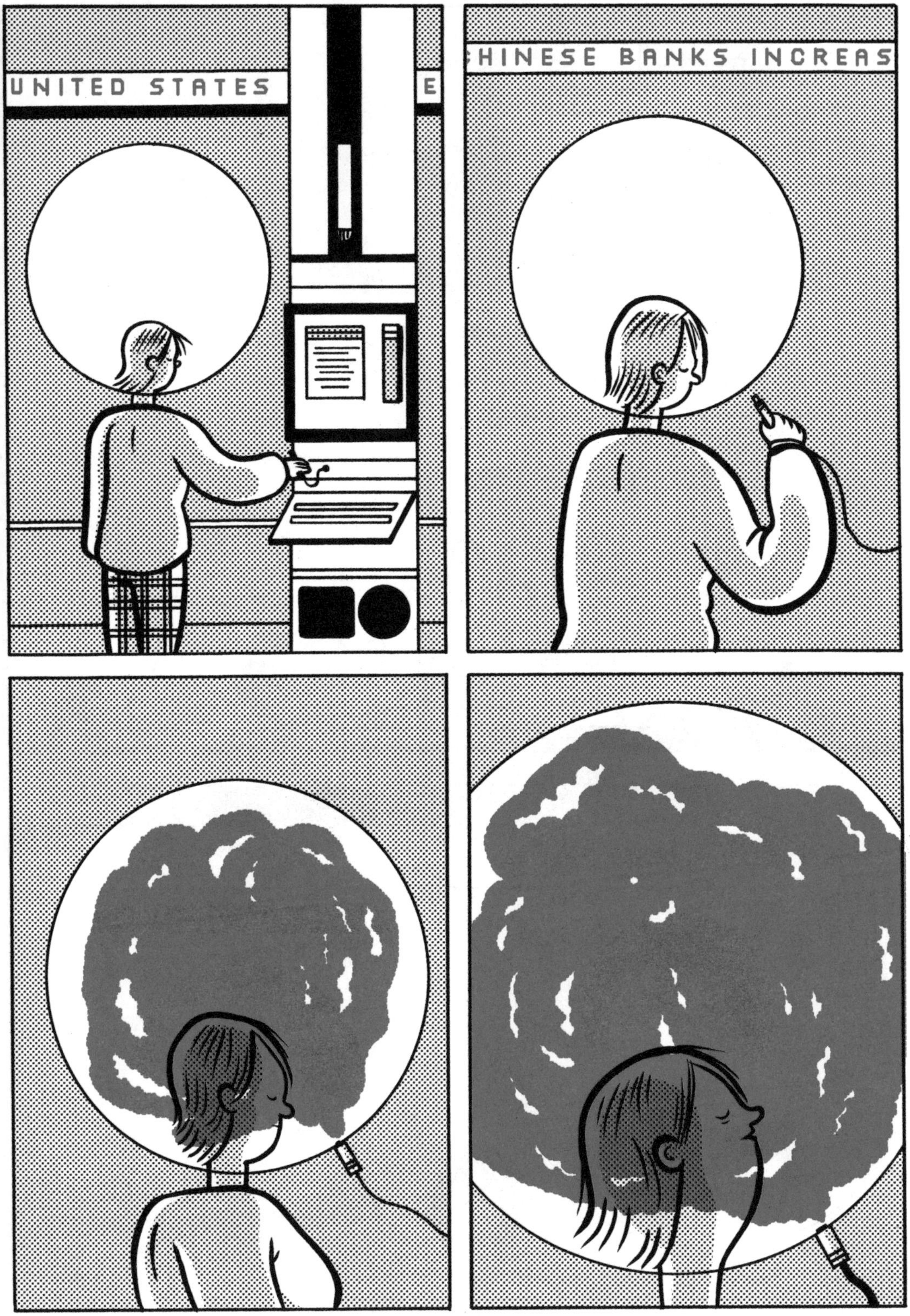
UNITED STATES
E
HINESE BANKS INCREAS

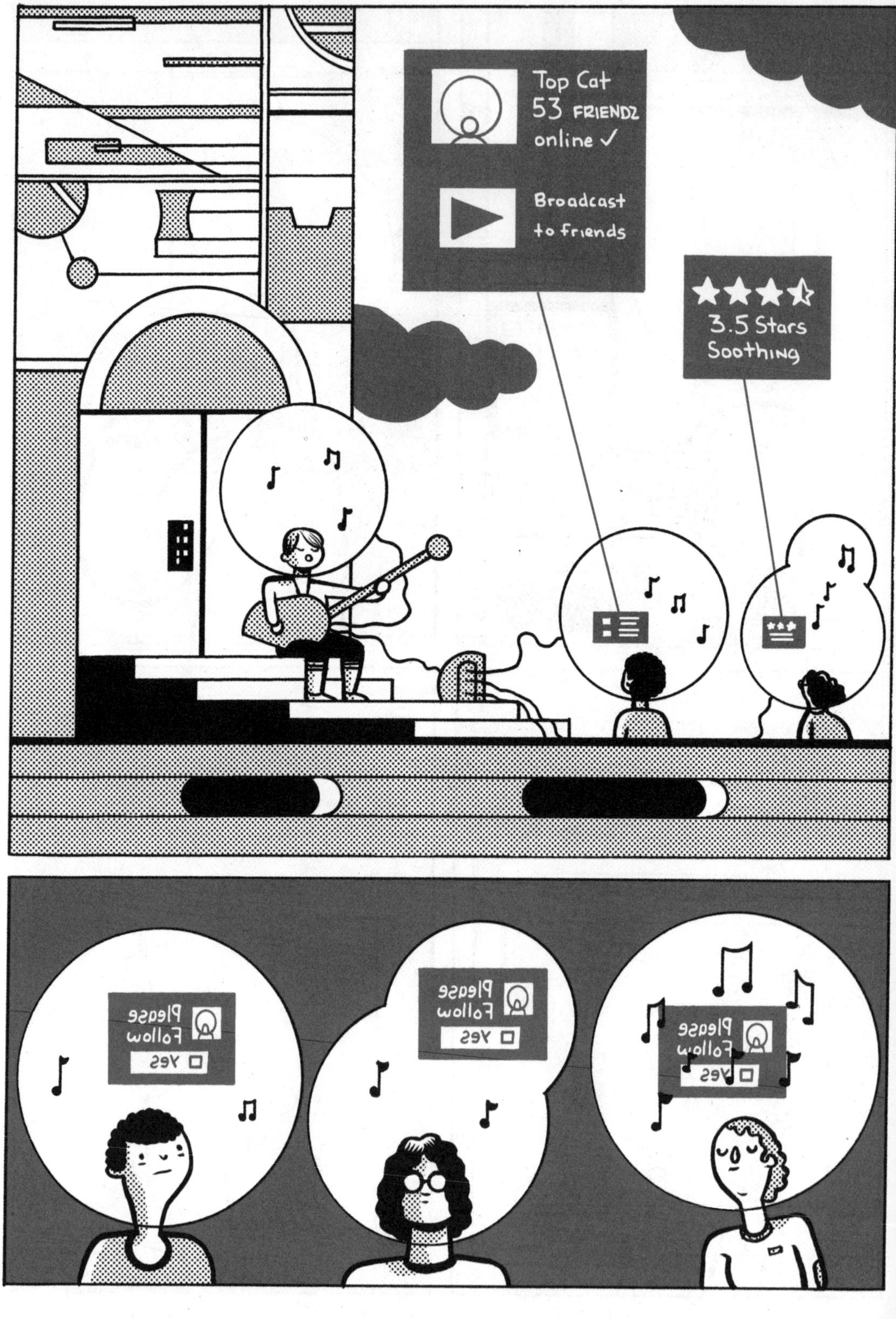
Top Cat
53 FRIENDZ
online ✓
Broadcast to friends
3.5 Stars
Soothing
Please Follow
Yes
Please Follow
Yes
Please Follow
Yes

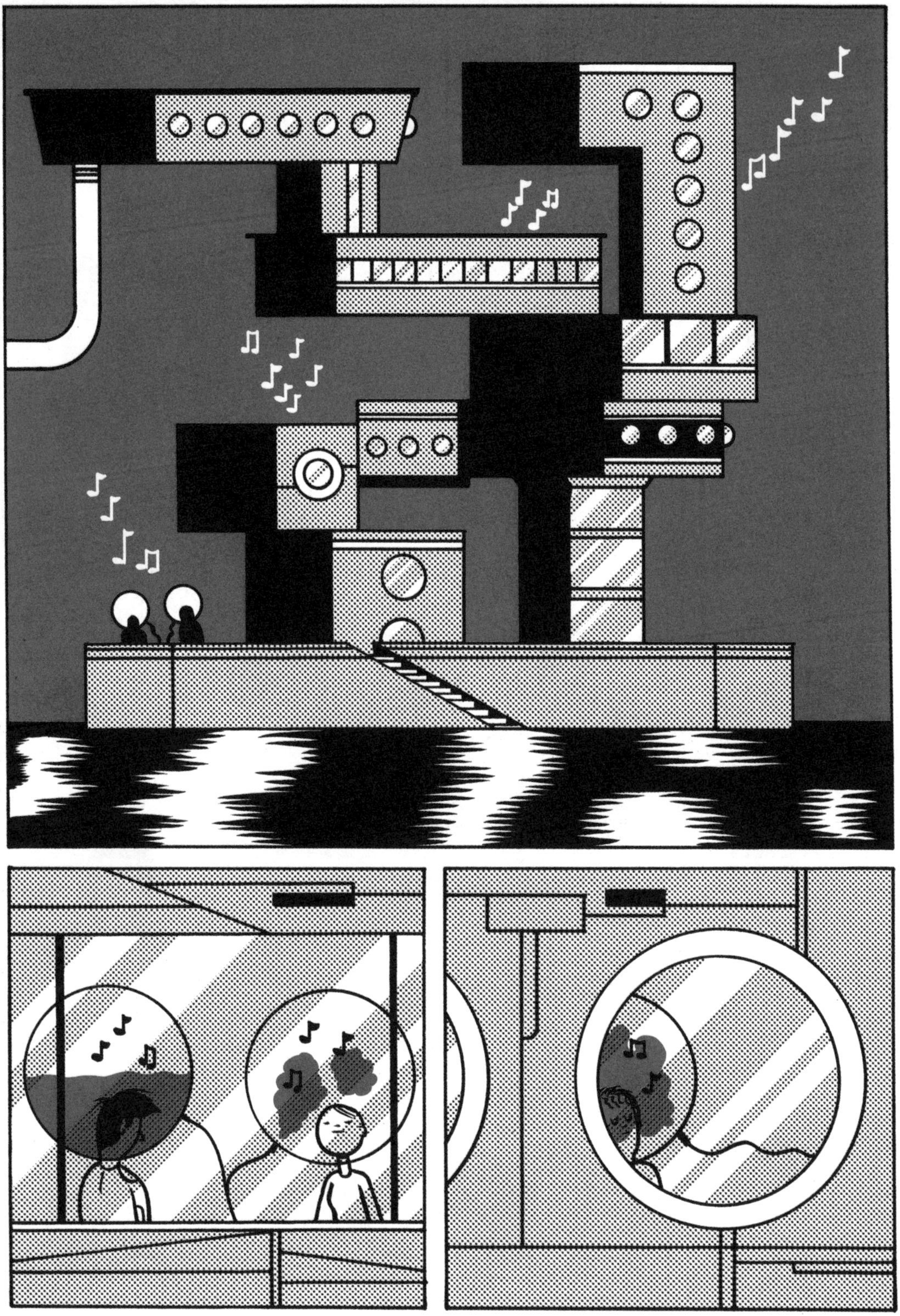

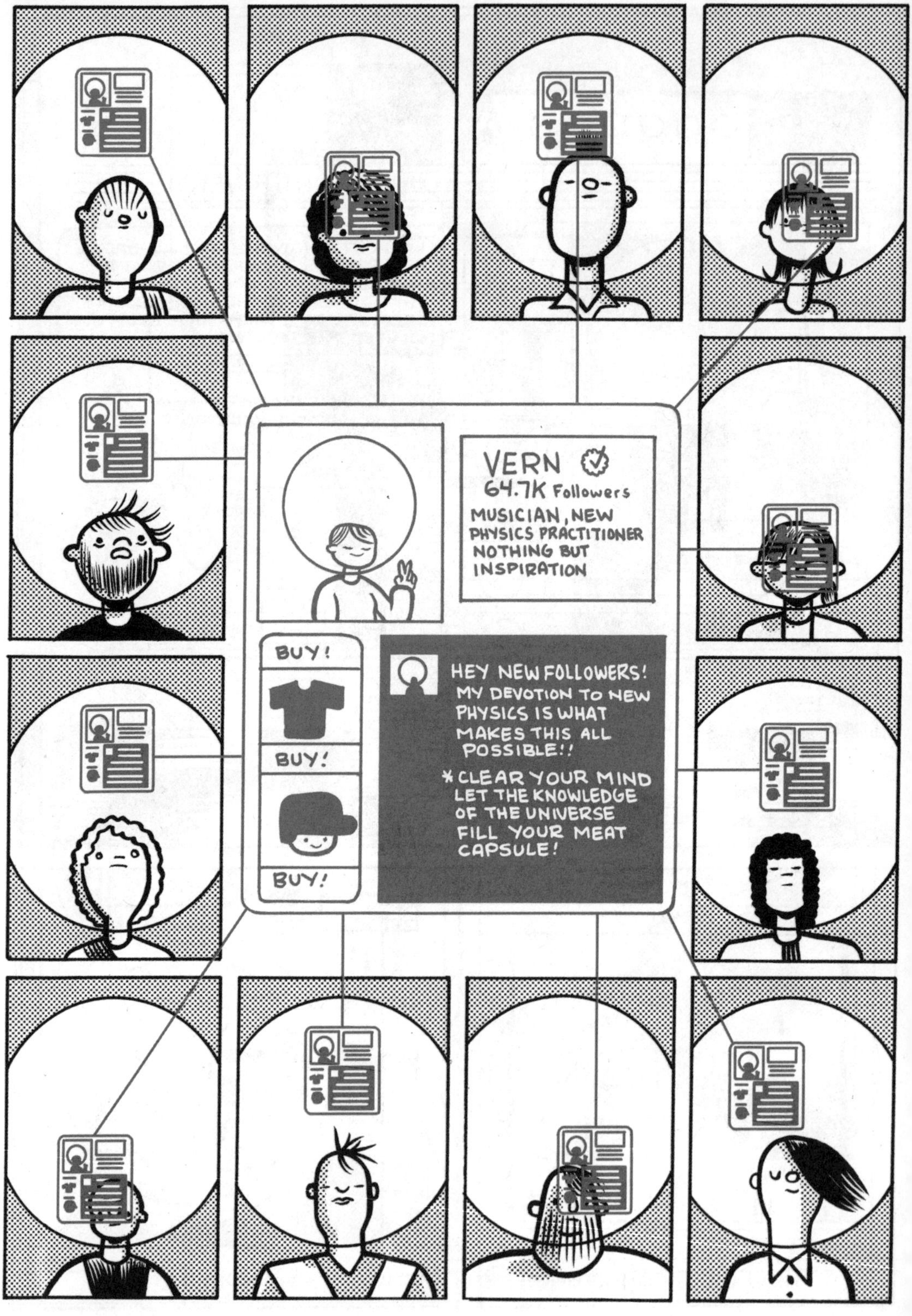

VERN
64.7K Followers
MUSICIAN, NEW PHYSICS PRACTITIONER NOTHING BUT INSPIRATION
BUY!
BUY!
BUY!
HEY NEW FOLLOWERS! MY DEVOTION TO NEW PHYSICS IS WHAT MAKES THIS ALL POSSIBLE!!
* CLEAR YOUR MIND LET THE KNOWLEDGE OF THE UNIVERSE FILL YOUR MEAT CAPSULE!

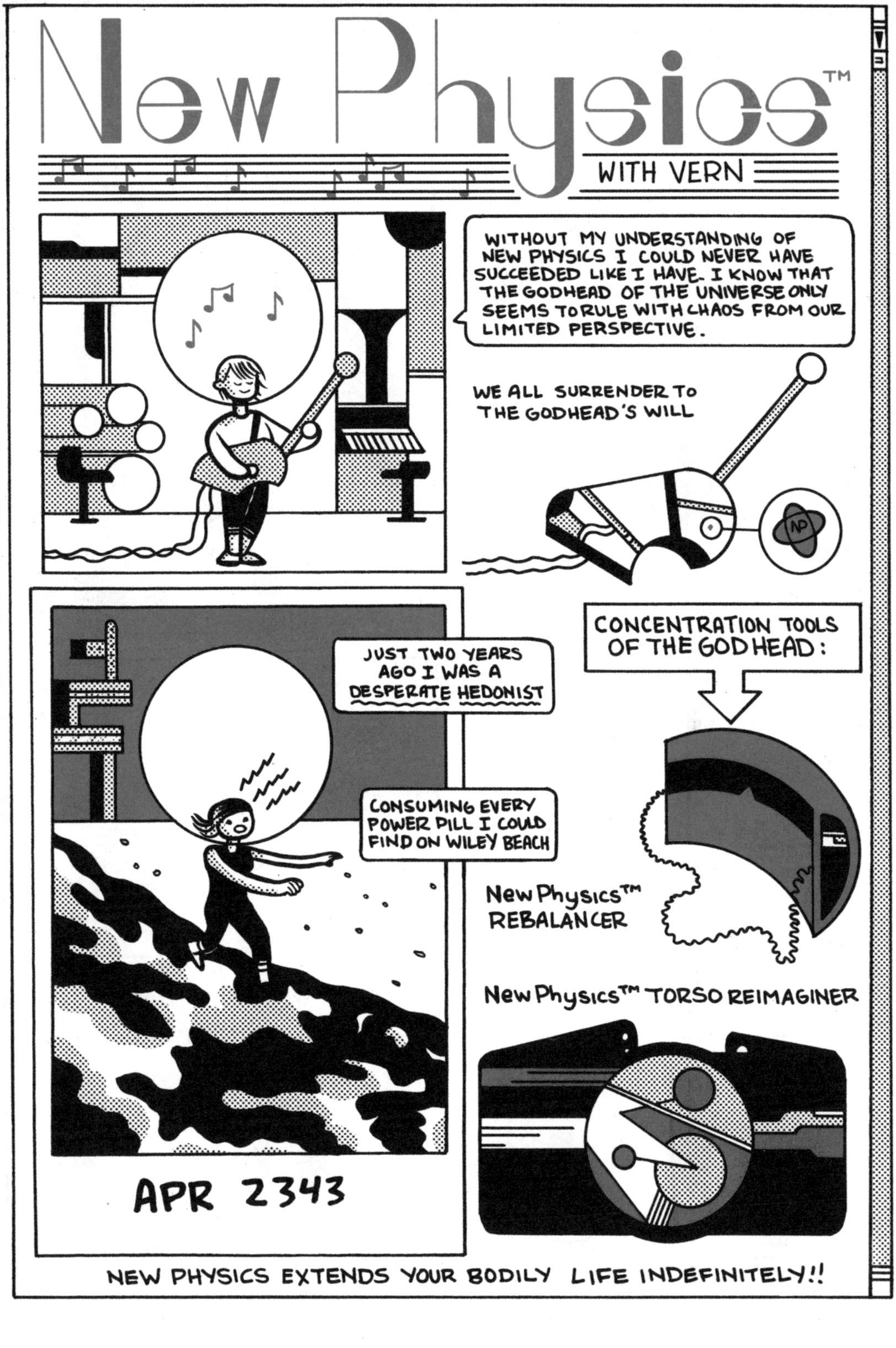

New Physics™
WITH VERN
WITHOUT MY UNDERSTANDING OF NEW PHYSICS I COULD NEVER HAVE SUCCEEDED LIKE I HAVE. I KNOW THAT THE GODHEAD OF THE UNIVERSE ONLY SEEMS TO RULE WITH CHAOS FROM OUR LIMITED PERSPECTIVE.
WE ALL SURRENDER TO THE GODHEAD'S WILL
JUST TWO YEARS AGO I WAS A DESPERATE HEDONIST
CONSUMING EVERY POWER PILL I COULD FIND ON WILEY BEACH
APR 2343
CONCENTRATION TOOLS OF THE GODHEAD:
New Physics™ REBALANCER
New Physics™ TORSO REIMAGINER
NEW PHYSICS EXTENDS YOUR BODILY LIFE INDEFINITELY!!

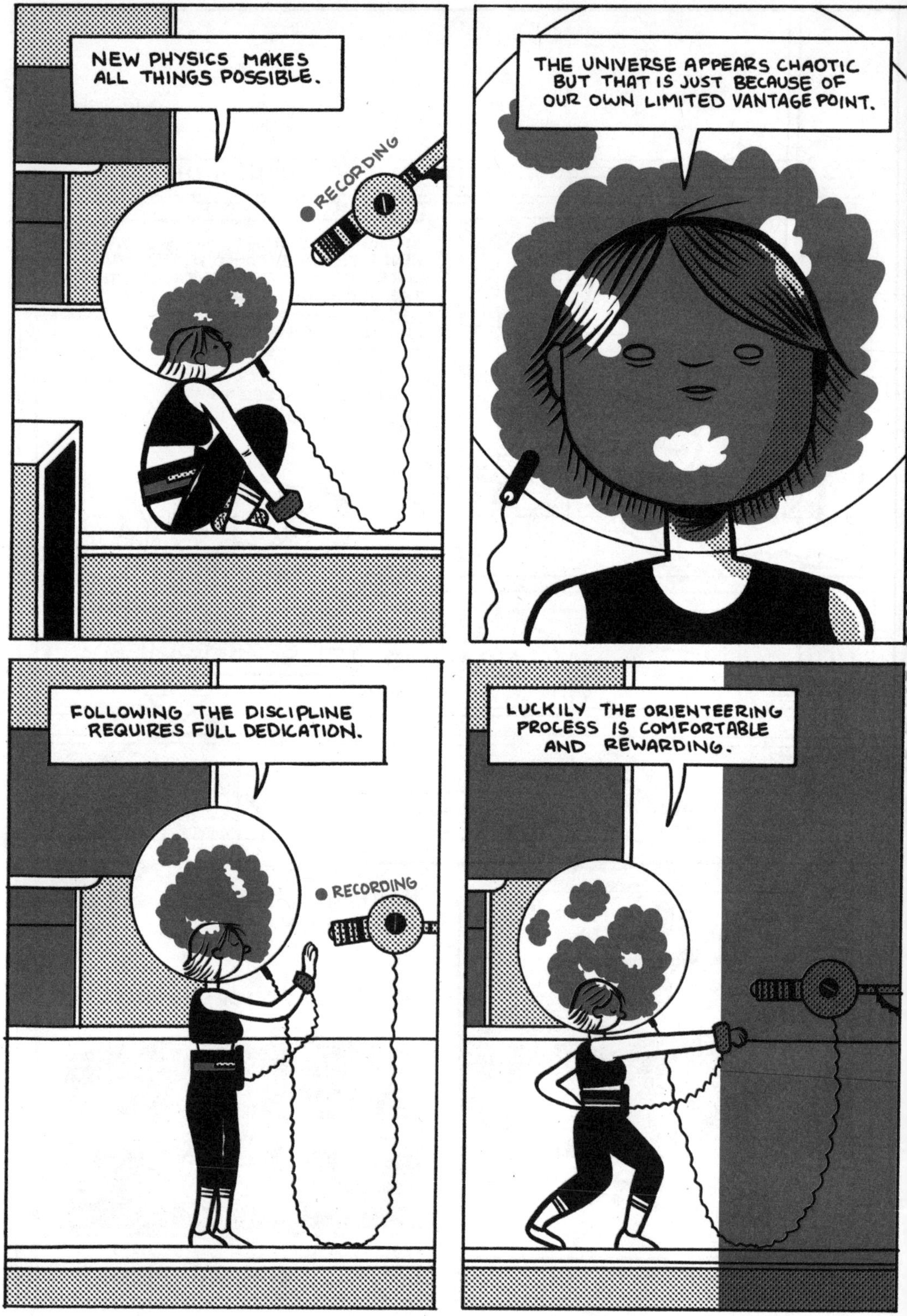
NEW PHYSICS MAKES ALL THINGS POSSIBLE.
RECORDING
THE UNIVERSE APPEARS CHAOTIC BUT THAT IS JUST BECAUSE OF OUR OWN LIMITED VANTAGE POINT.
FOLLOWING THE DISCIPLINE REQUIRES FULL DEDICATION.
RECORDING
LUCKILY THE ORIENTEERING PROCESS IS COMFORTABLE AND REWARDING.

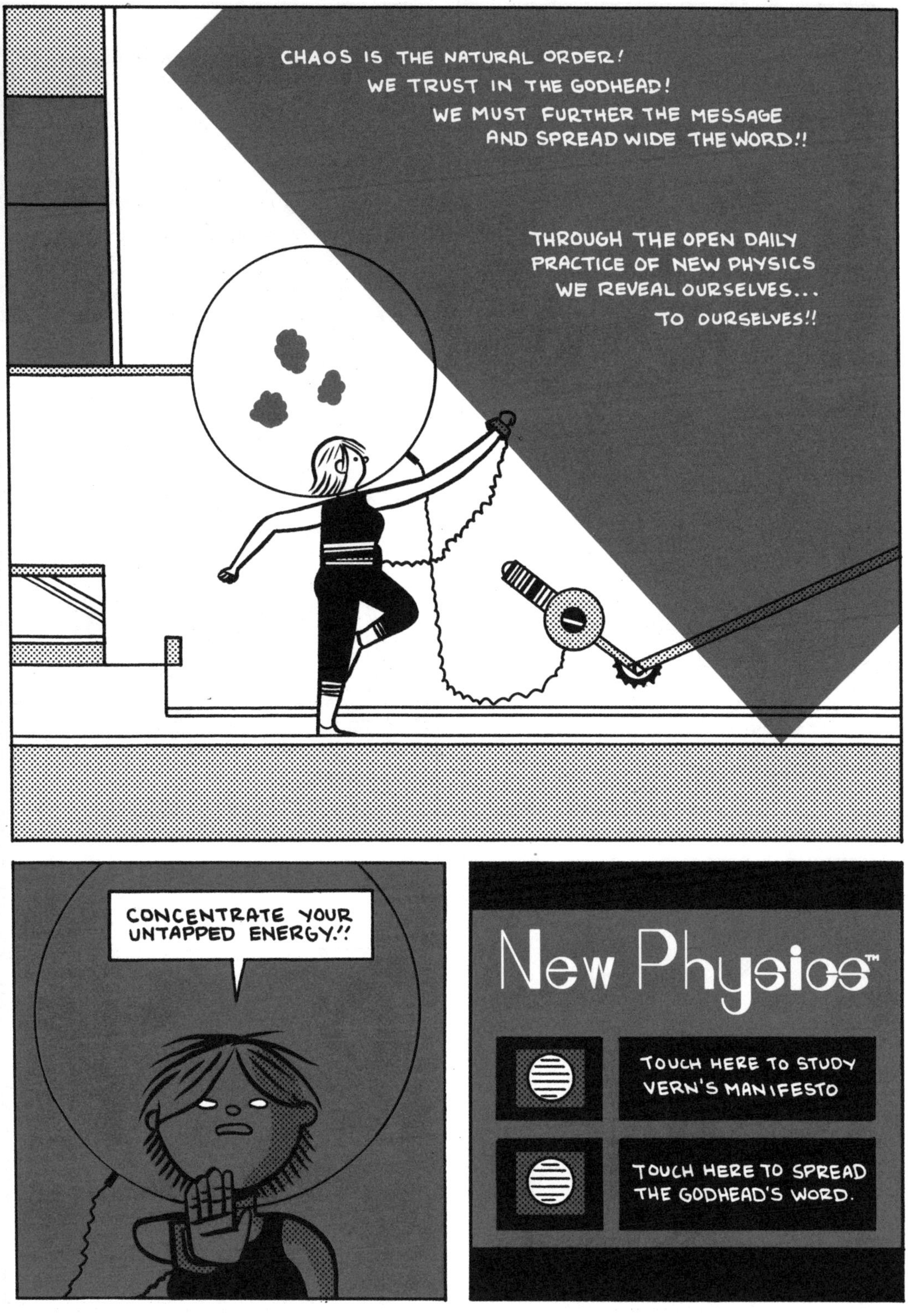

CHAOS IS THE NATURAL ORDER!
WE TRUST IN THE GODHEAD!
WE MUST FURTHER THE MESSAGE AND SPREAD WIDE THE WORD!!
THROUGH THE OPEN DAILY PRACTICE OF NEW PHYSICS WE REVEAL OURSELVES... TO OURSELVES!!
CONCENTRATE YOUR UNTAPPED ENERGY!!
New Physics™
TOUCH HERE TO STUDY VERN'S MANIFESTO
TOUCH HERE TO SPREAD THE GODHEAD'S WORD.

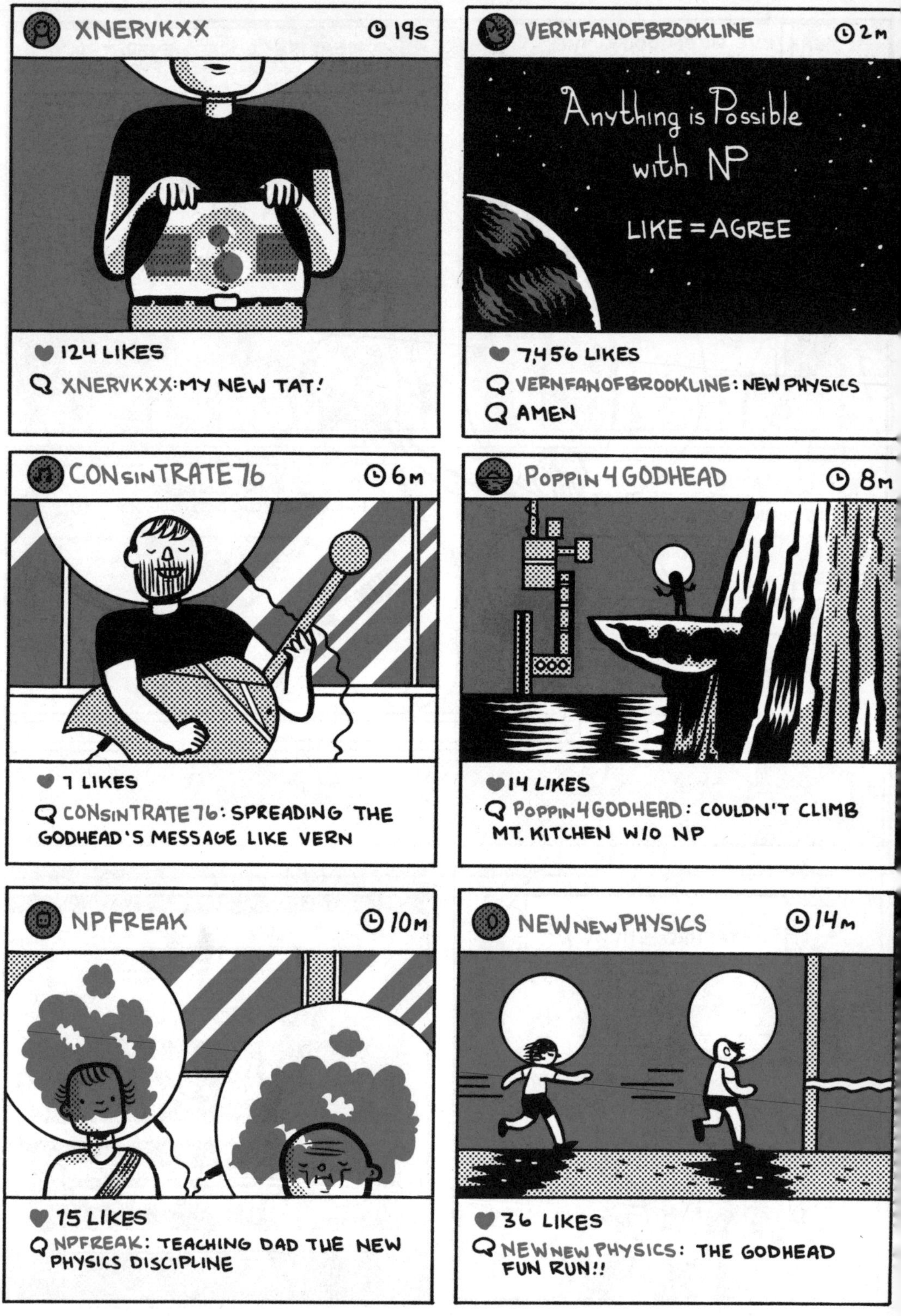
XNERVKXX
19S
124 LIKES
XNERVKXX: MY NEW TAT!
VERNFANOFBROOKLINE
2M
Anything is Possible with NP
LIKE = AGREE
7,456 LIKES
VERNFANOFBROOKLINE: NEW PHYSICS
AMEN
CONsinTRATE76
6M
7 LIKES
CONsinTRATE76: SPREADING THE GODHEAD'S MESSAGE LIKE VERN
Poppin4GODHEAD
8M
14 LIKES
Poppin4GODHEAD: COULDN'T CLIMB MT. KITCHEN W/O NP
NPFREAK
10M
15 LIKES
NPFREAK: TEACHING DAD THE NEW PHYSICS DISCIPLINE
NEWnewPHYSICS
14M
36 LIKES
NEWnewPHYSICS: THE GODHEAD FUN RUN!!

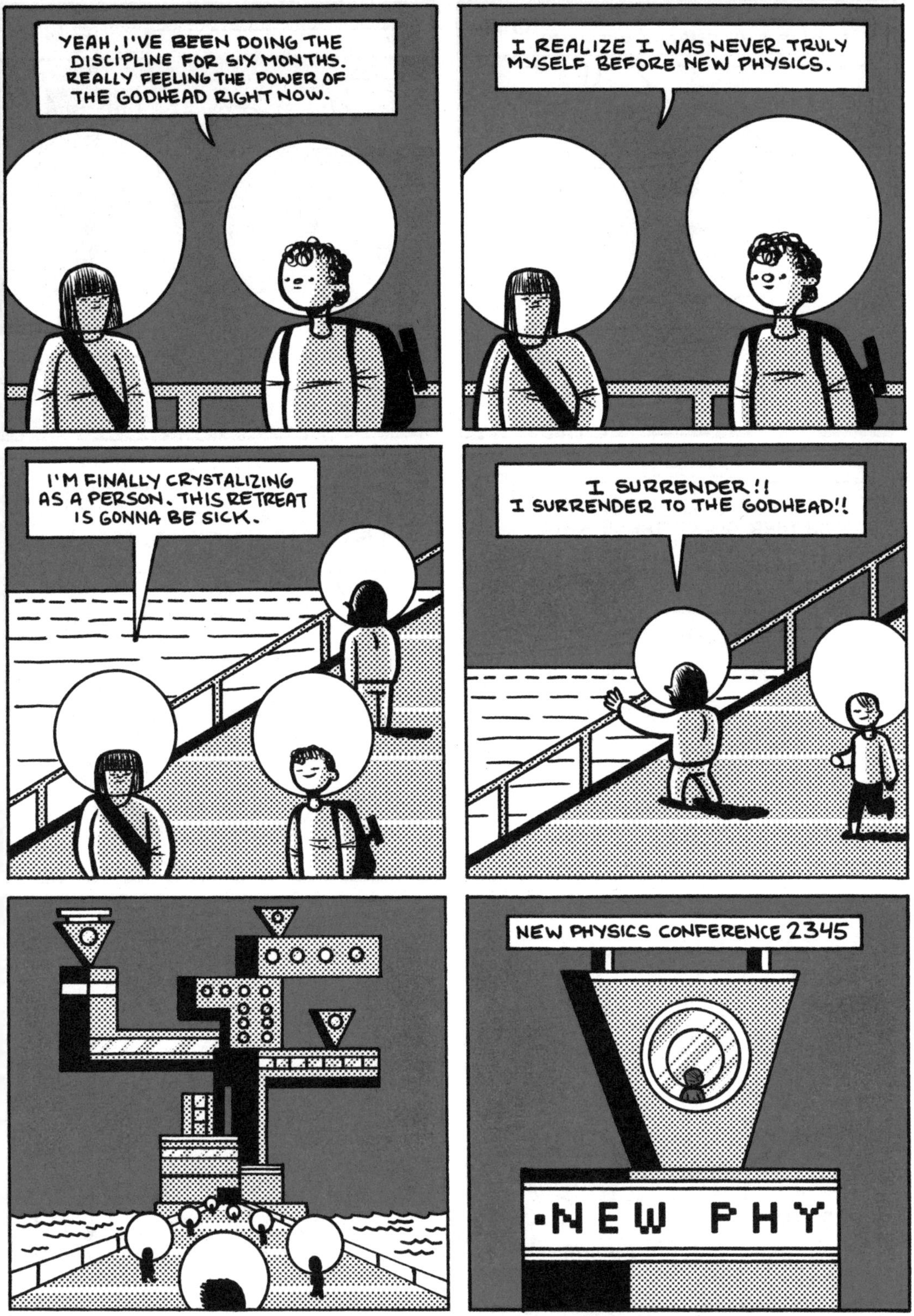
YEAH, I'VE BEEN DOING THE DISCIPLINE FOR SIX MONTHS. REALLY FEELING THE POWER OF THE GODHEAD RIGHT NOW.
I REALIZE I WAS NEVER TRULY MYSELF BEFORE NEW PHYSICS.
I'M FINALLY CRYSTALIZING AS A PERSON. THIS RETREAT IS GONNA BE SICK.
I SURRENDER!! I SURRENDER TO THE GODHEAD!!
NEW PHYSICS CONFERENCE 2345
•NEW PHY

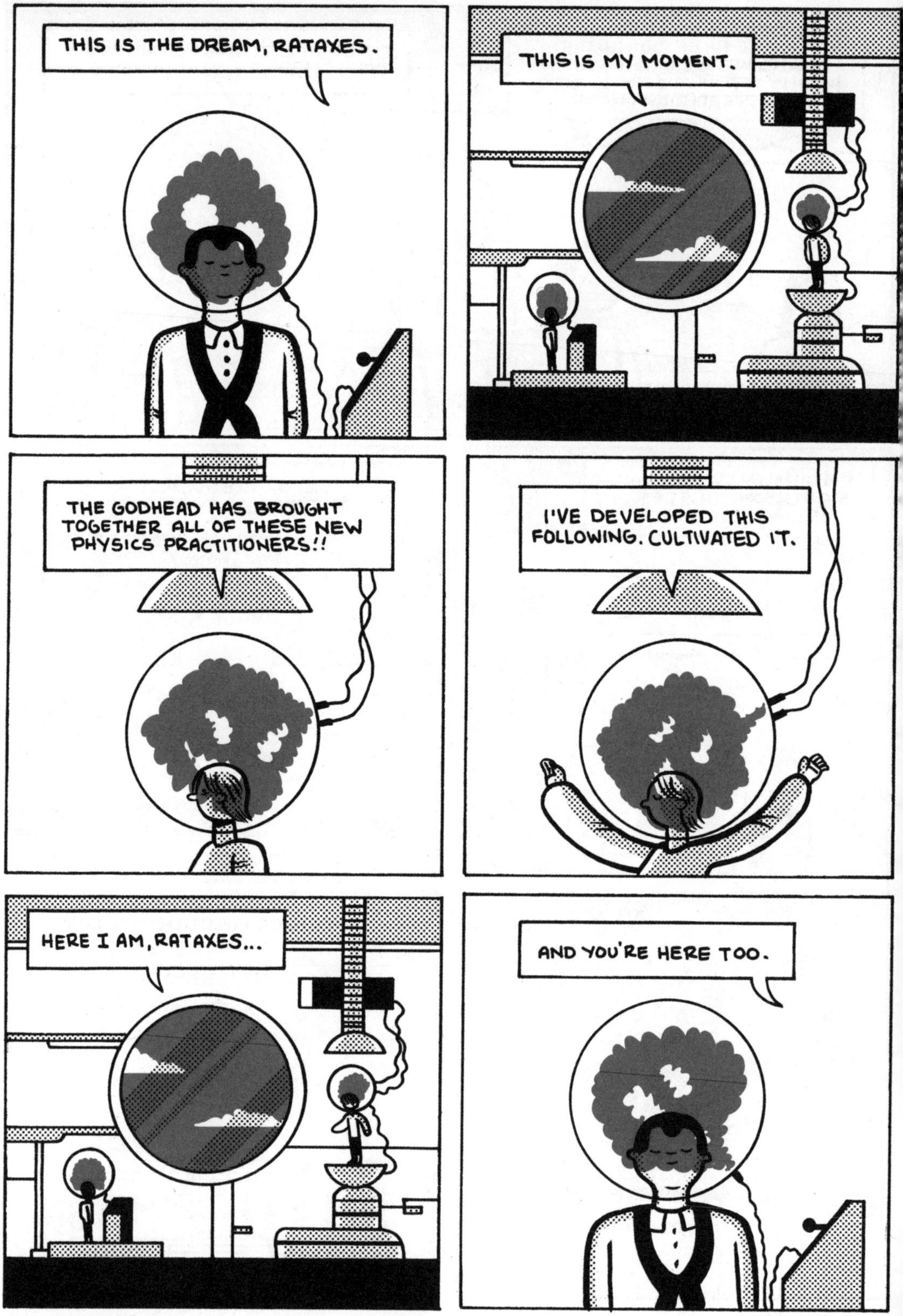
THIS IS THE DREAM, RATAXES.
THIS IS MY MOMENT.
THE GODHEAD HAS BROUGHT TOGETHER ALL OF THESE NEW PHYSICS PRACTITIONERS!!
I'VE DEVELOPED THIS FOLLOWING. CULTIVATED IT.
HERE I AM, RATAXES...
AND YOU'RE HERE TOO.

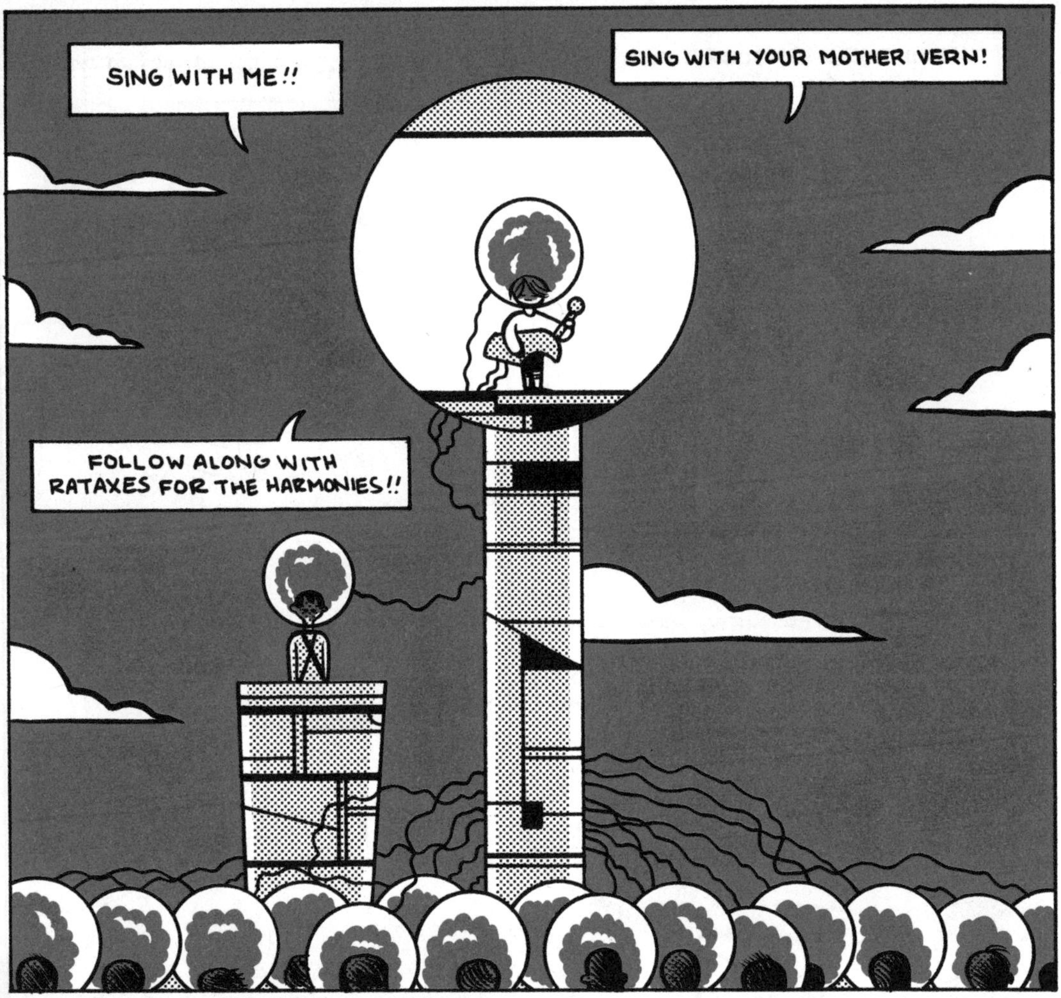
SING WITH ME!!
SING WITH YOUR MOTHER VERN!
FOLLOW ALONG WITH RATAXES FOR THE HARMONIES!!

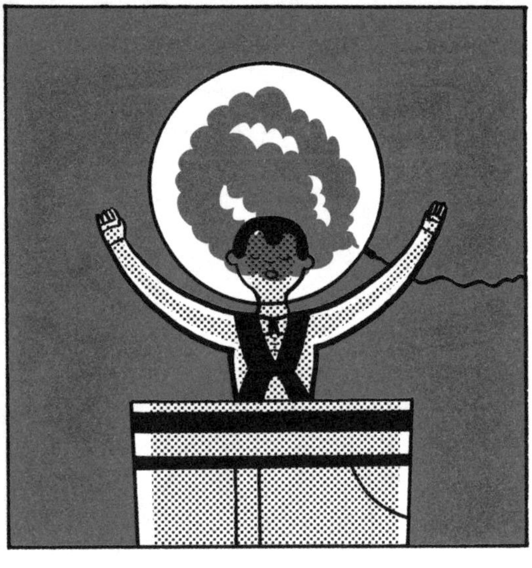

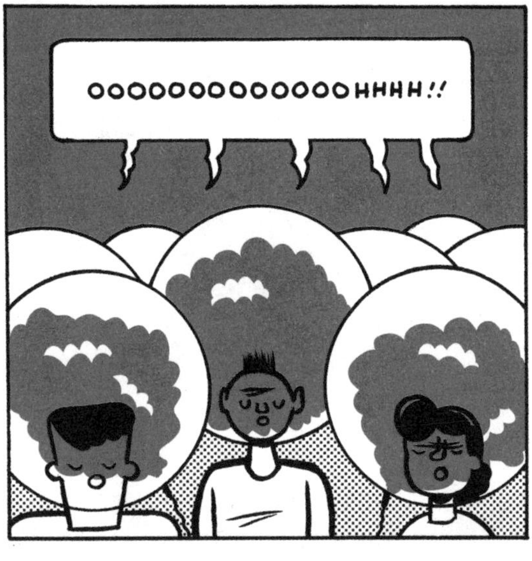
OOOOOOOOOOOOOHHHH!!

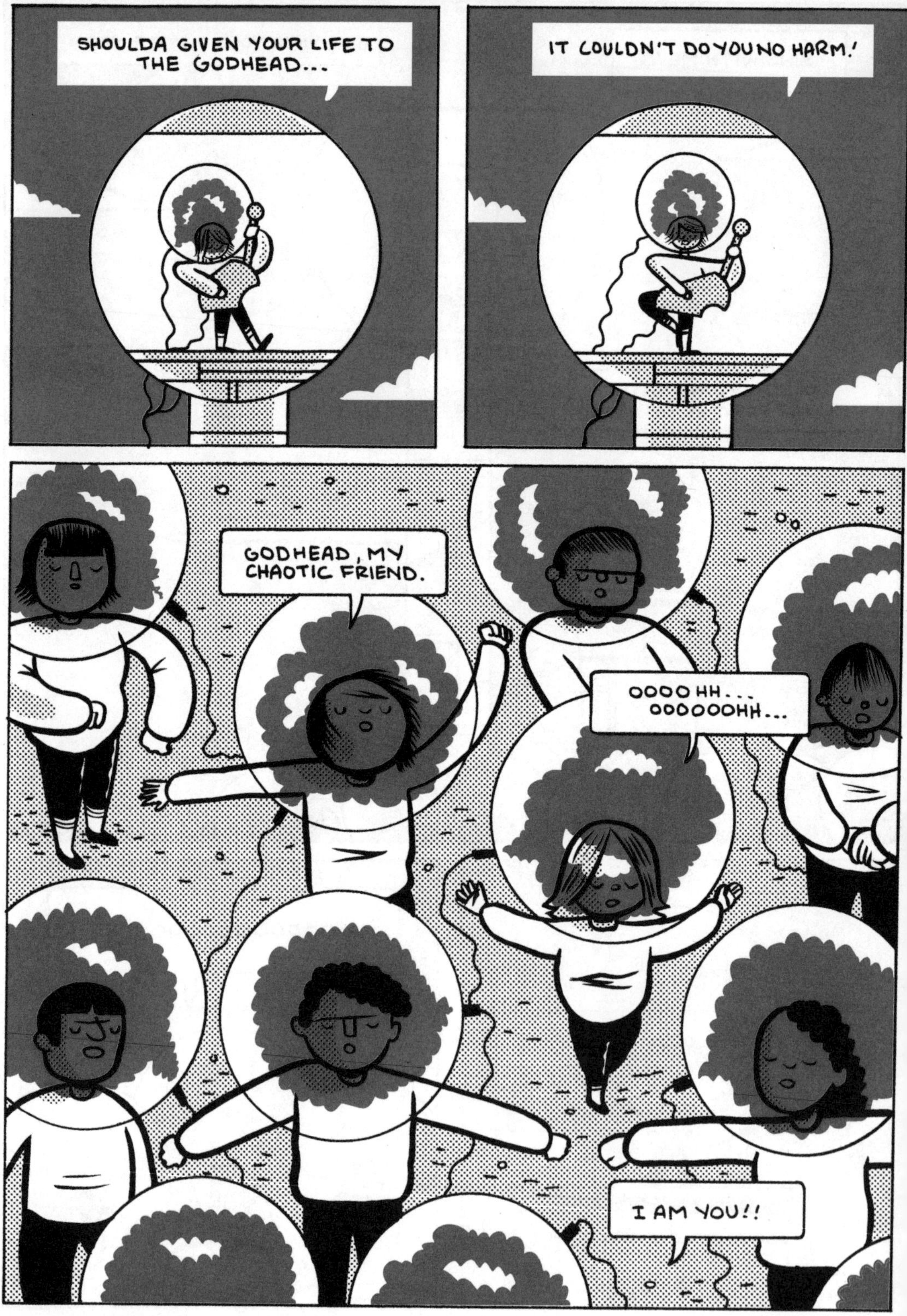

SHOULDA GIVEN YOUR LIFE TO THE GODHEAD...
IT COULDN'T DO YOU NO HARM!
GODHEAD, MY CHAOTIC FRIEND.
OOOOHH... OOOOOOHH...
I AM YOU!!

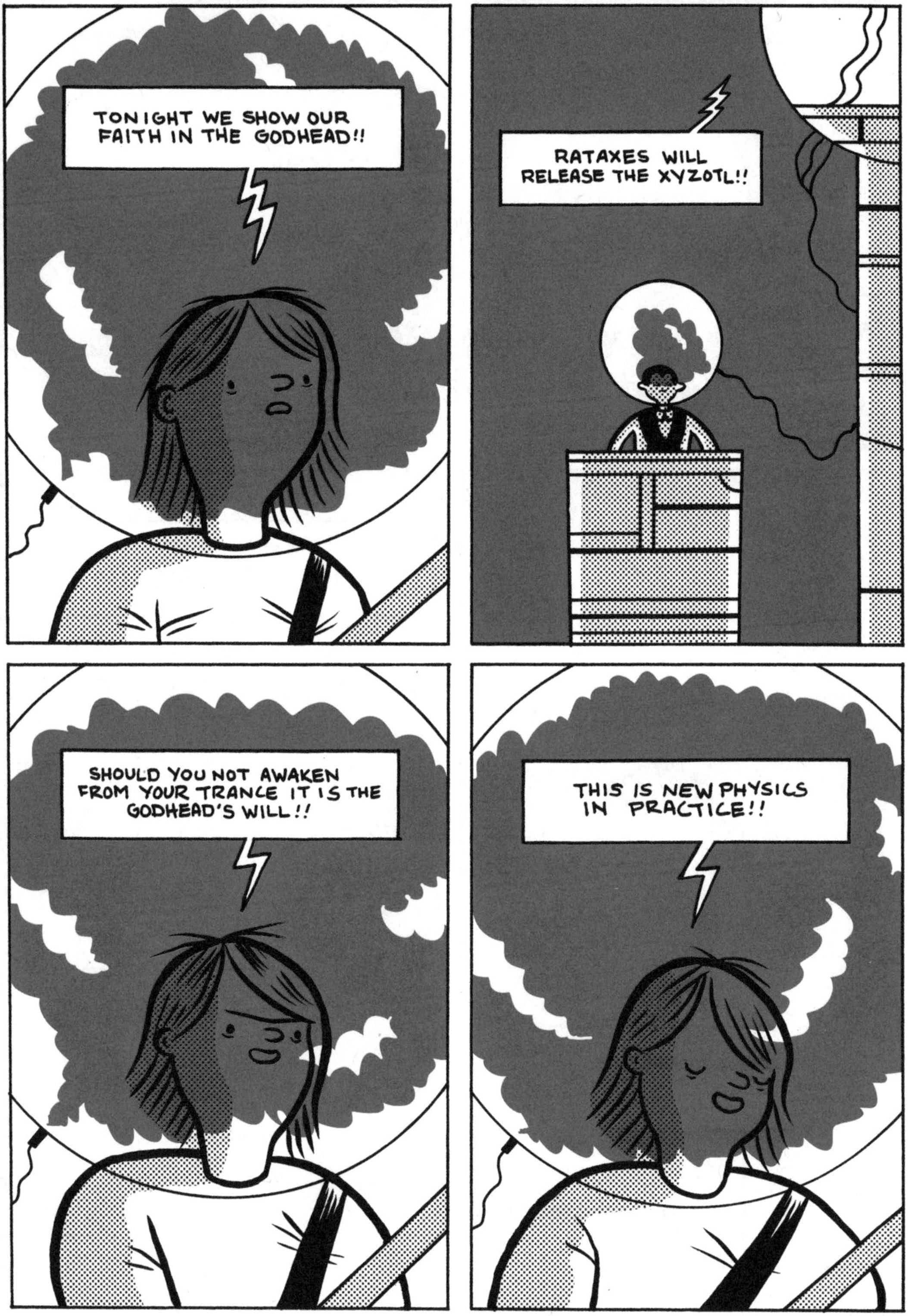
TONIGHT WE SHOW OUR FAITH IN THE GODHEAD!!
RATAXES WILL RELEASE THE XYZOTL!!
SHOULD YOU NOT AWAKEN FROM YOUR TRANCE IT IS THE GODHEAD'S WILL!!
THIS IS NEW PHYSICS IN PRACTICE!!

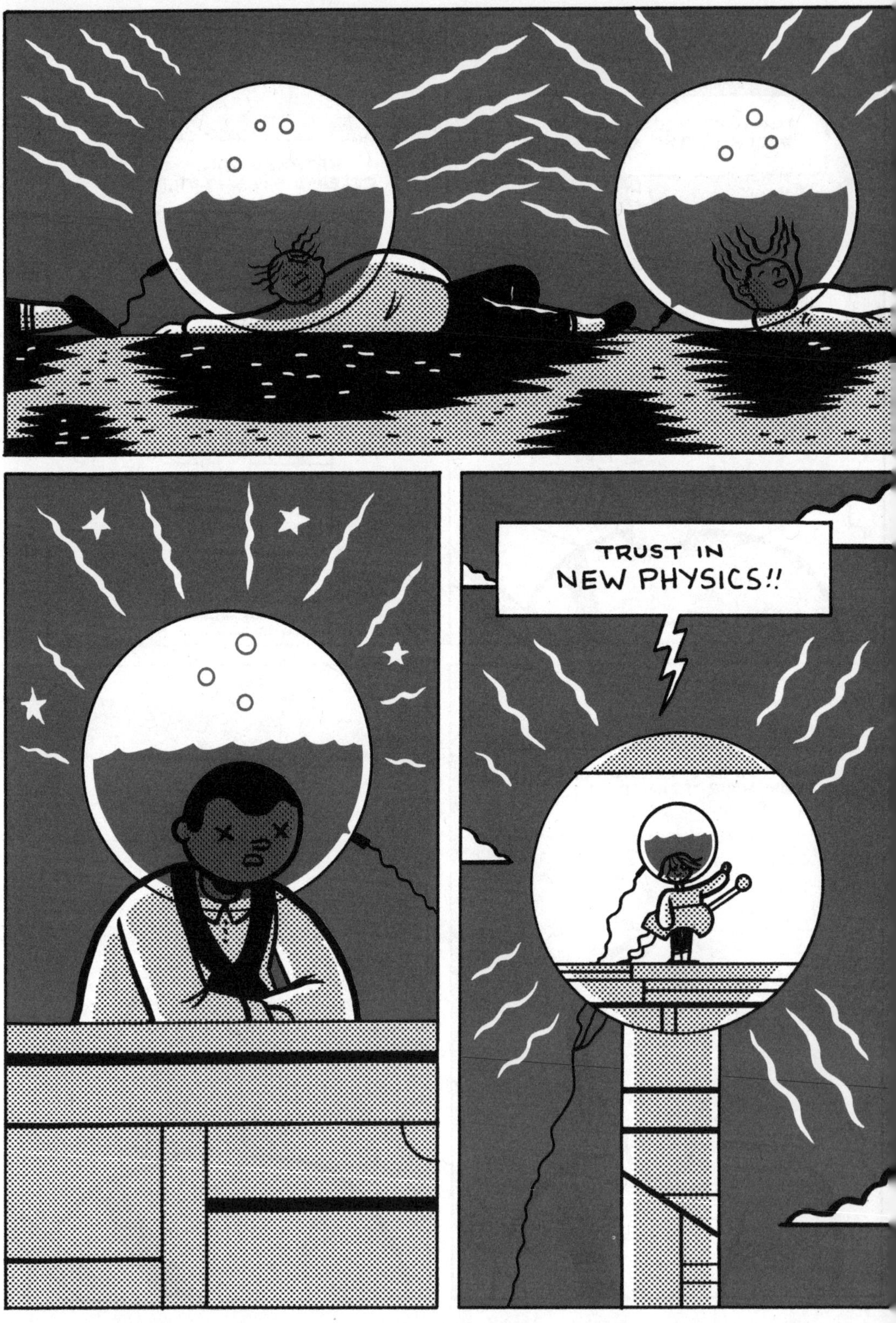
TRUST IN
NEW PHYSICS!!

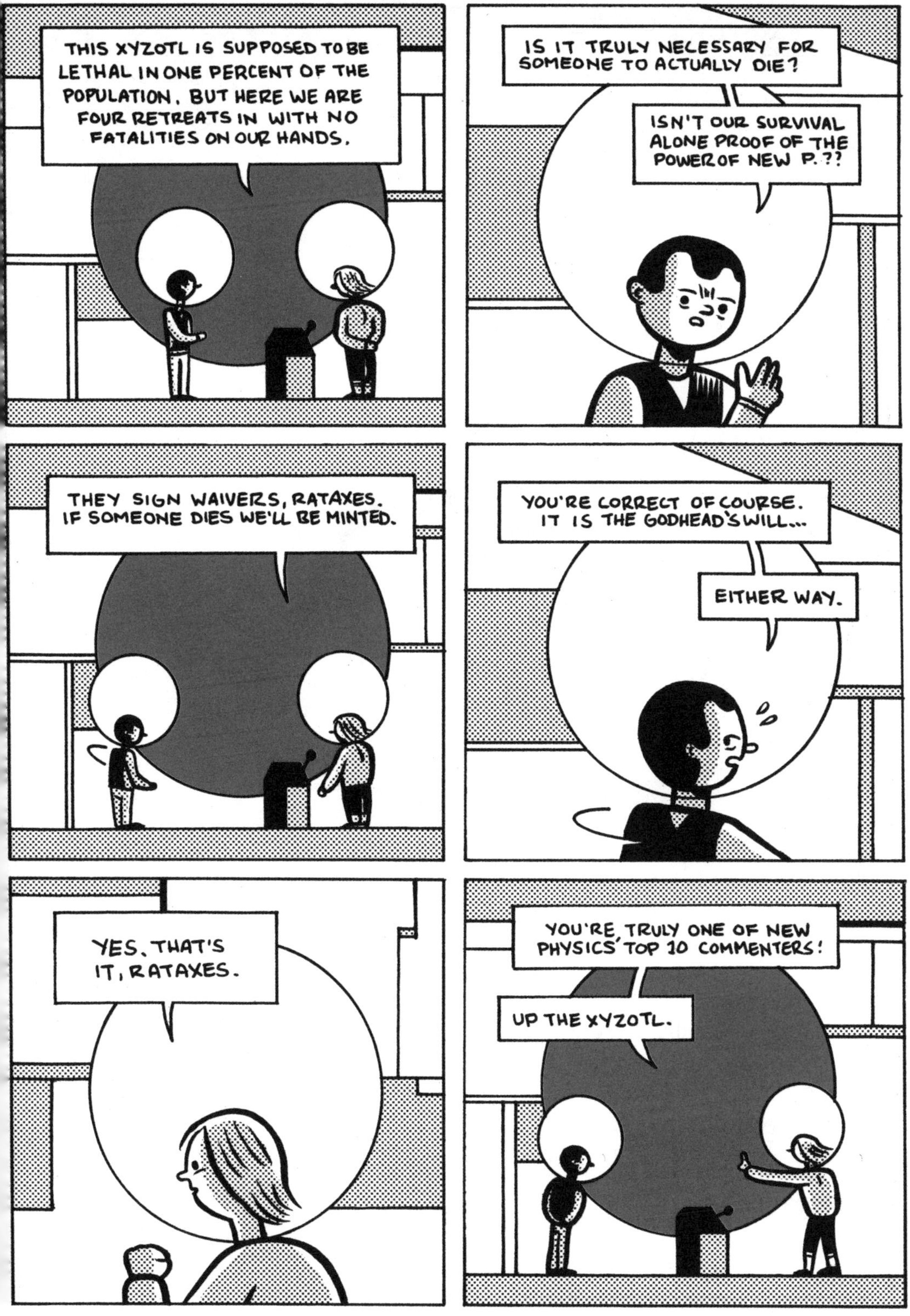
THIS XYZOTL IS SUPPOSED TO BE LETHAL IN ONE PERCENT OF THE POPULATION. BUT HERE WE ARE FOUR RETREATS IN WITH NO FATALITIES ON OUR HANDS.
IS IT TRULY NECESSARY FOR SOMEONE TO ACTUALLY DIE?
ISN'T OUR SURVIVAL ALONE PROOF OF THE POWER OF NEW P.??
THEY SIGN WAIVERS, RATAXES. IF SOMEONE DIES WE'LL BE MINTED.
YOU'RE CORRECT OF COURSE. IT IS THE GODHEAD'S WILL...
EITHER WAY.
YES. THAT'S IT, RATAXES.
YOU'RE, TRULY ONE OF NEW PHYSICS' TOP 10 COMMENTERS!
UP THE XYZOTL.

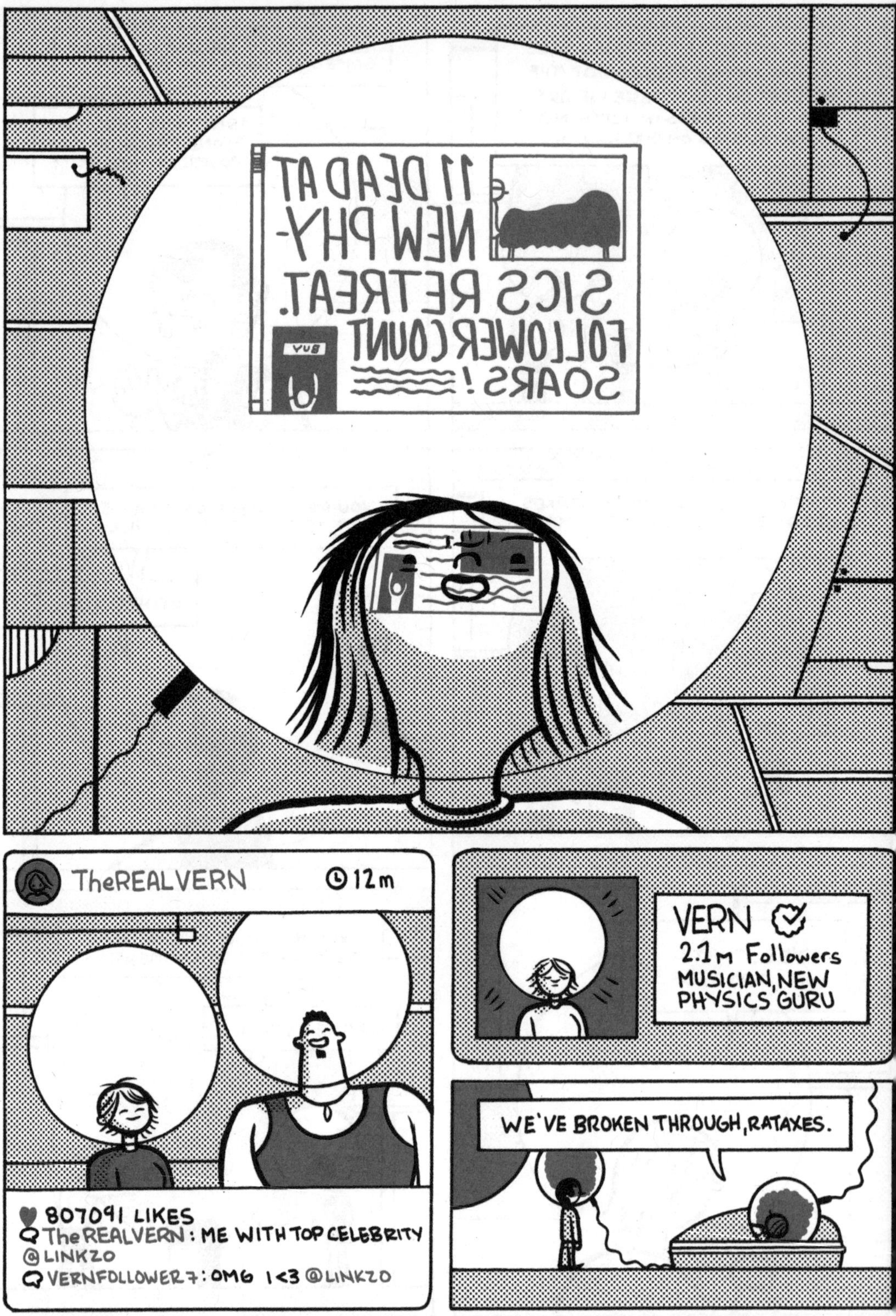
11 DEAD AT NEW PHY-SICS RETREAT. FOLLOWER COUNT SOARS!
TheREALVERN
12m
807091 LIKES
TheREALVERN : ME WITH TOP CELEBRITY @LINKZO
VERNFOLLOWER7 : OMG I<3 @LINKZO
VERN
2.1m Followers
MUSICIAN, NEW PHYSICS GURU
WE'VE BROKEN THROUGH, RATAXES.

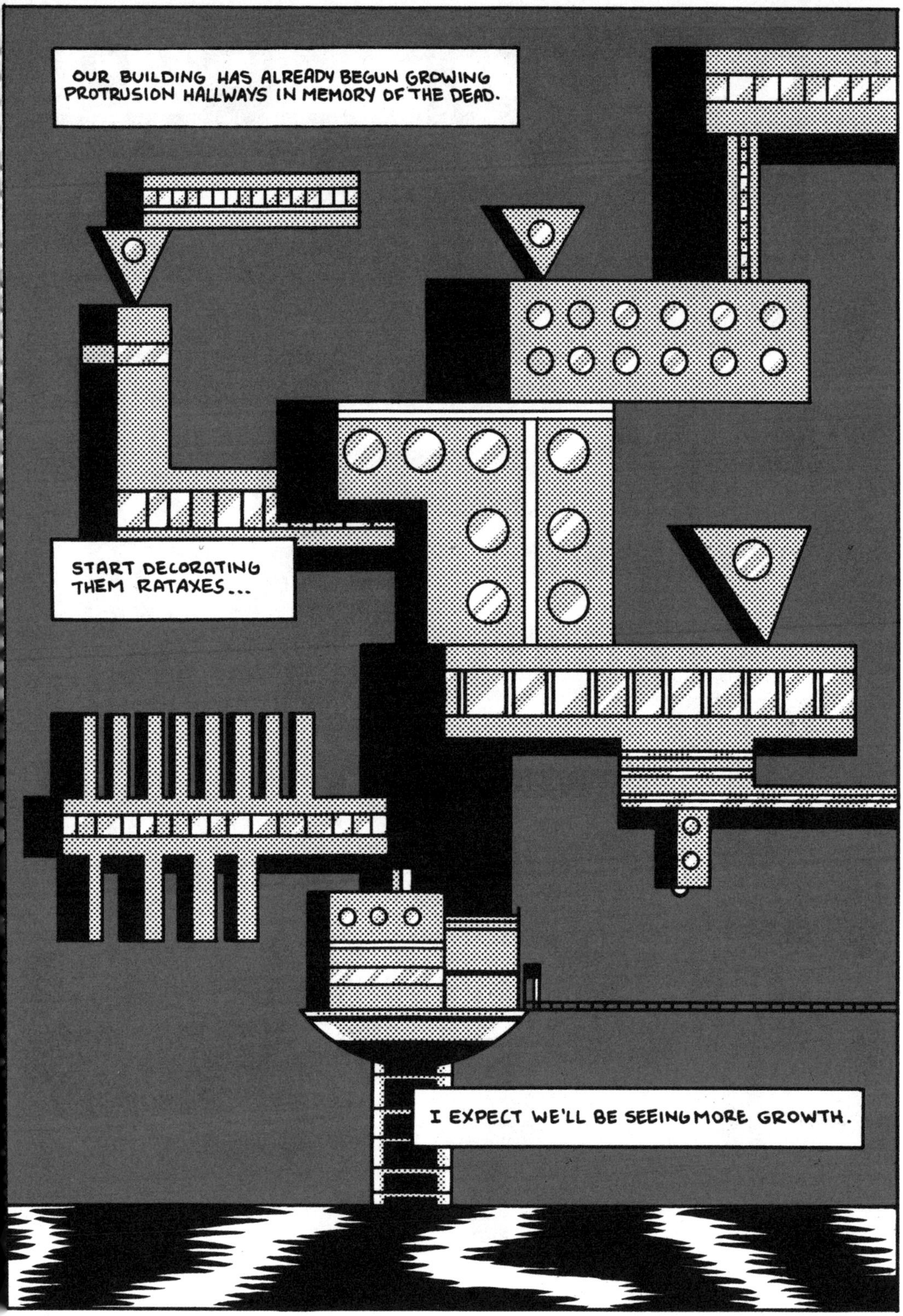
OUR BUILDING HAS ALREADY BEGUN GROWING PROTRUSION HALLWAYS IN MEMORY OF THE DEAD.
START DECORATING THEM RATAXES...
I EXPECT WE'LL BE SEEING MORE GROWTH.

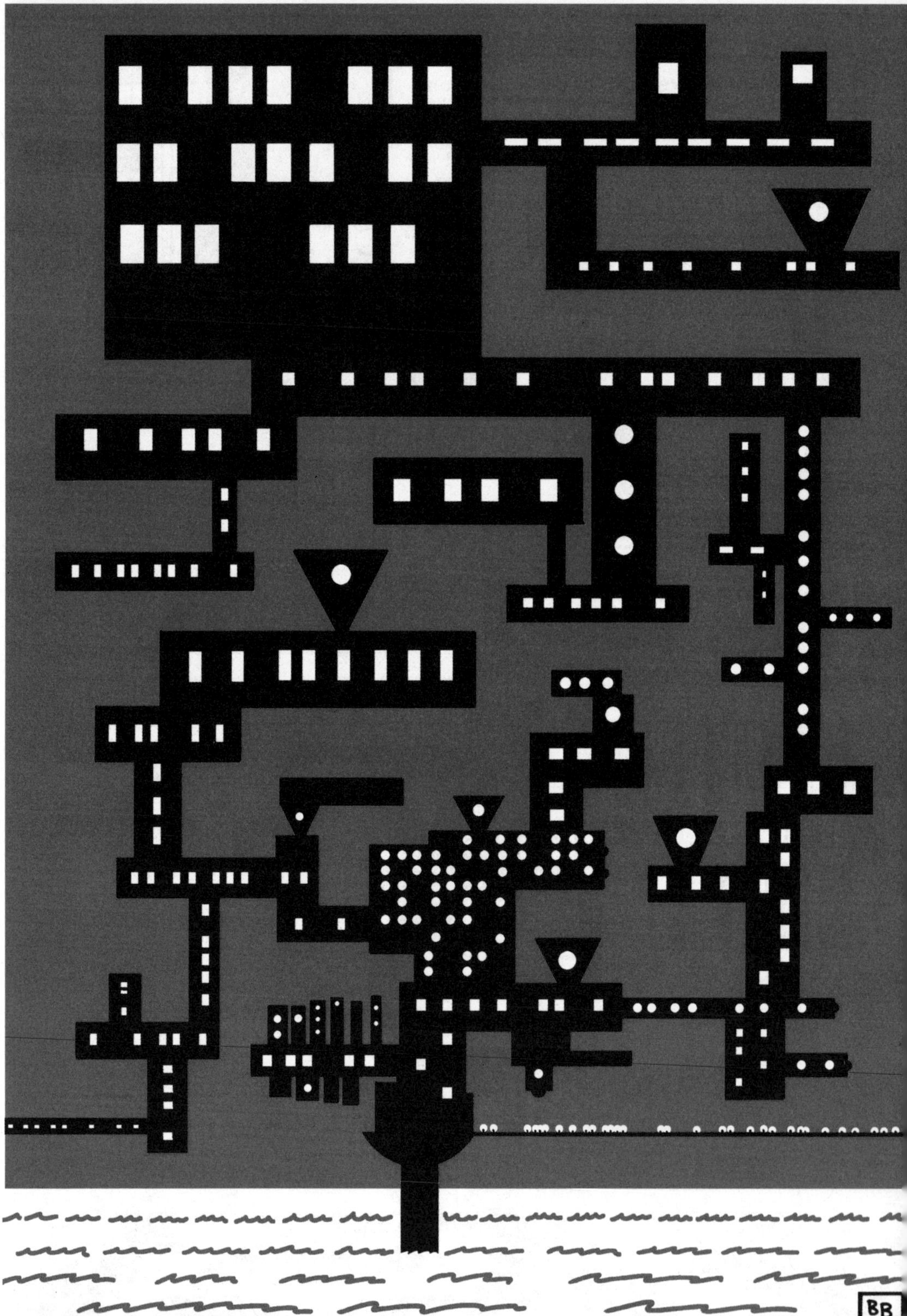
BB

THE SYSTEM CORPUS

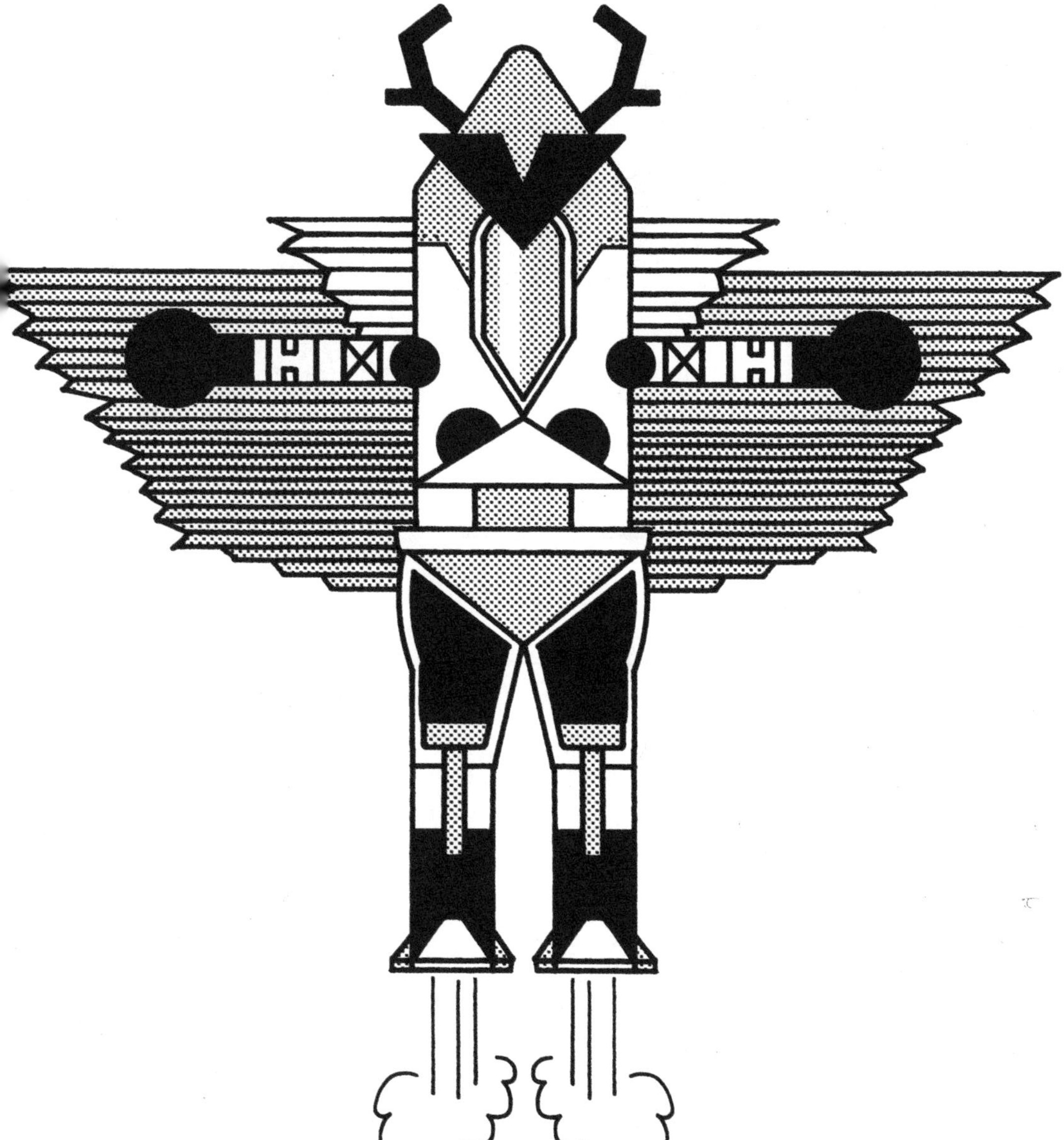

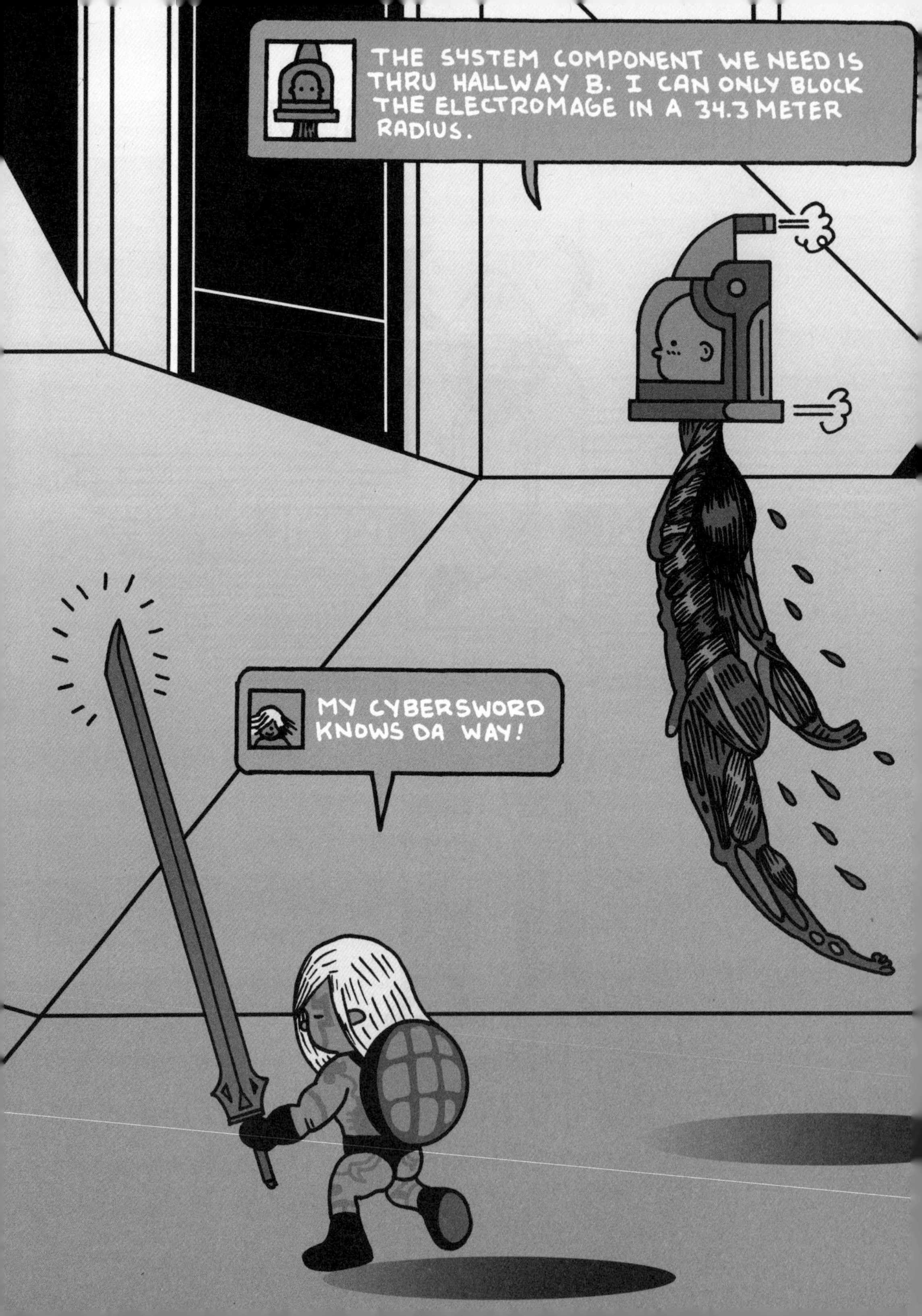
THE SYSTEM COMPONENT WE NEED IS THRU HALLWAY B. I CAN ONLY BLOCK THE ELECTROMAGE IN A 34.3 METER RADIUS.
MY CYBERSWORD KNOWS DA WAY!

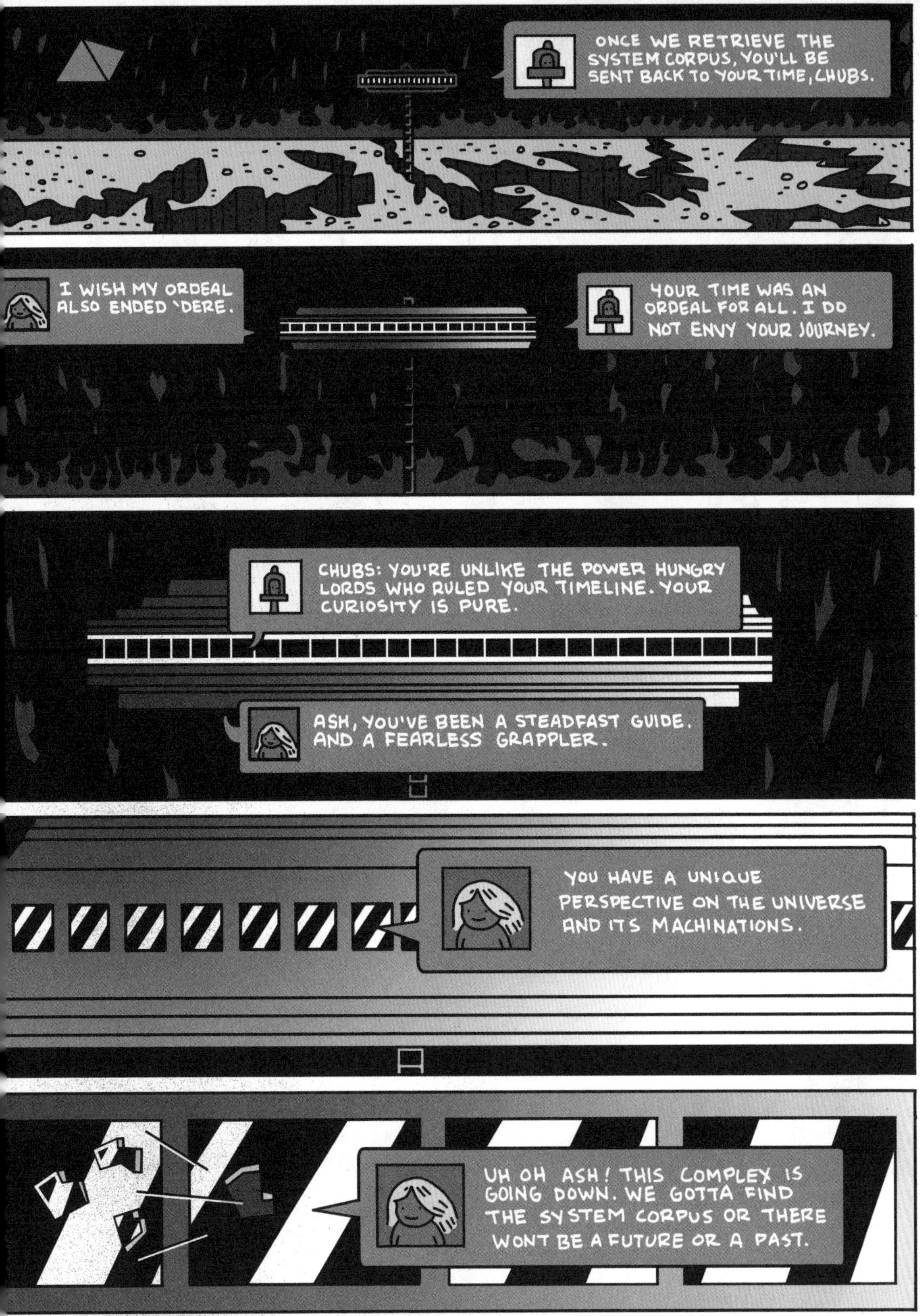
ONCE WE RETRIEVE THE SYSTEM CORPUS, YOU'LL BE SENT BACK TO YOUR TIME, CHUBS.
I WISH MY ORDEAL ALSO ENDED 'DERE.
YOUR TIME WAS AN ORDEAL FOR ALL. I DO NOT ENVY YOUR JOURNEY.
CHUBS: YOU'RE UNLIKE THE POWER HUNGRY LORDS WHO RULED YOUR TIMELINE. YOUR CURIOSITY IS PURE.
ASH, YOU'VE BEEN A STEADFAST GUIDE. AND A FEARLESS GRAPPLER.
YOU HAVE A UNIQUE PERSPECTIVE ON THE UNIVERSE AND ITS MACHINATIONS.
UH OH ASH! THIS COMPLEX IS GOING DOWN. WE GOTTA FIND THE SYSTEM CORPUS OR THERE WONT BE A FUTURE OR A PAST.

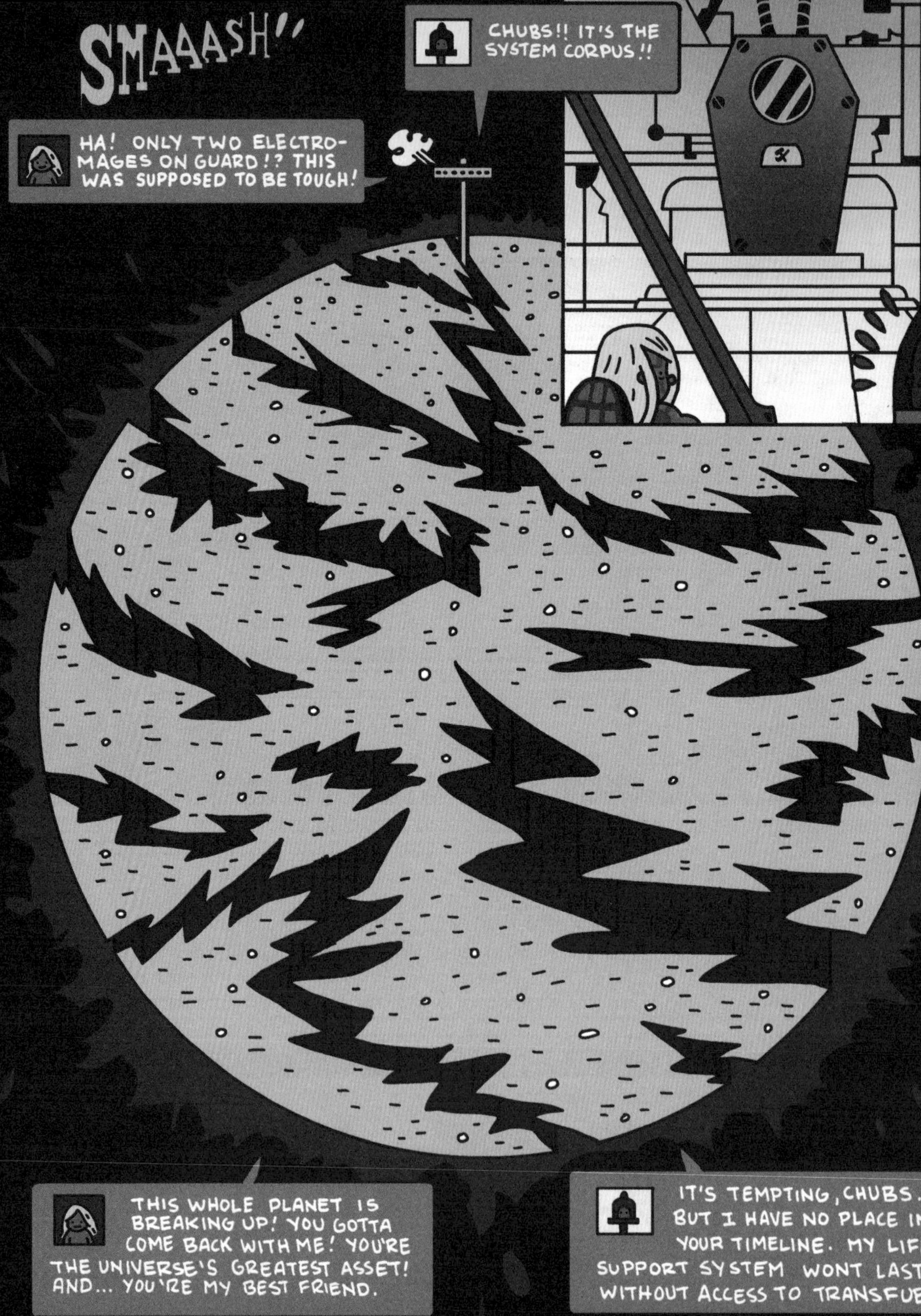
SMAAASH!!
CHUBS!! IT'S THE SYSTEM CORPUS!!
HA! ONLY TWO ELECTRO-MAGES ON GUARD!? THIS WAS SUPPOSED TO BE TOUGH!
THIS WHOLE PLANET IS BREAKING UP! YOU GOTTA COME BACK WITH ME! YOU'RE THE UNIVERSE'S GREATEST ASSET! AND... YOU'RE MY BEST FRIEND.
IT'S TEMPTING, CHUBS... BUT I HAVE NO PLACE IN YOUR TIMELINE. MY LIFE SUPPORT SYSTEM WONT LAST WITHOUT ACCESS TO TRANSFU

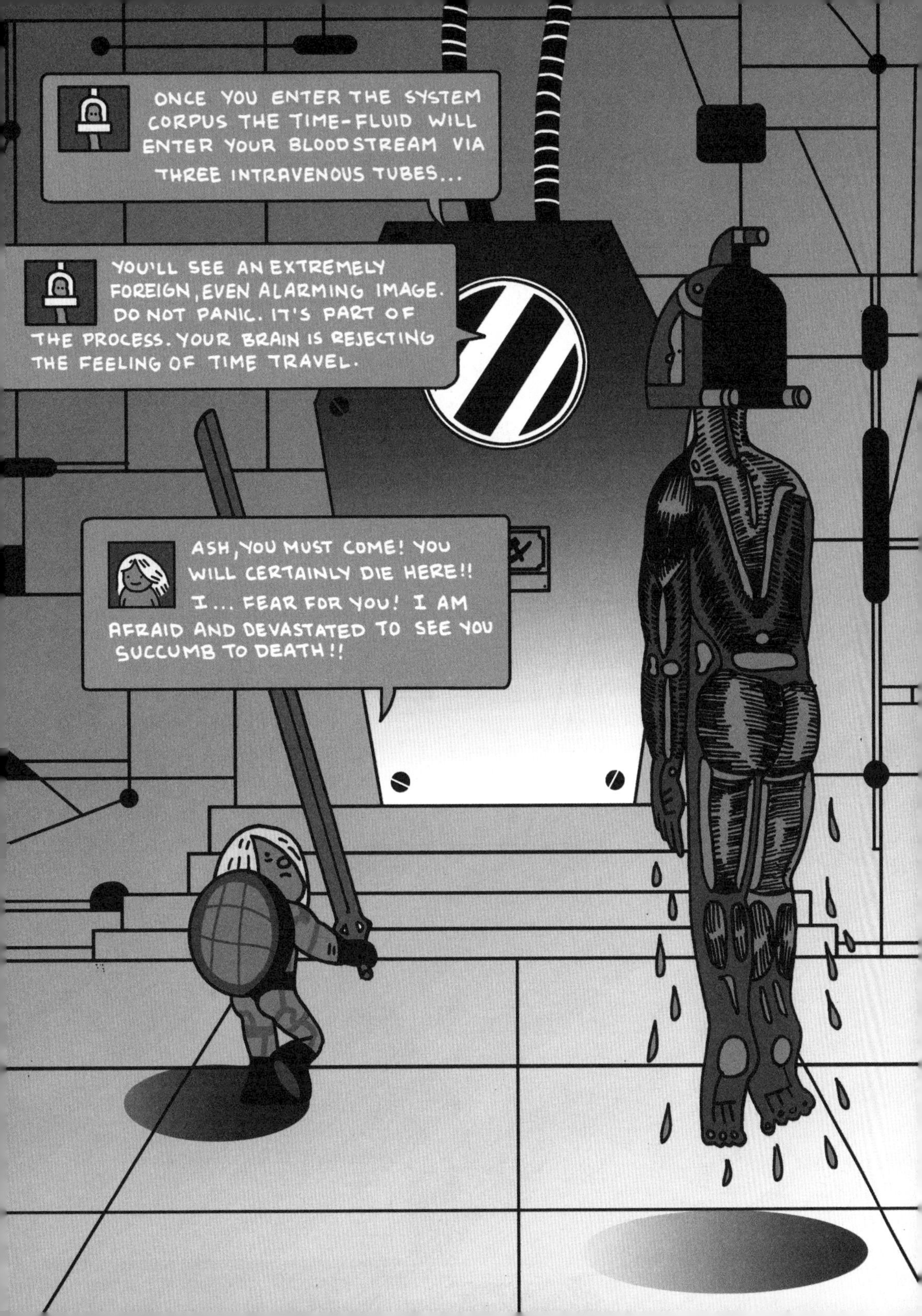
ONCE YOU ENTER THE SYSTEM CORPUS THE TIME-FLUID WILL ENTER YOUR BLOODSTREAM VIA THREE INTRAVENOUS TUBES...
YOU'LL SEE AN EXTREMELY FOREIGN, EVEN ALARMING IMAGE. DO NOT PANIC. IT'S PART OF THE PROCESS. YOUR BRAIN IS REJECTING THE FEELING OF TIME TRAVEL.
ASH, YOU MUST COME! YOU WILL CERTAINLY DIE HERE!! I... FEAR FOR YOU! I AM AFRAID AND DEVASTATED TO SEE YOU SUCCUMB TO DEATH!!

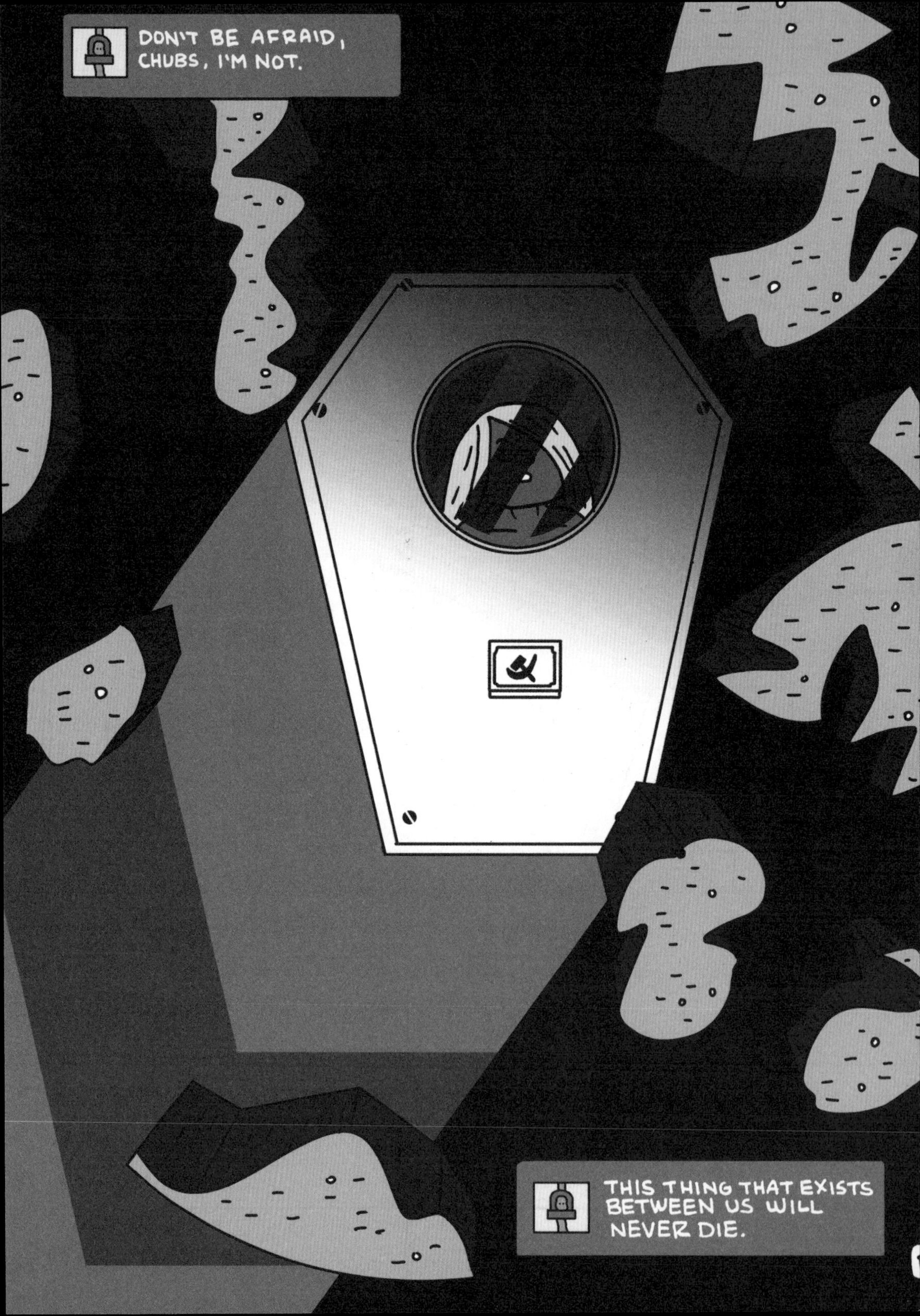

DON'T BE AFRAID, CHUBS, I'M NOT.
THIS THING THAT EXISTS BETWEEN US WILL NEVER DIE.

COMMUNION OF THE STAR WARRIORS

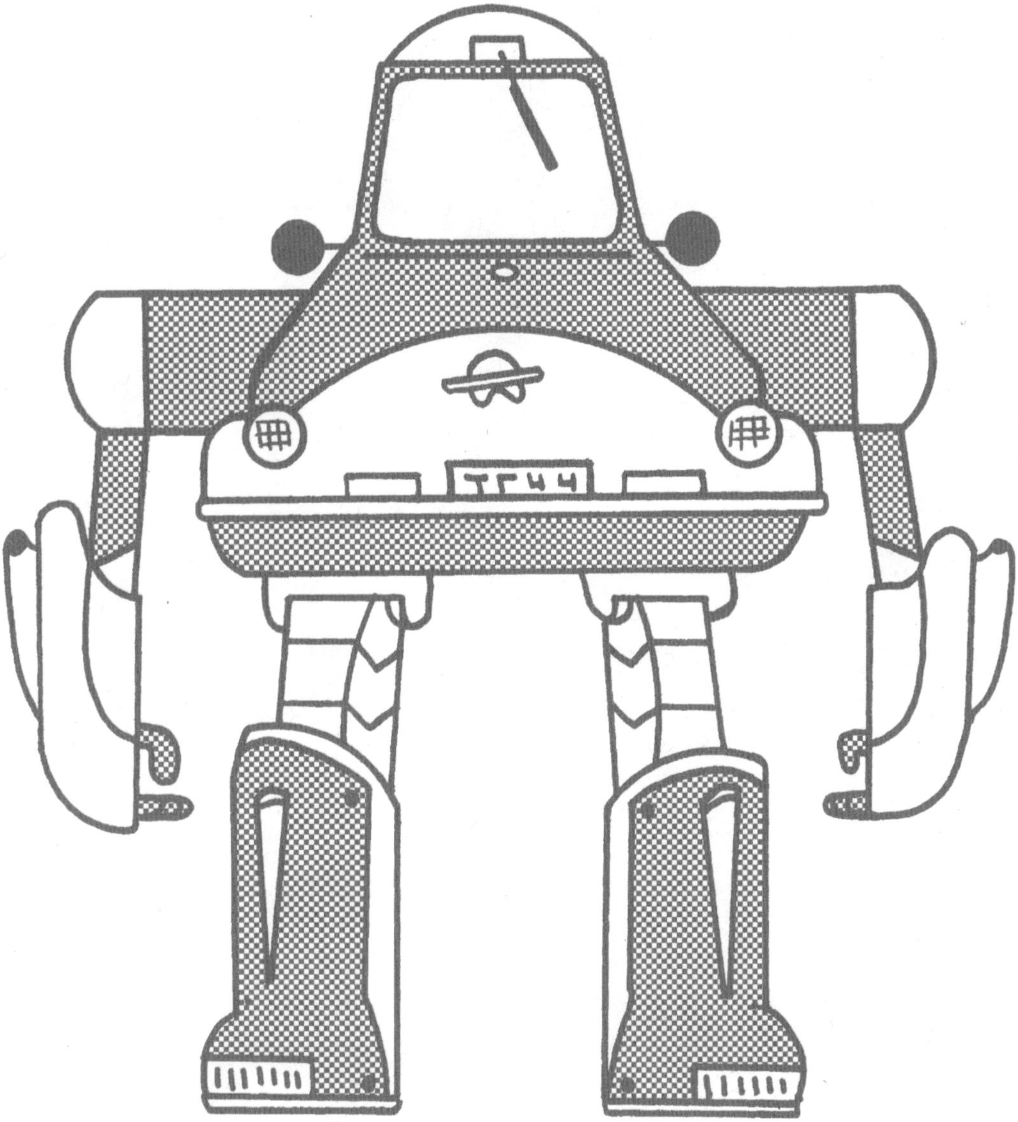

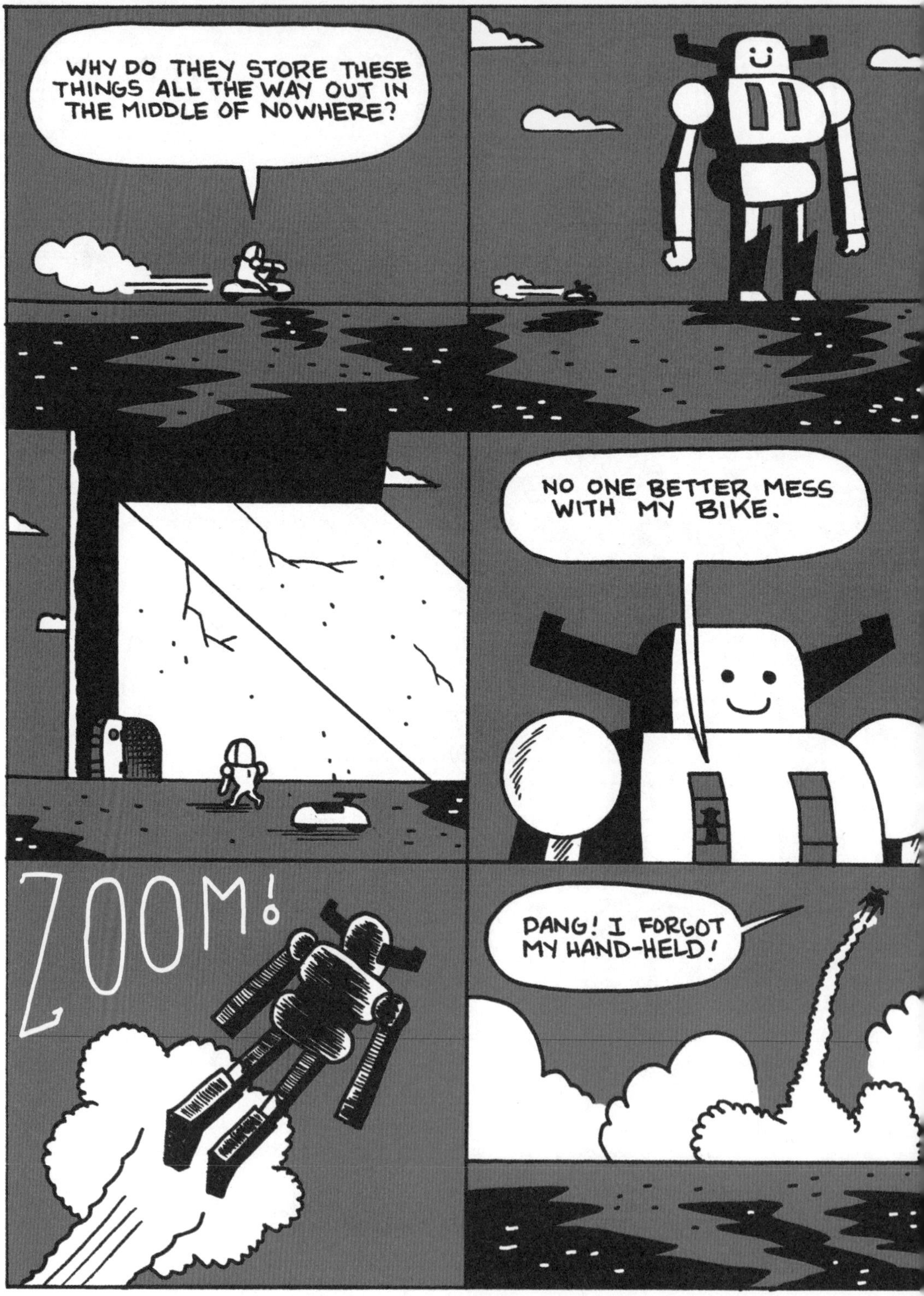
WHY DO THEY STORE THESE THINGS ALL THE WAY OUT IN THE MIDDLE OF NOWHERE?
NO ONE BETTER MESS WITH MY BIKE.
ZOOM!
DANG! I FORGOT MY HAND-HELD!

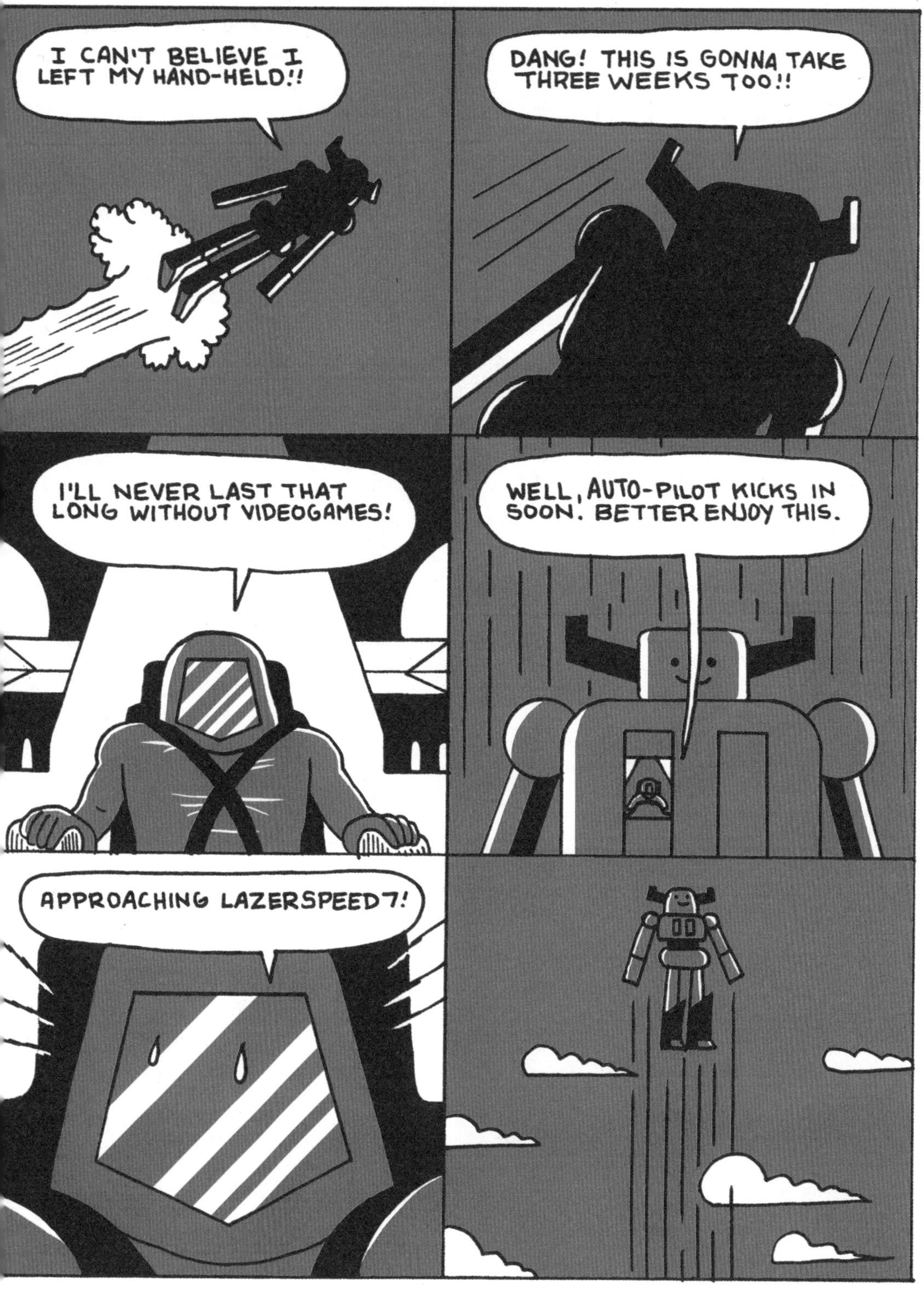
I CAN'T BELIEVE I LEFT MY HAND-HELD!!
DANG! THIS IS GONNA TAKE THREE WEEKS TOO!!
I'LL NEVER LAST THAT LONG WITHOUT VIDEOGAMES!
WELL, AUTO-PILOT KICKS IN SOON. BETTER ENJOY THIS.
APPROACHING LAZERSPEED 7!

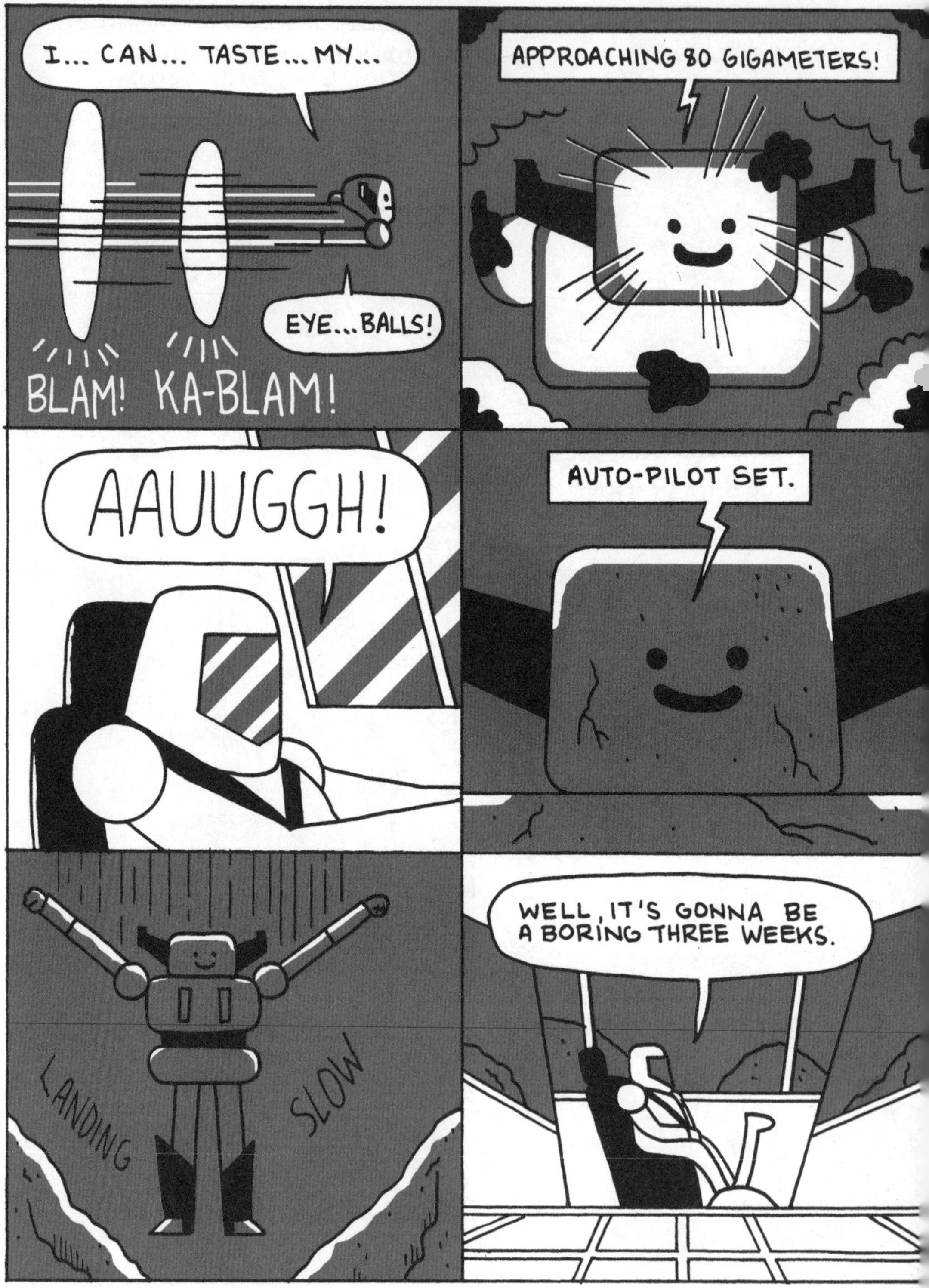
I... CAN... TASTE... MY...
EYE... BALLS!
BLAM! KA-BLAM!
APPROACHING 80 GIGAMETERS!
AAUUGGH!
AUTO-PILOT SET.
LANDING
SLOW
WELL, IT'S GONNA BE A BORING THREE WEEKS.

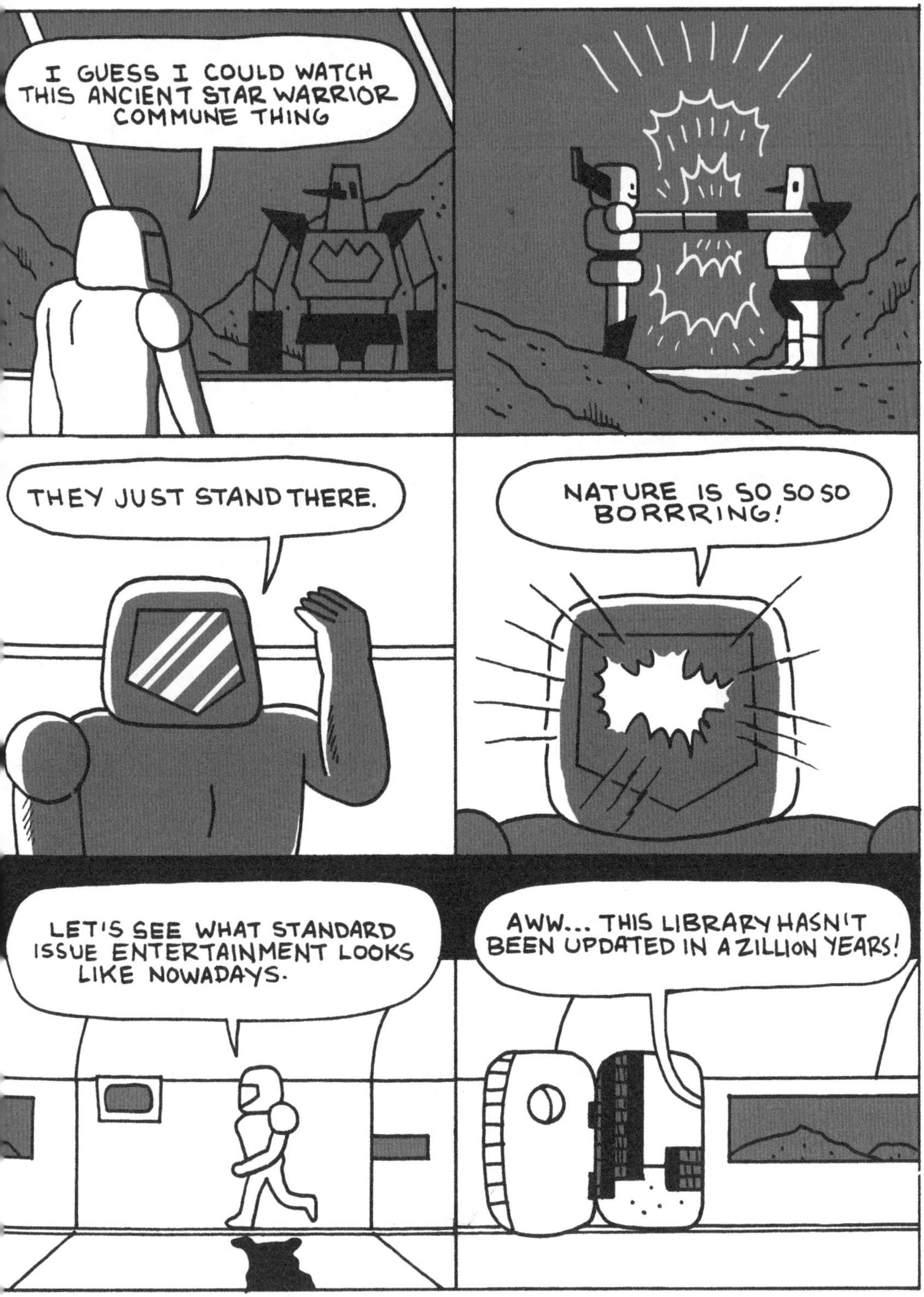

I GUESS I COULD WATCH THIS ANCIENT STAR WARRIOR COMMUNE THING
THEY JUST STAND THERE.
NATURE IS SO SO SO BORRRING!
LET'S SEE WHAT STANDARD ISSUE ENTERTAINMENT LOOKS LIKE NOWADAYS.
AWW... THIS LIBRARY HASN'T BEEN UPDATED IN A ZILLION YEARS!

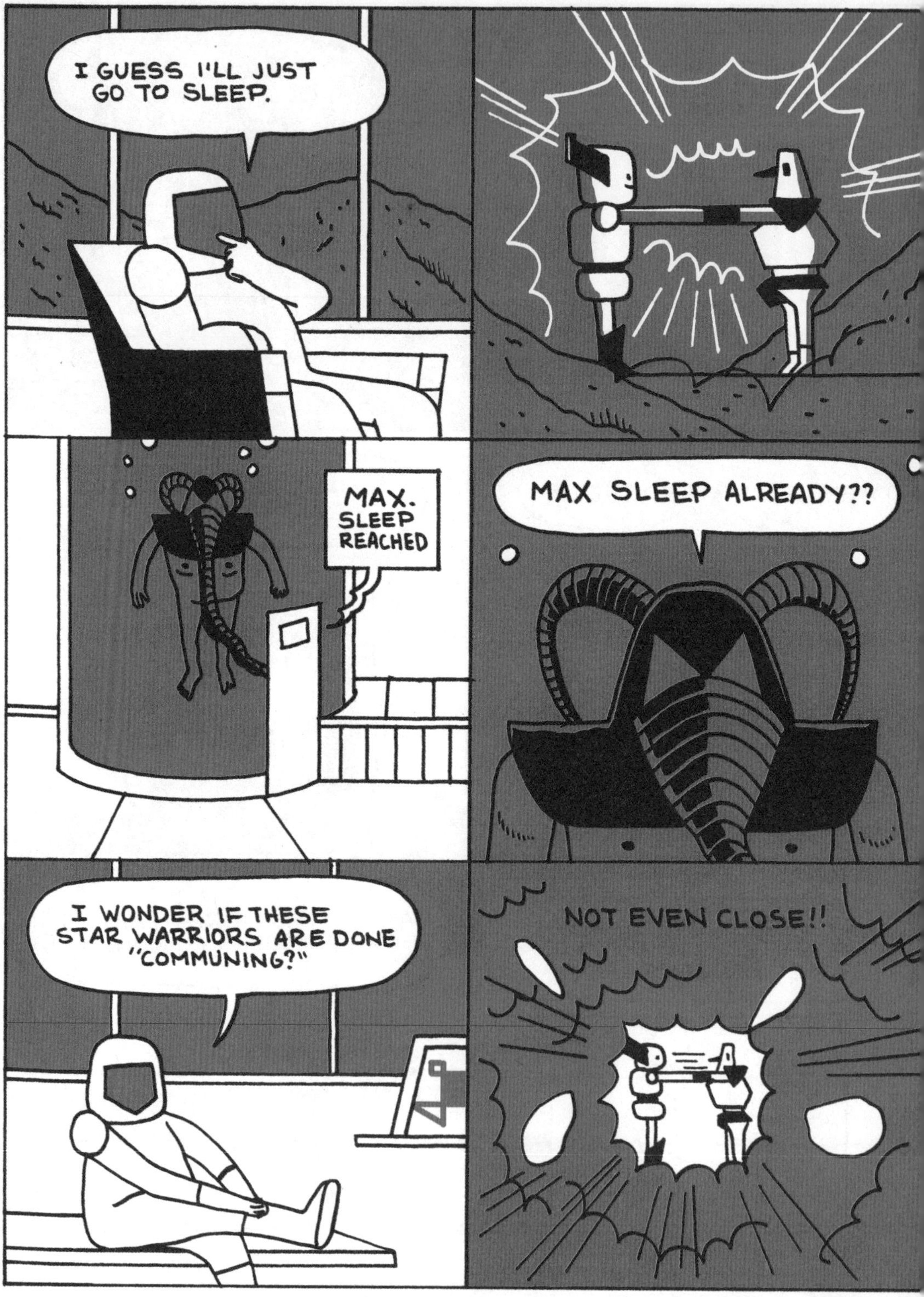
I GUESS I'LL JUST GO TO SLEEP.
MAX. SLEEP REACHED
MAX SLEEP ALREADY??
I WONDER IF THESE STAR WARRIORS ARE DONE "COMMUNING?"
NOT EVEN CLOSE!!

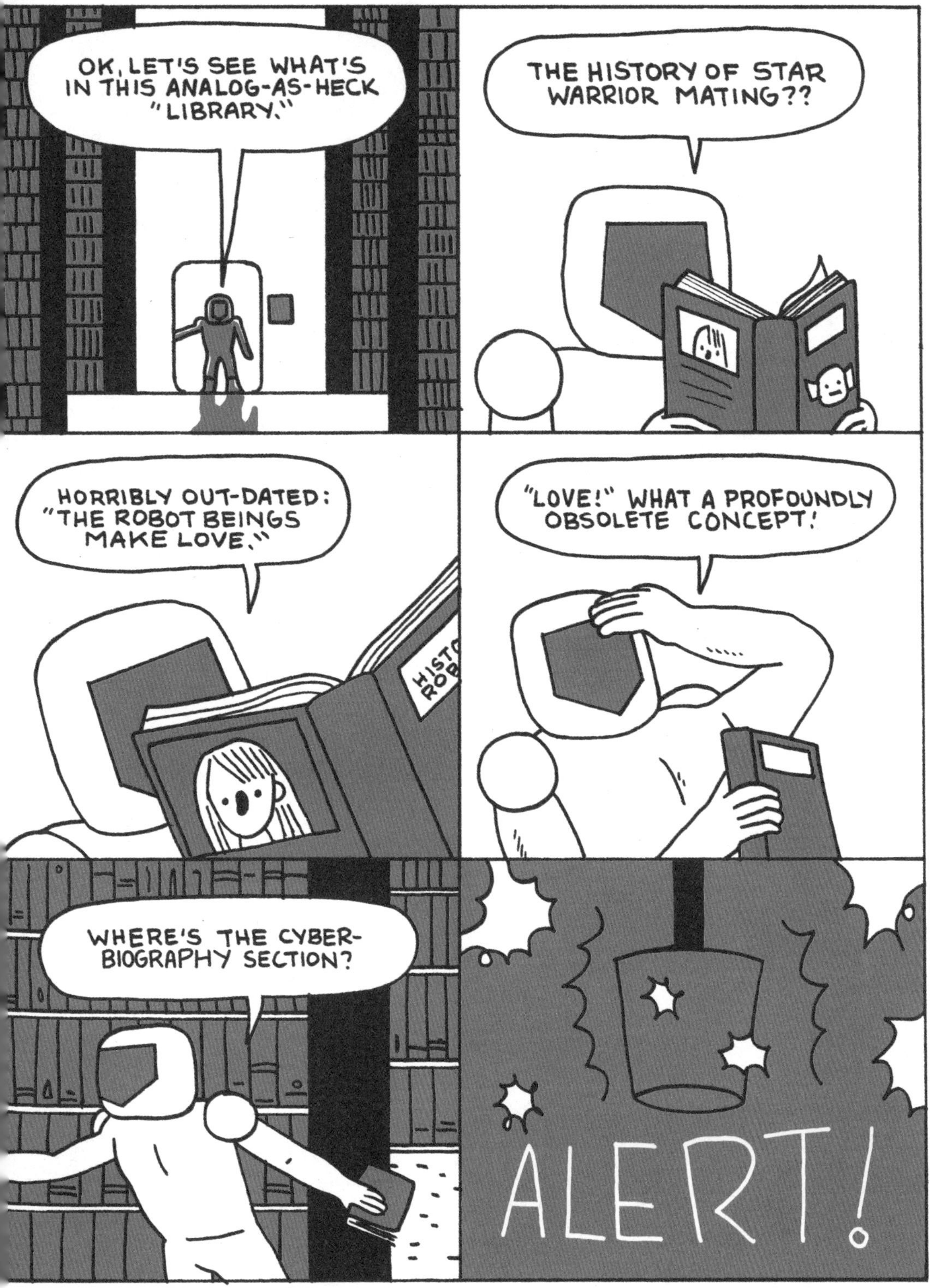

OK, LET'S SEE WHAT'S IN THIS ANALOG-AS-HECK "LIBRARY."
THE HISTORY OF STAR WARRIOR MATING??
HORRIBLY OUT-DATED: "THE ROBOT BEINGS MAKE LOVE."
"LOVE!" WHAT A PROFOUNDLY OBSOLETE CONCEPT!
WHERE'S THE CYBER-BIOGRAPHY SECTION?
ALERT!

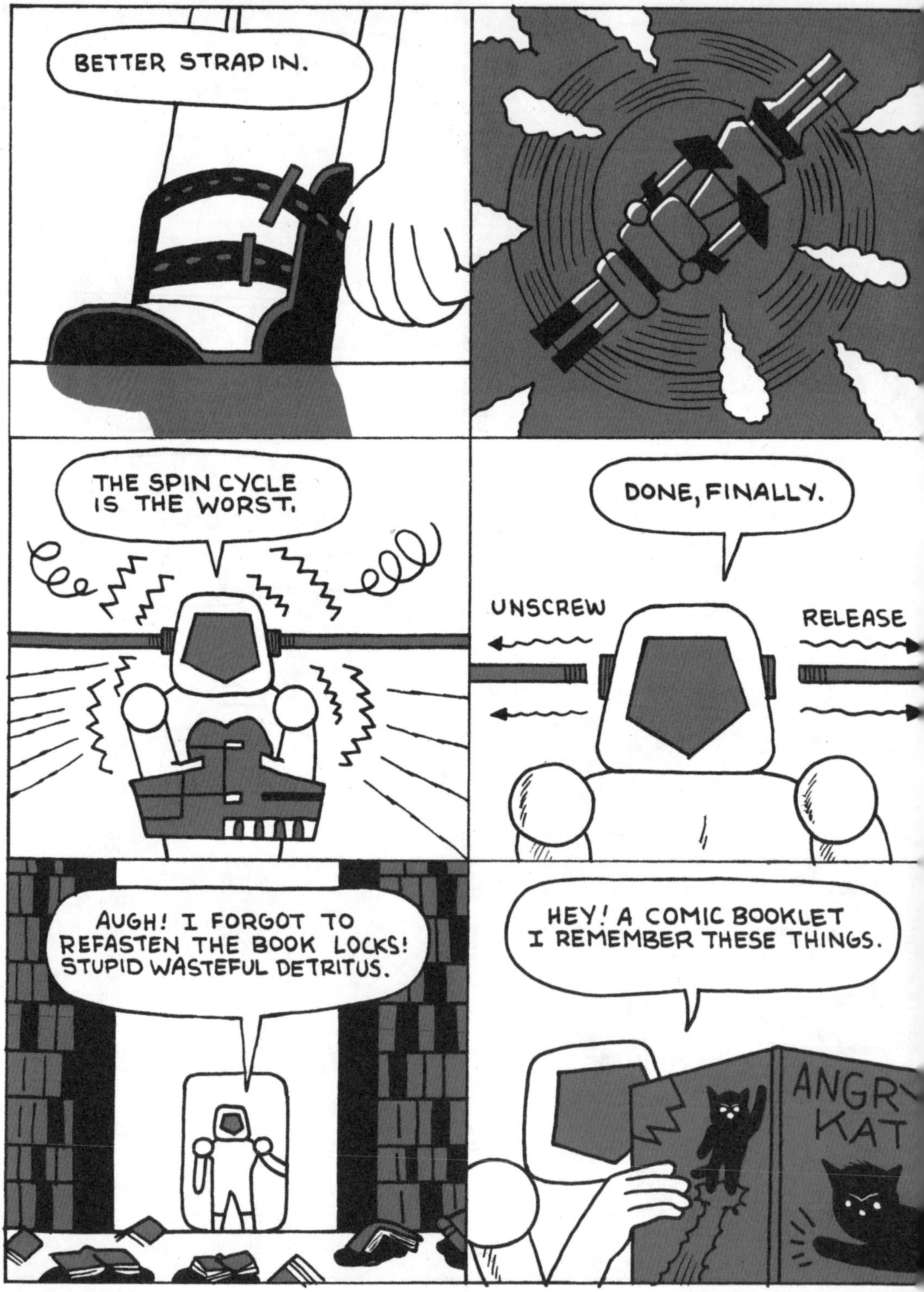
BETTER STRAP IN.
THE SPIN CYCLE IS THE WORST.
DONE, FINALLY.
UNSCREW
RELEASE
AUGH! I FORGOT TO REFASTEN THE BOOK LOCKS! STUPID WASTEFUL DETRITUS.
HEY! A COMIC BOOKLET I REMEMBER THESE THINGS.
ANGRY KAT

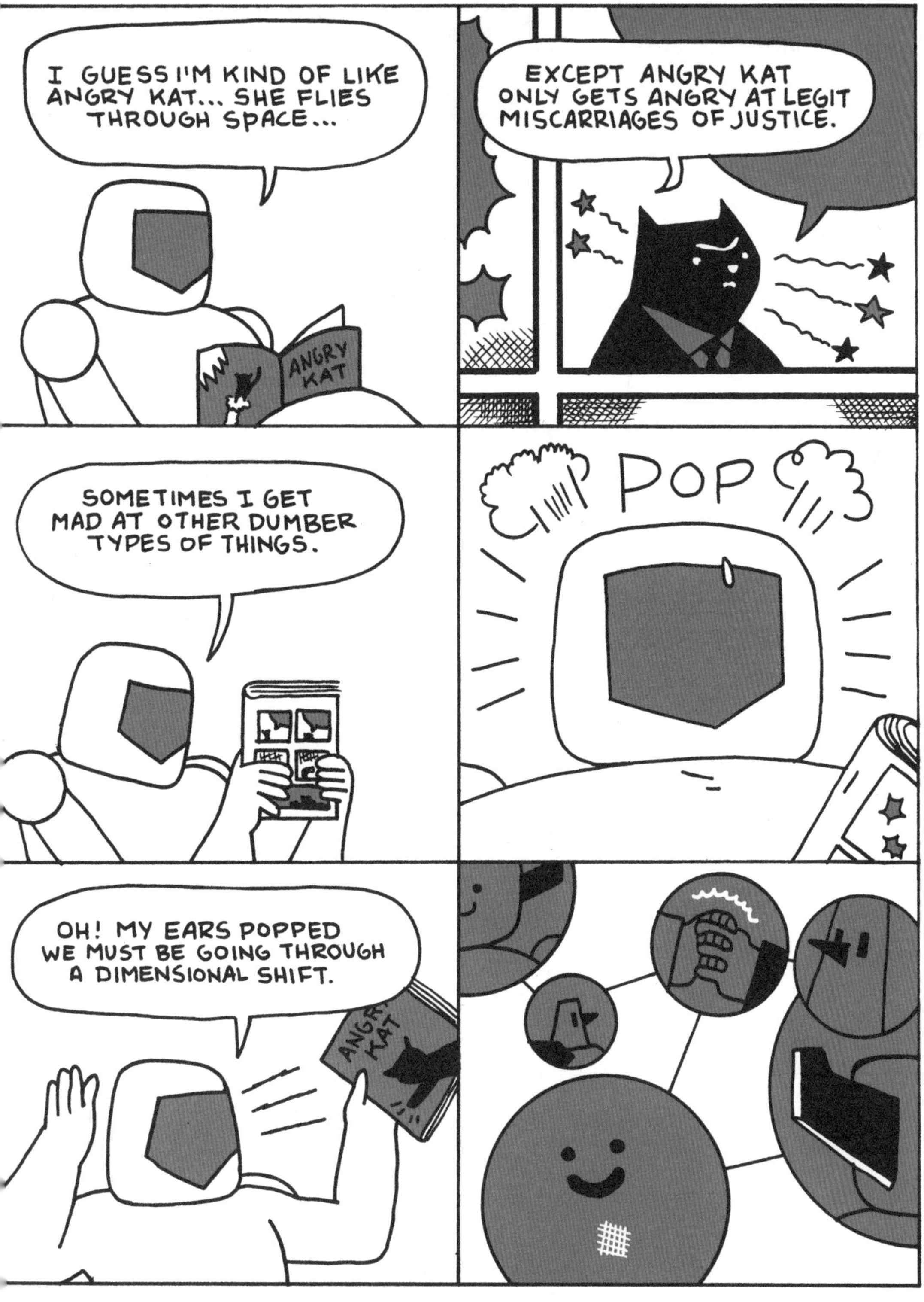
I GUESS I'M KIND OF LIKE ANGRY KAT... SHE FLIES THROUGH SPACE...
ANGRY KAT
EXCEPT ANGRY KAT ONLY GETS ANGRY AT LEGIT MISCARRIAGES OF JUSTICE.
SOMETIMES I GET MAD AT OTHER DUMBER TYPES OF THINGS.
POP
OH! MY EARS POPPED WE MUST BE GOING THROUGH A DIMENSIONAL SHIFT.
ANGRY KAT

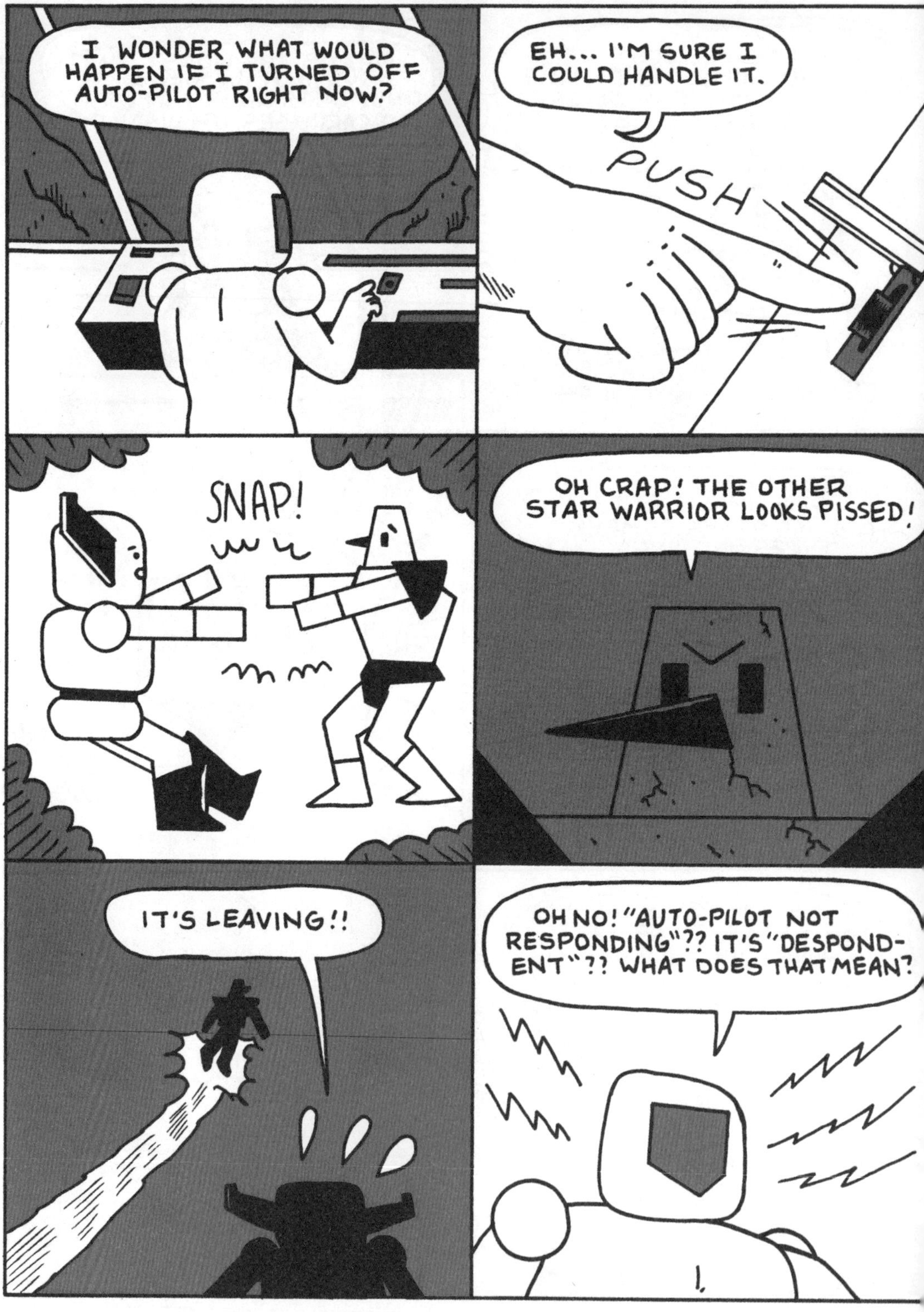
I WONDER WHAT WOULD HAPPEN IF I TURNED OFF AUTO-PILOT RIGHT NOW?
EH... I'M SURE I COULD HANDLE IT.
PUSH
SNAP!
OH CRAP! THE OTHER STAR WARRIOR LOOKS PISSED!
IT'S LEAVING!!
OH NO! "AUTO-PILOT NOT RESPONDING"?? IT'S "DESPONDENT"?? WHAT DOES THAT MEAN?

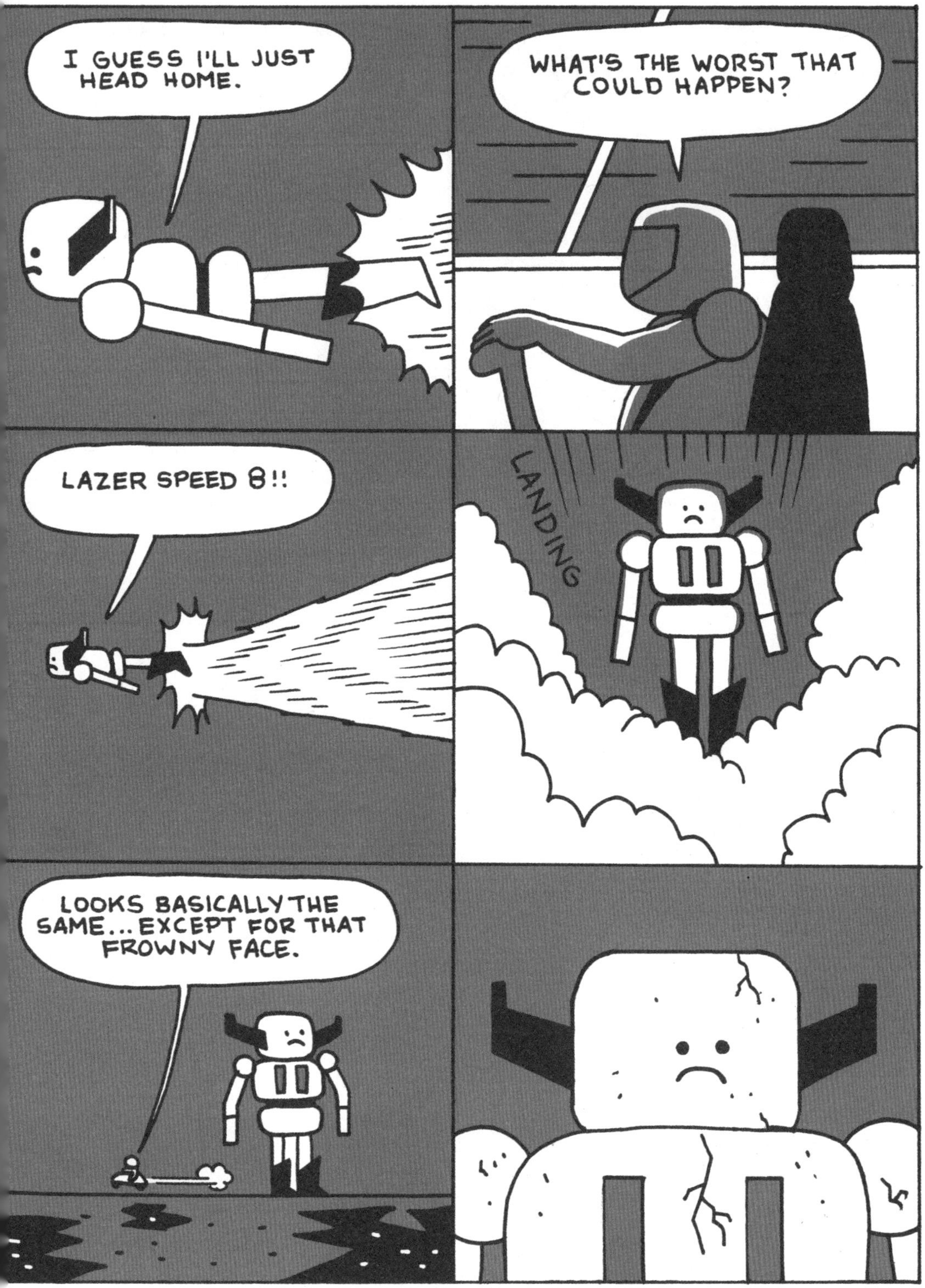
I GUESS I'LL JUST HEAD HOME.
WHAT'S THE WORST THAT COULD HAPPEN?
LAZER SPEED 8!!
LANDING
LOOKS BASICALLY THE SAME... EXCEPT FOR THAT FROWNY FACE.

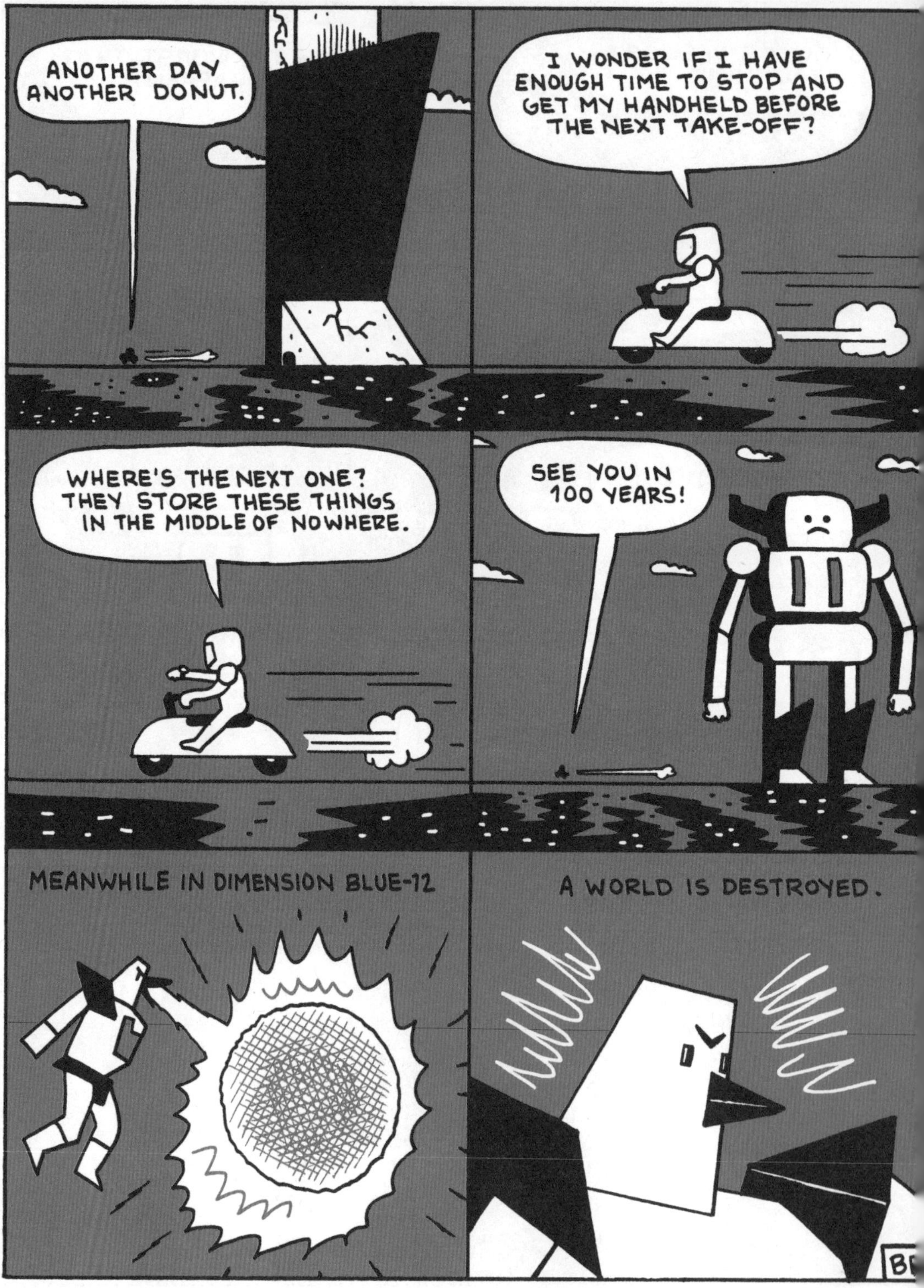
ANOTHER DAY ANOTHER DONUT.
I WONDER IF I HAVE ENOUGH TIME TO STOP AND GET MY HANDHELD BEFORE THE NEXT TAKE-OFF?
WHERE'S THE NEXT ONE? THEY STORE THESE THINGS IN THE MIDDLE OF NOWHERE.
SEE YOU IN 100 YEARS!
MEANWHILE IN DIMENSION BLUE-12
A WORLD IS DESTROYED.

THE LIZARD

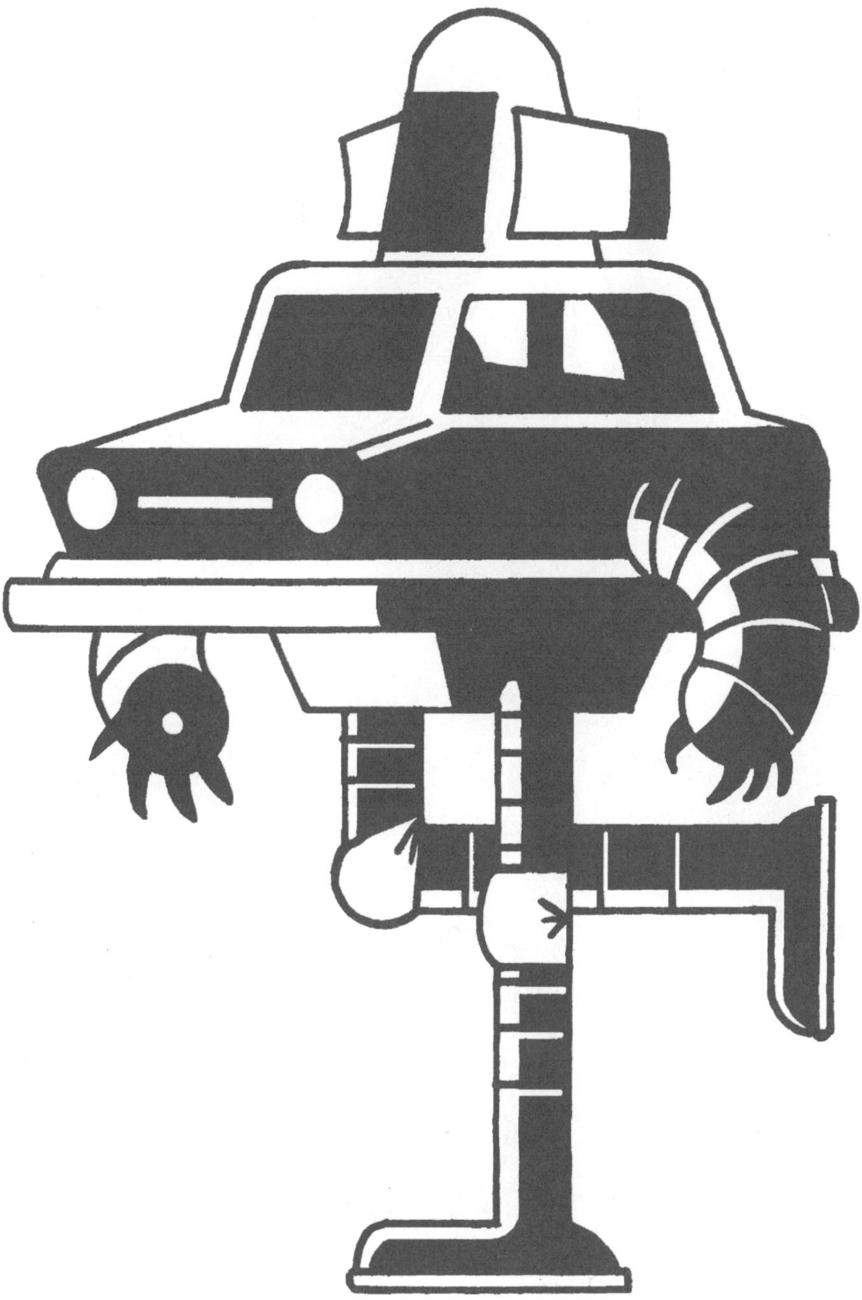

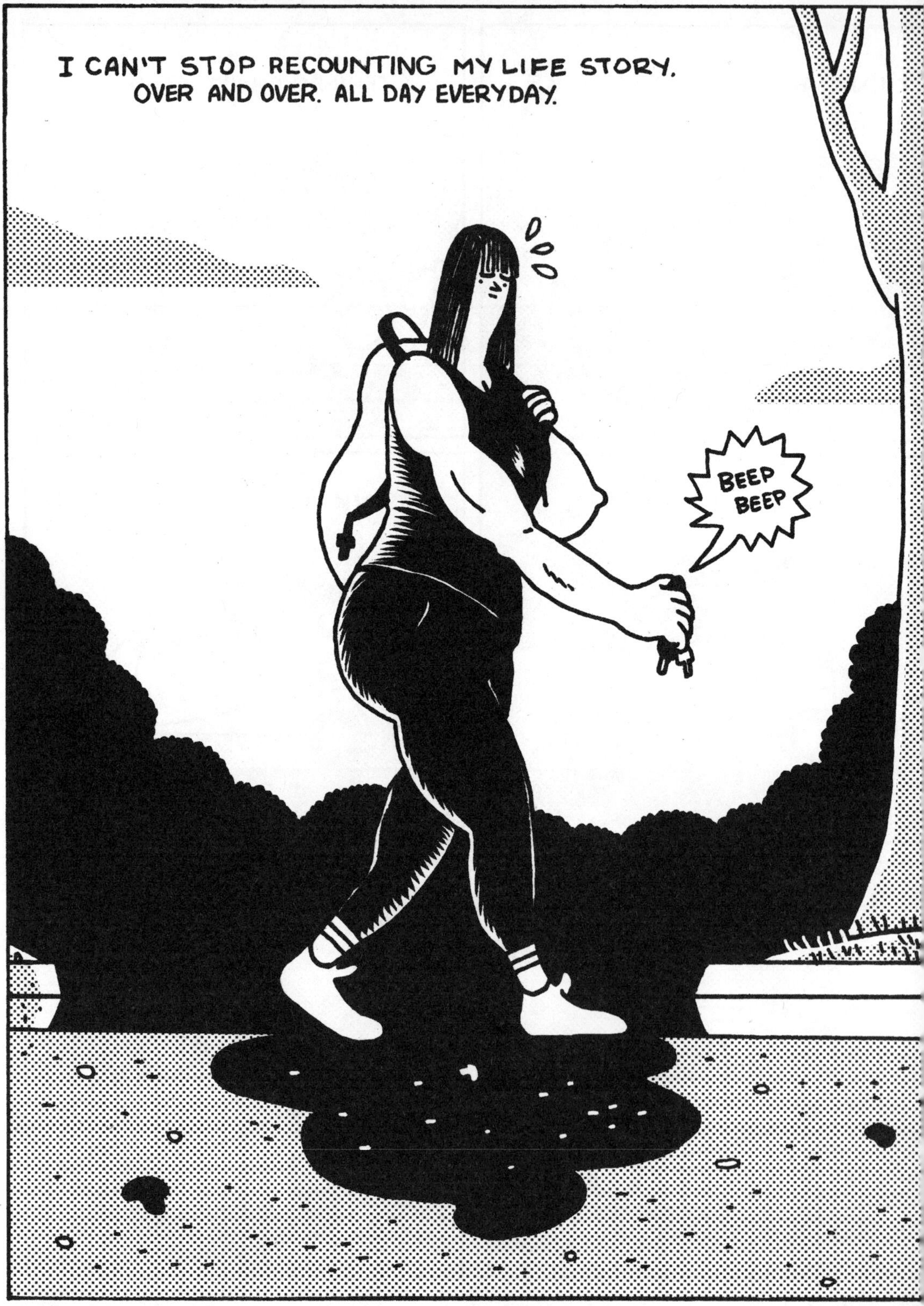
I CAN'T STOP RECOUNTING MY LIFE STORY. OVER AND OVER. ALL DAY EVERYDAY.
BEEP BEEP

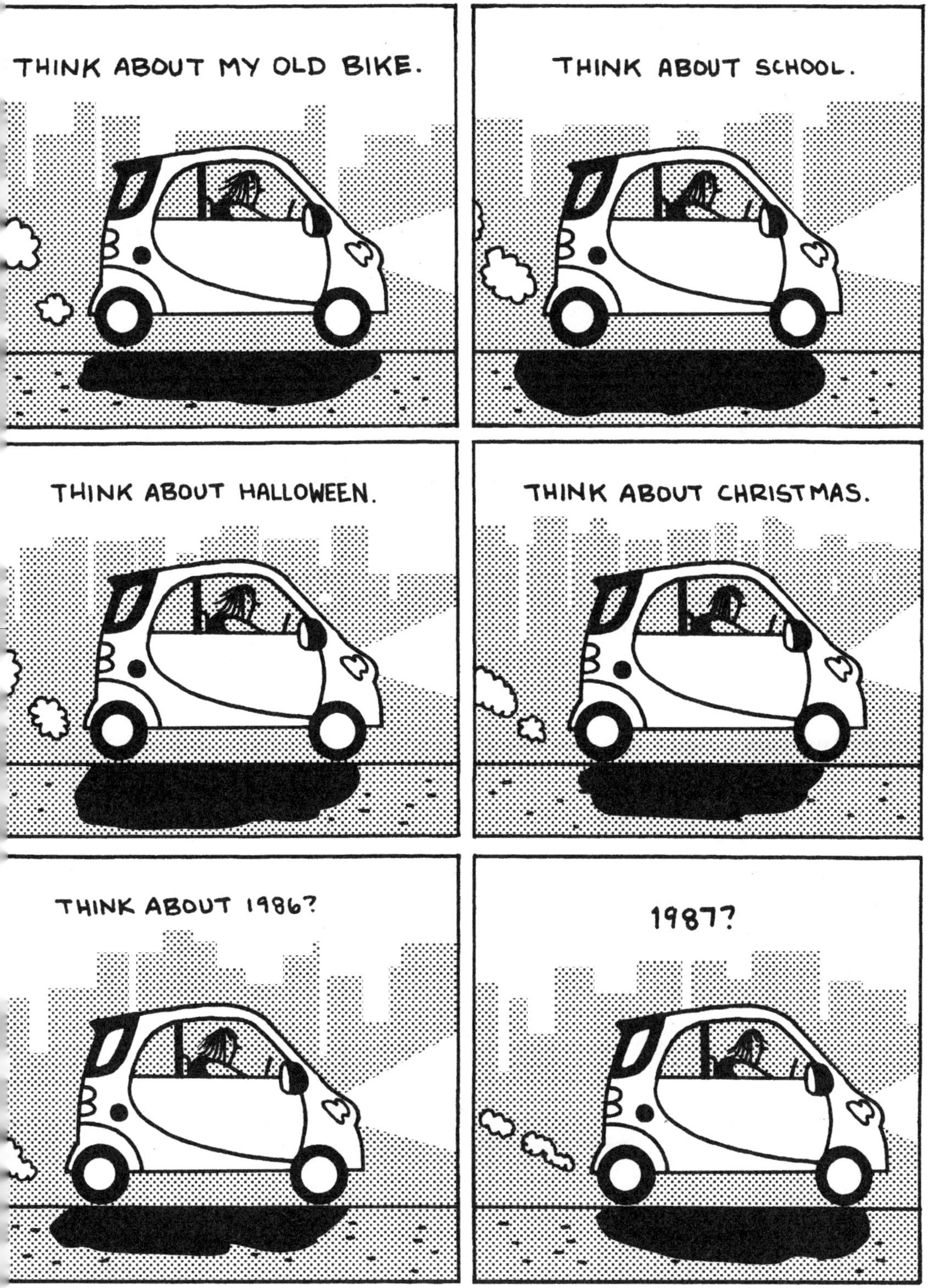
THINK ABOUT MY OLD BIKE.
THINK ABOUT SCHOOL.
THINK ABOUT HALLOWEEN.
THINK ABOUT CHRISTMAS.
THINK ABOUT 1986?
1987?

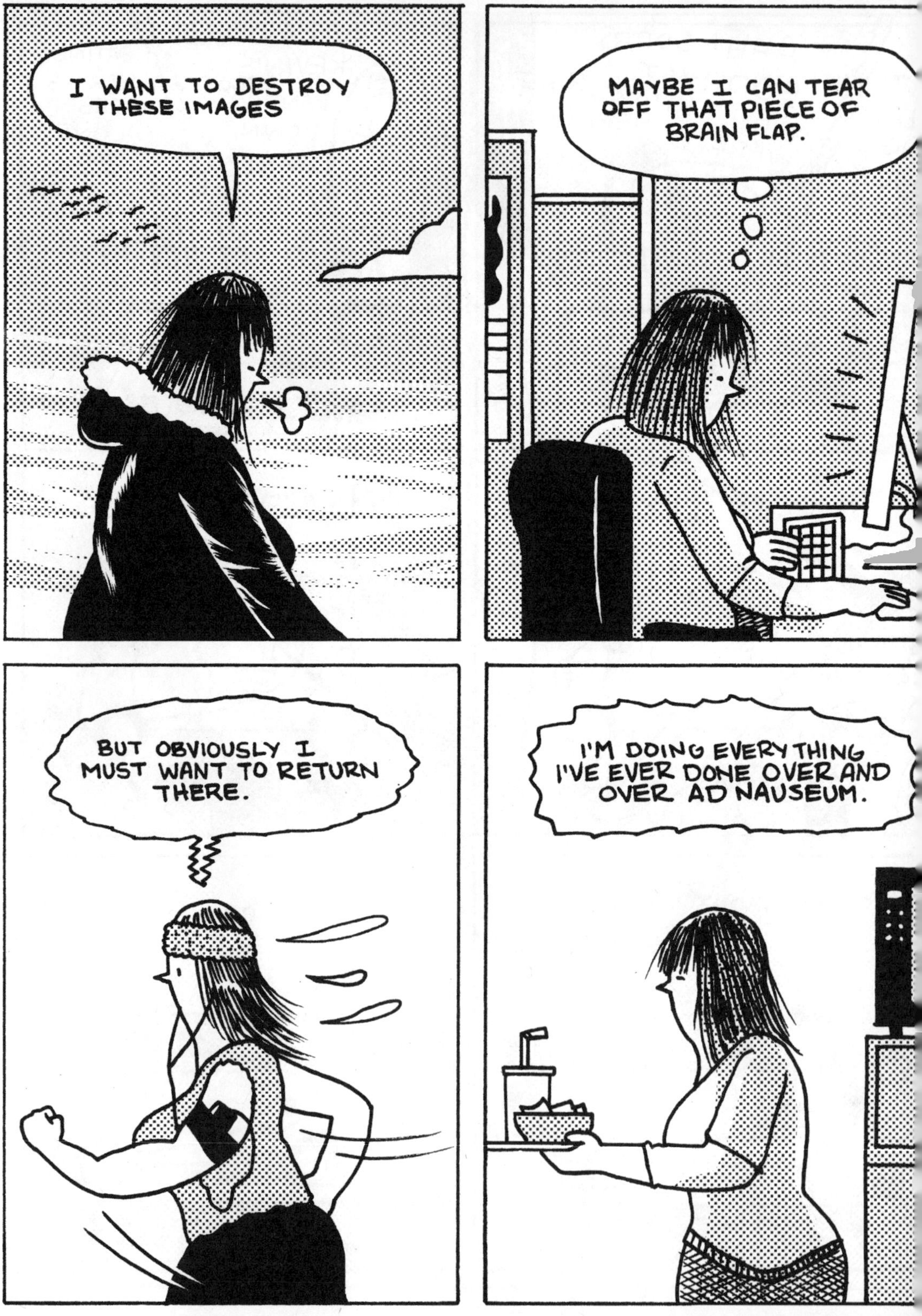
I WANT TO DESTROY THESE IMAGES
MAYBE I CAN TEAR OFF THAT PIECE OF BRAIN FLAP.
BUT OBVIOUSLY I MUST WANT TO RETURN THERE.
I'M DOING EVERYTHING I'VE EVER DONE OVER AND OVER AD NAUSEUM.

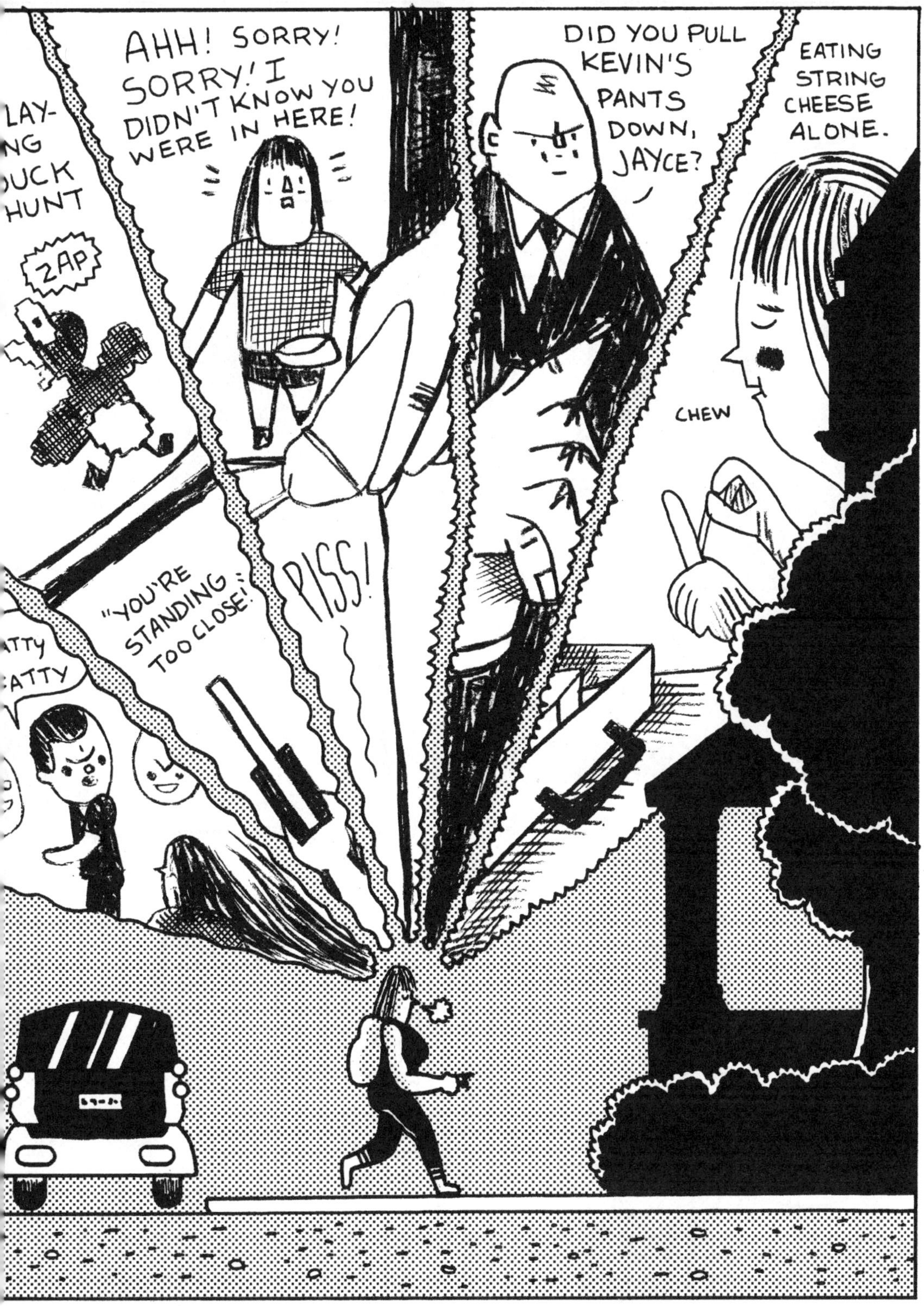

LAY-
NG
UCK
HUNT
ZAP
AHH! SORRY! SORRY! I DIDN'T KNOW YOU WERE IN HERE!
DID YOU PULL KEVIN'S PANTS DOWN, JAYCE?
EATING STRING CHEESE ALONE.
CHEW
"YOU'RE STANDING TOO CLOSE!
PISS!
ATTY
ATTY

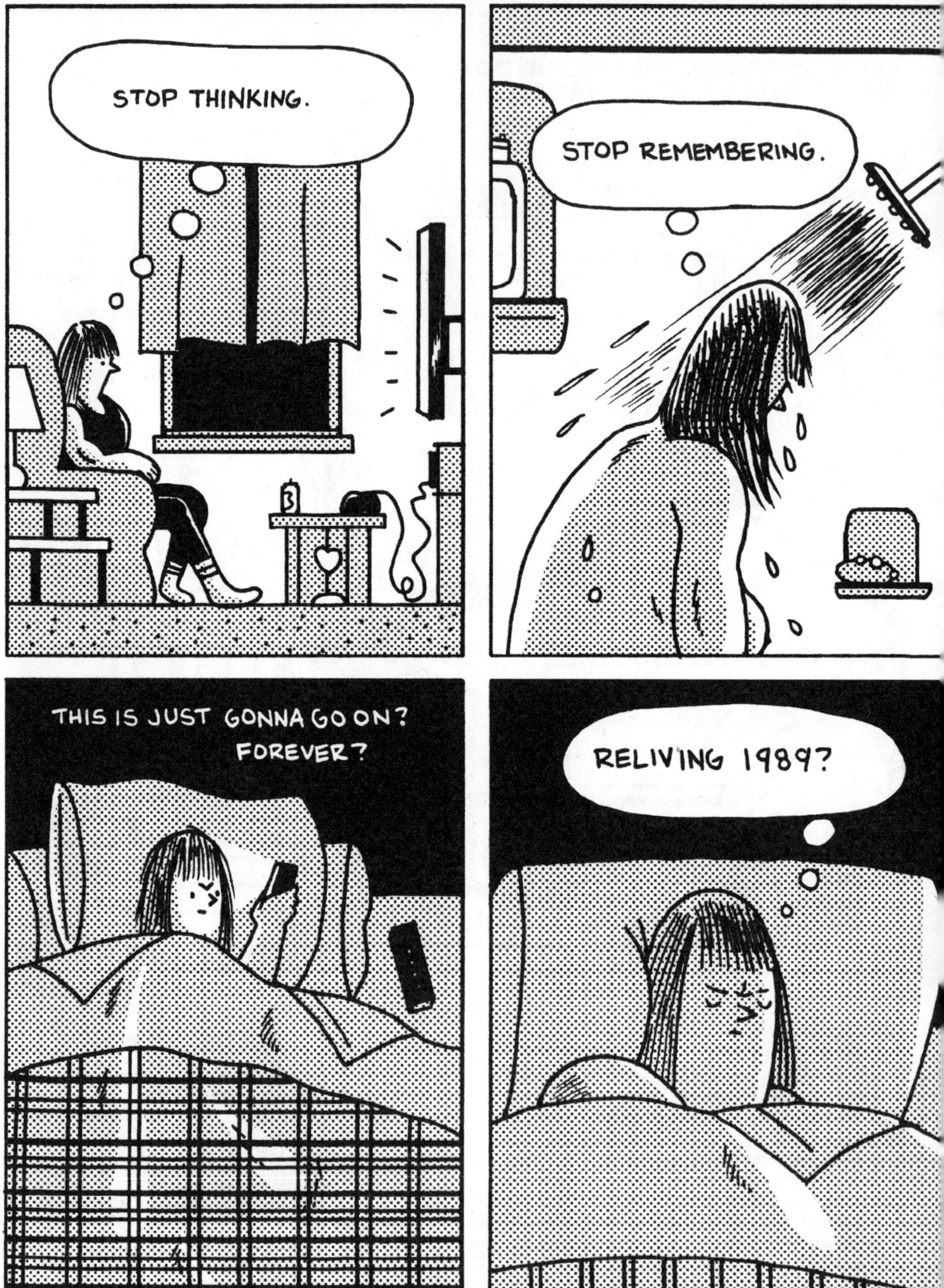
STOP THINKING.
STOP REMEMBERING.
THIS IS JUST GONNA GO ON? FOREVER?
RELIVING 1989?

I'M IN A SCHOOL OR COLLEGE DORM MAYBE.
BUT IT FEELS LIKE A MAZE.

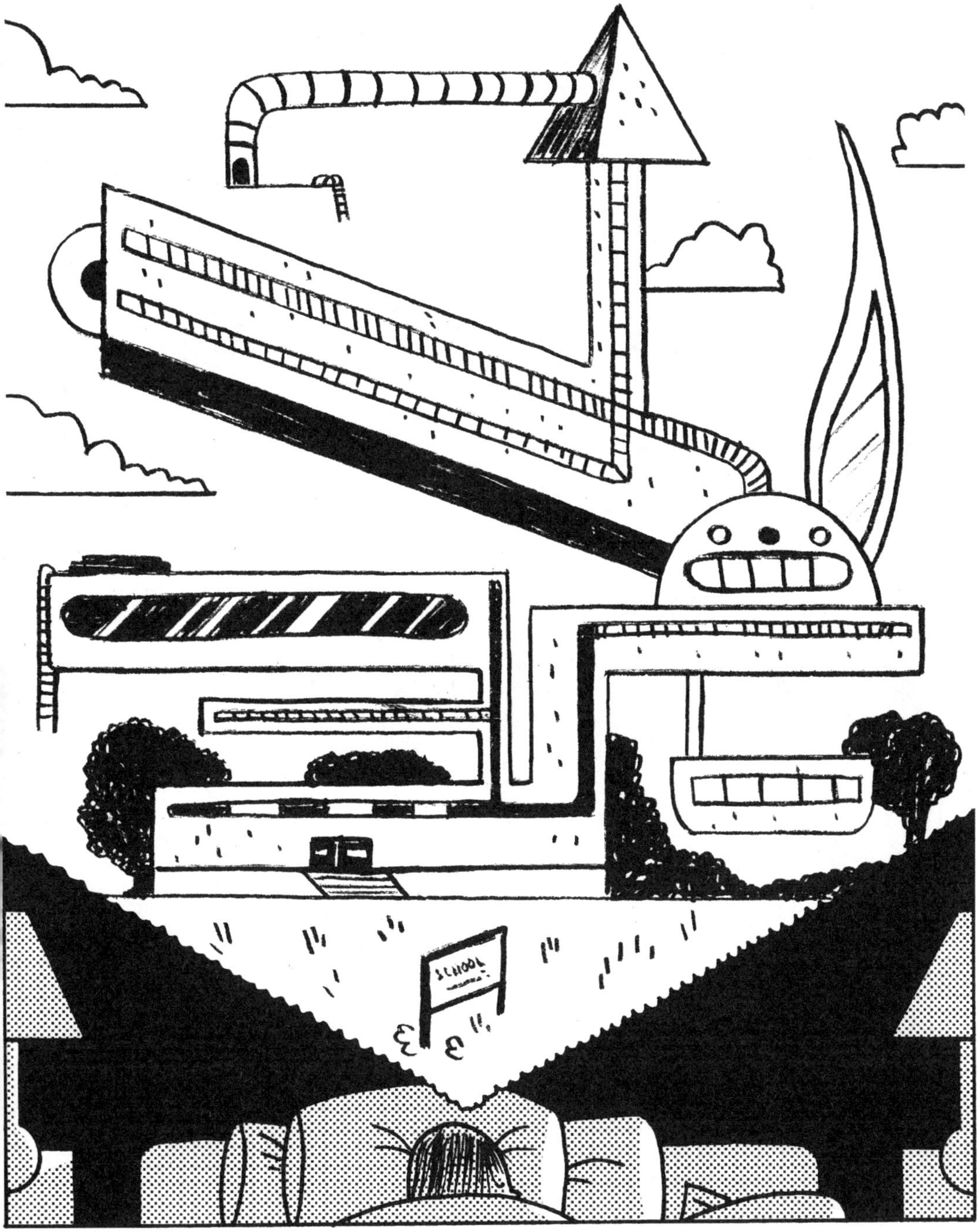
SCHOOL

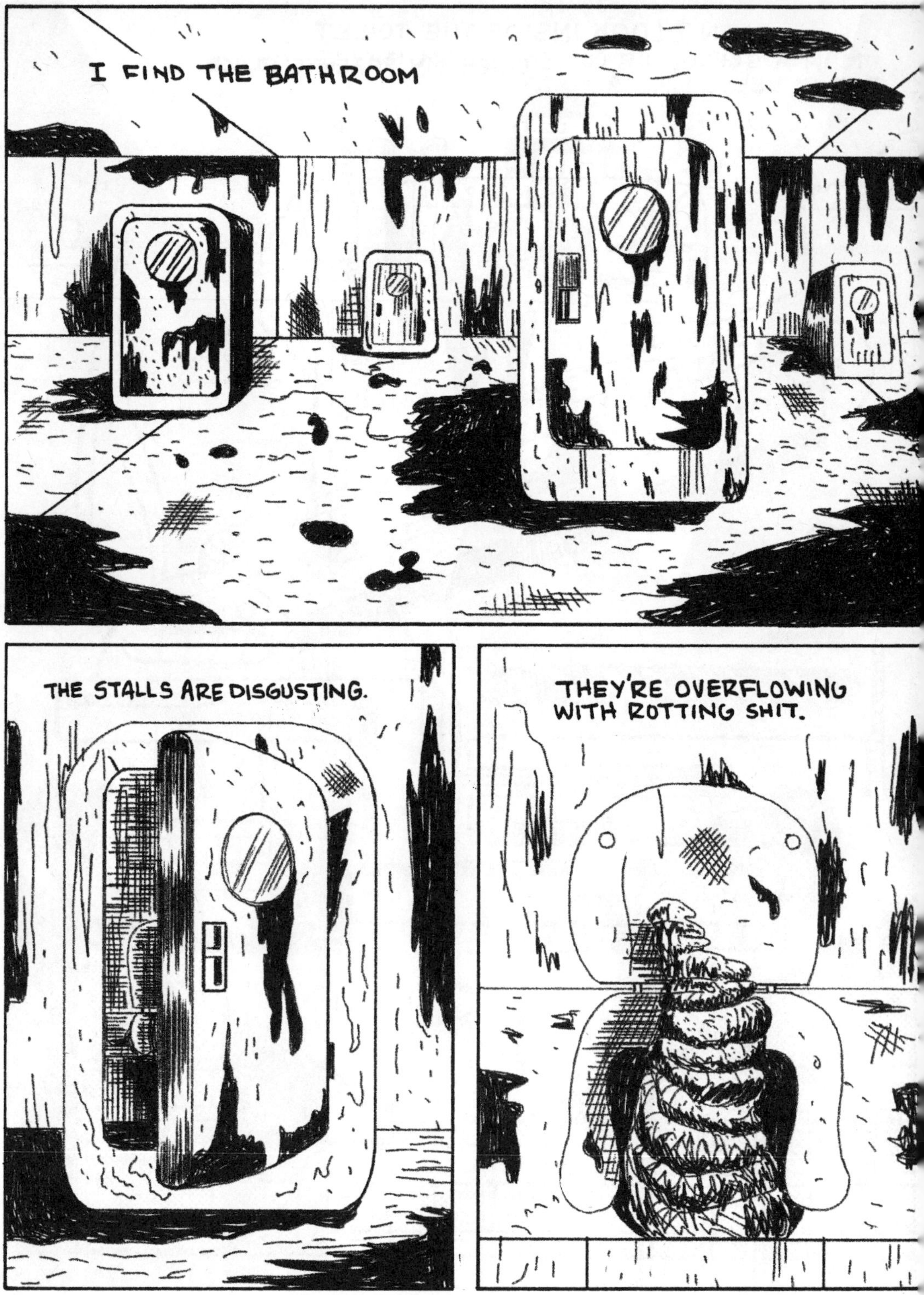
I FIND THE BATHROOM
THE STALLS ARE DISGUSTING.
THEY'RE OVERFLOWING WITH ROTTING SHIT.

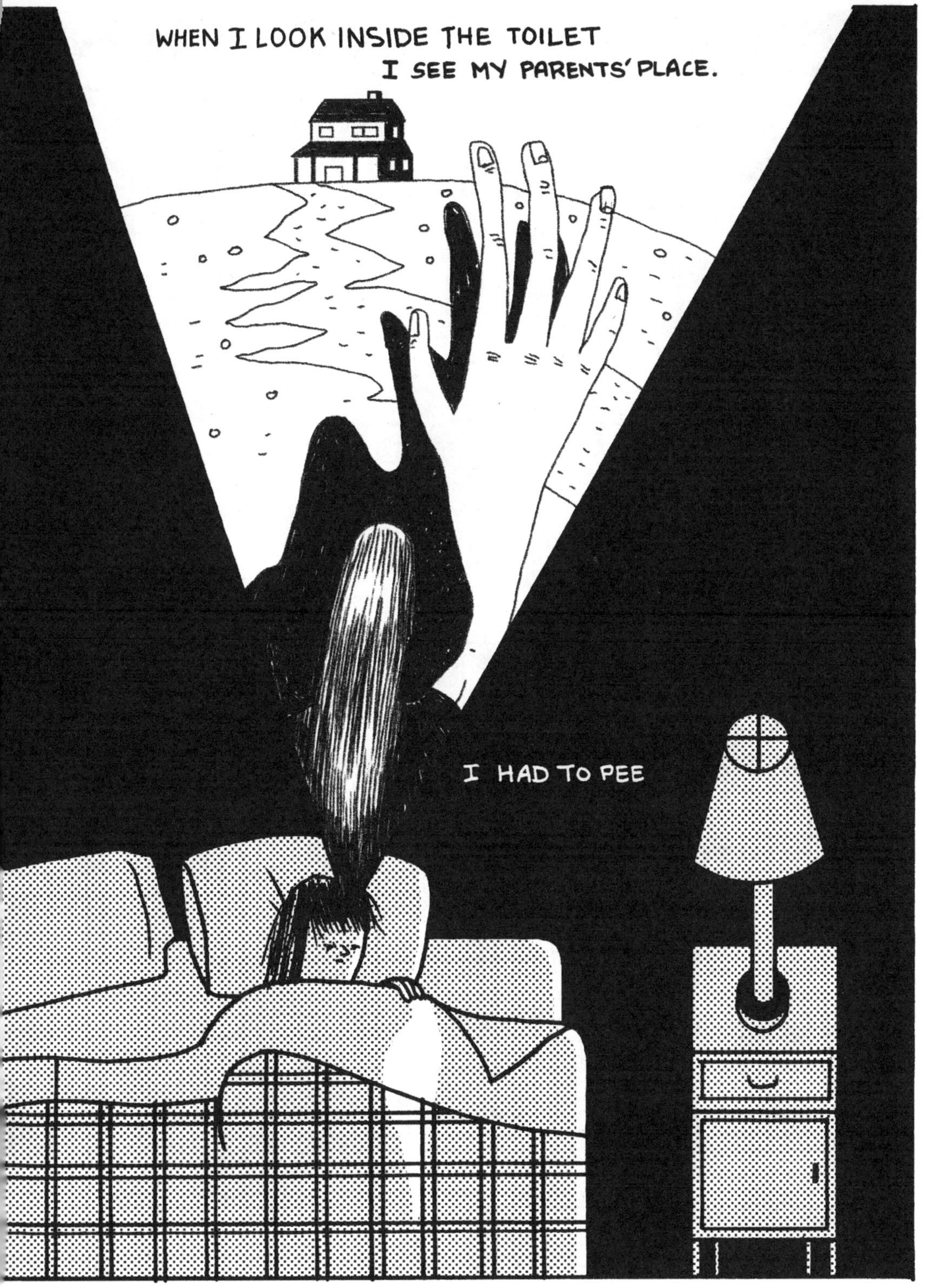
WHEN I LOOK INSIDE THE TOILET
I SEE MY PARENTS' PLACE.
I HAD TO PEE

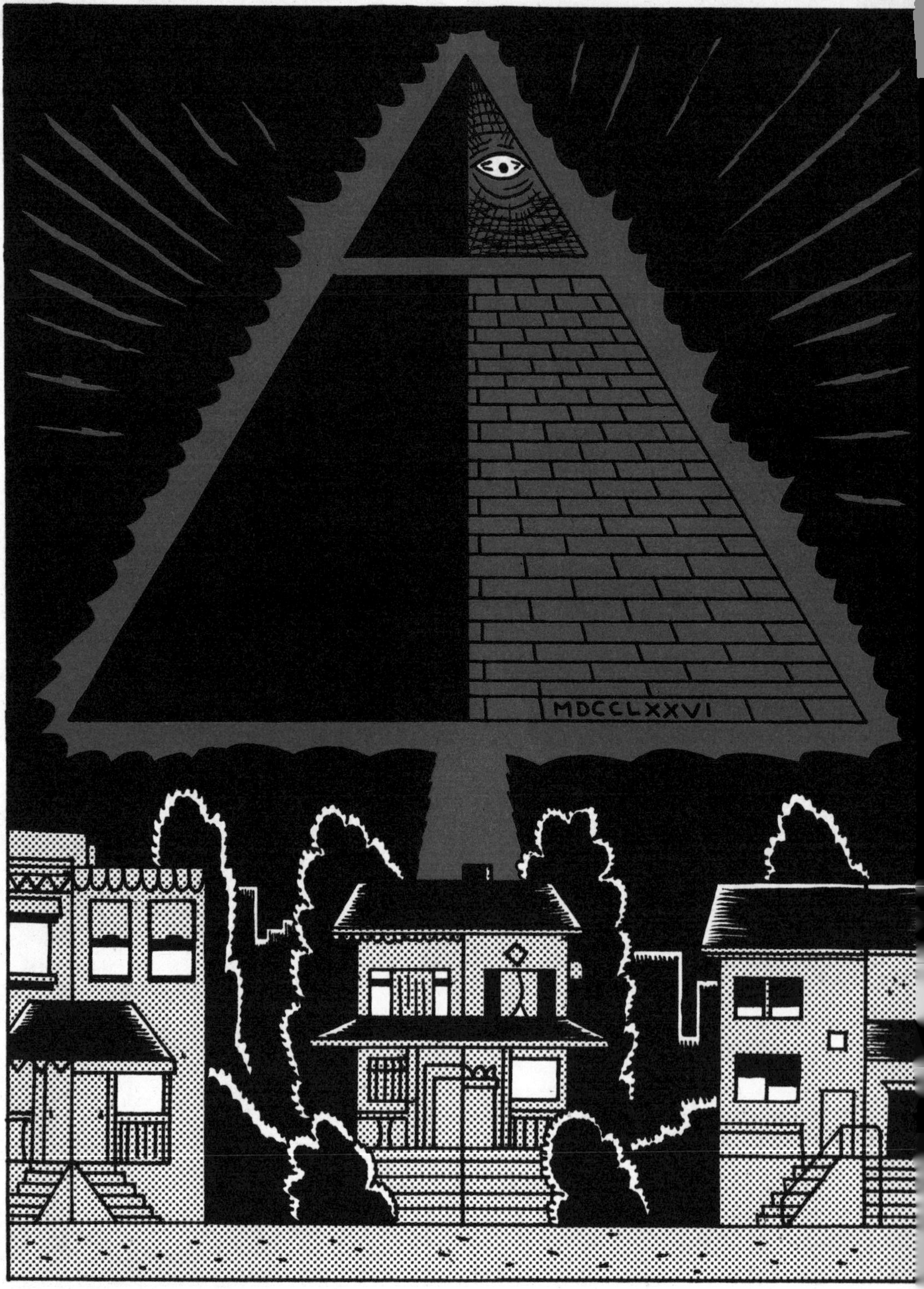
MDCCLXXVI

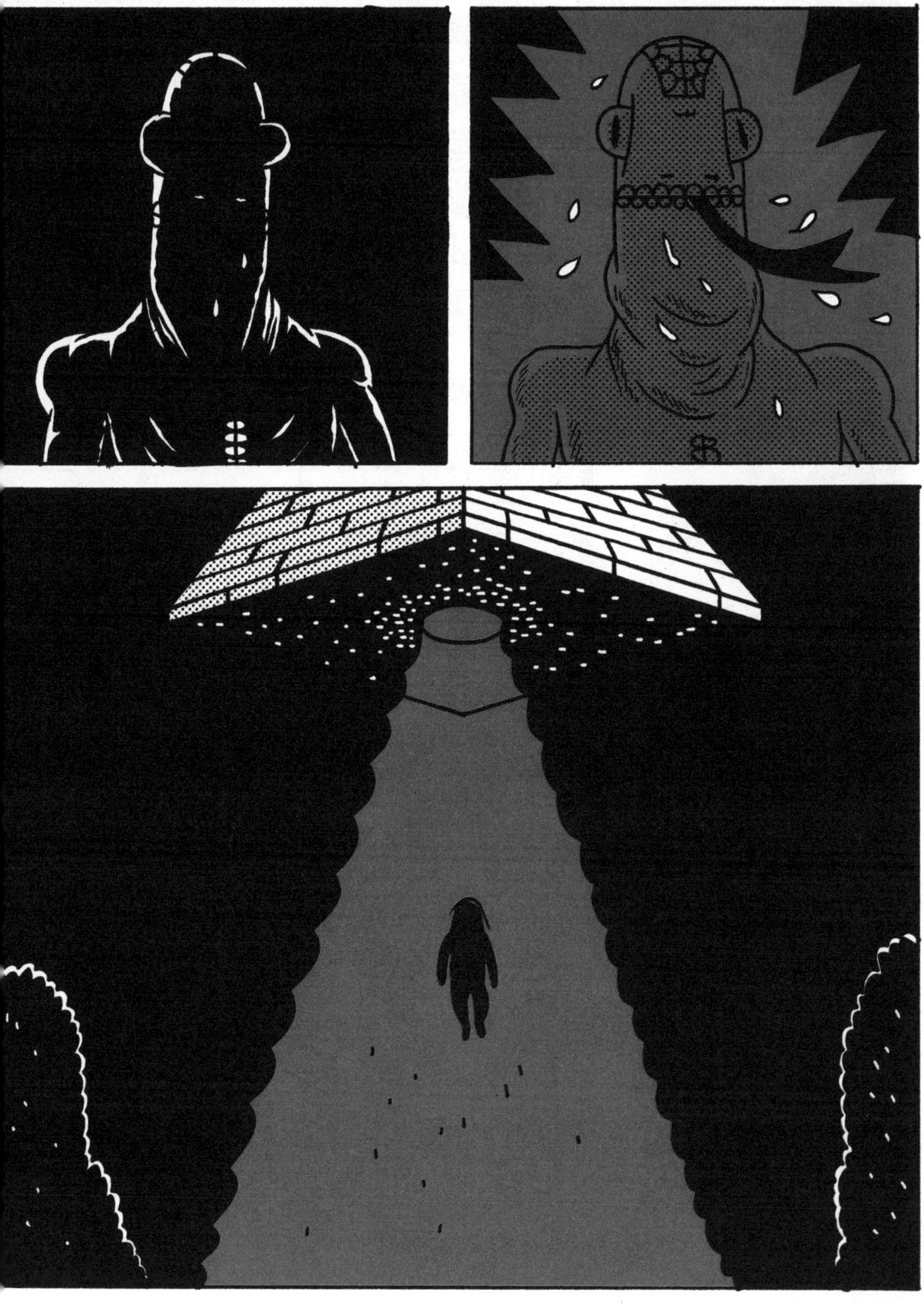

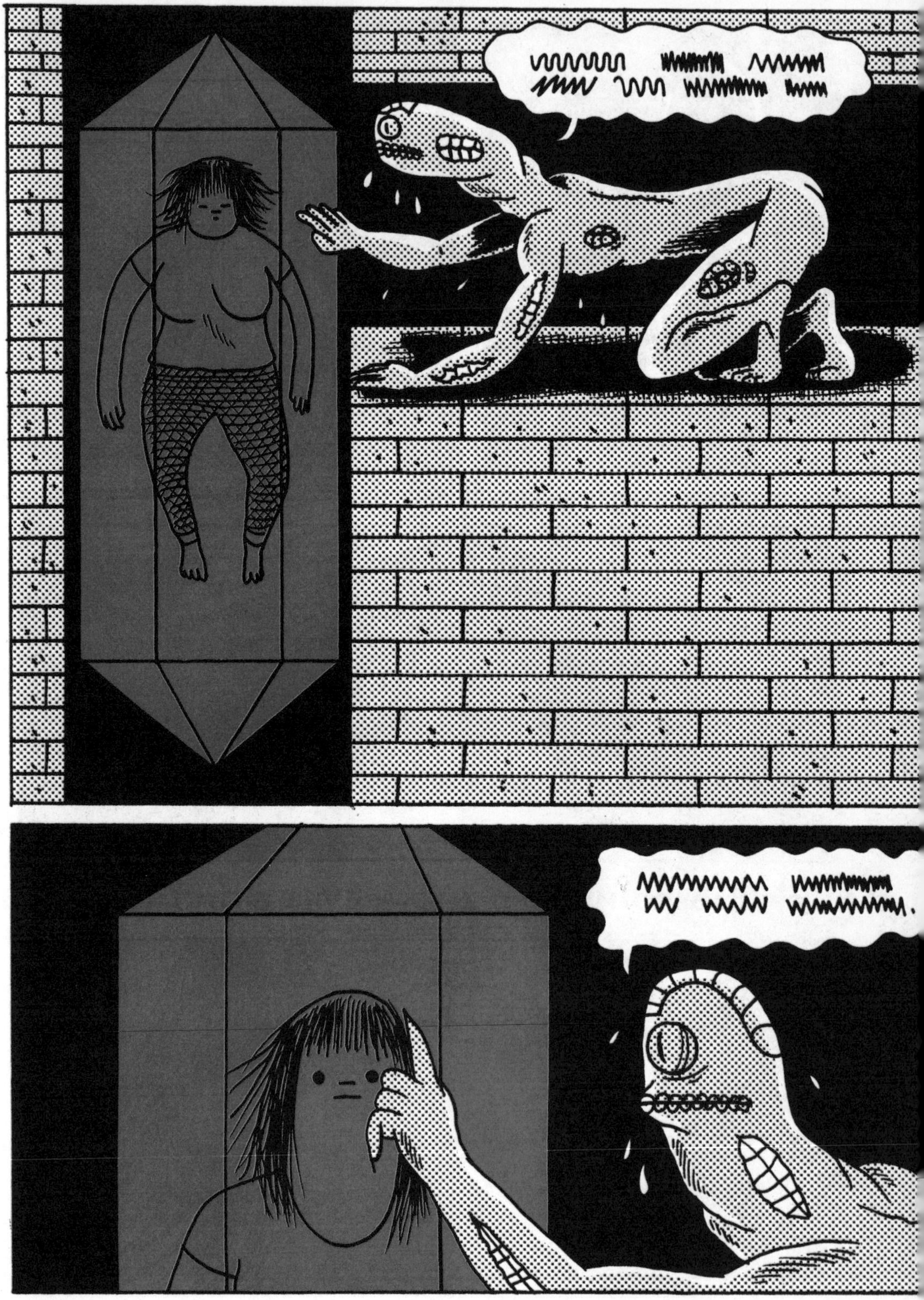

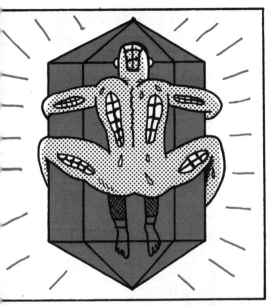

THE ALIEN ENTERED ME.

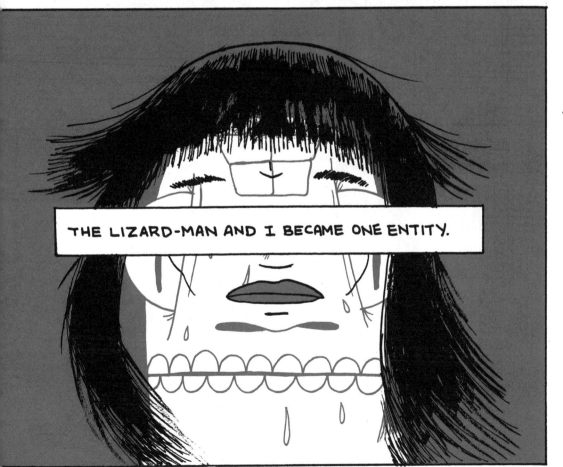

THE LIZARD-MAN AND I BECAME ONE ENTITY.

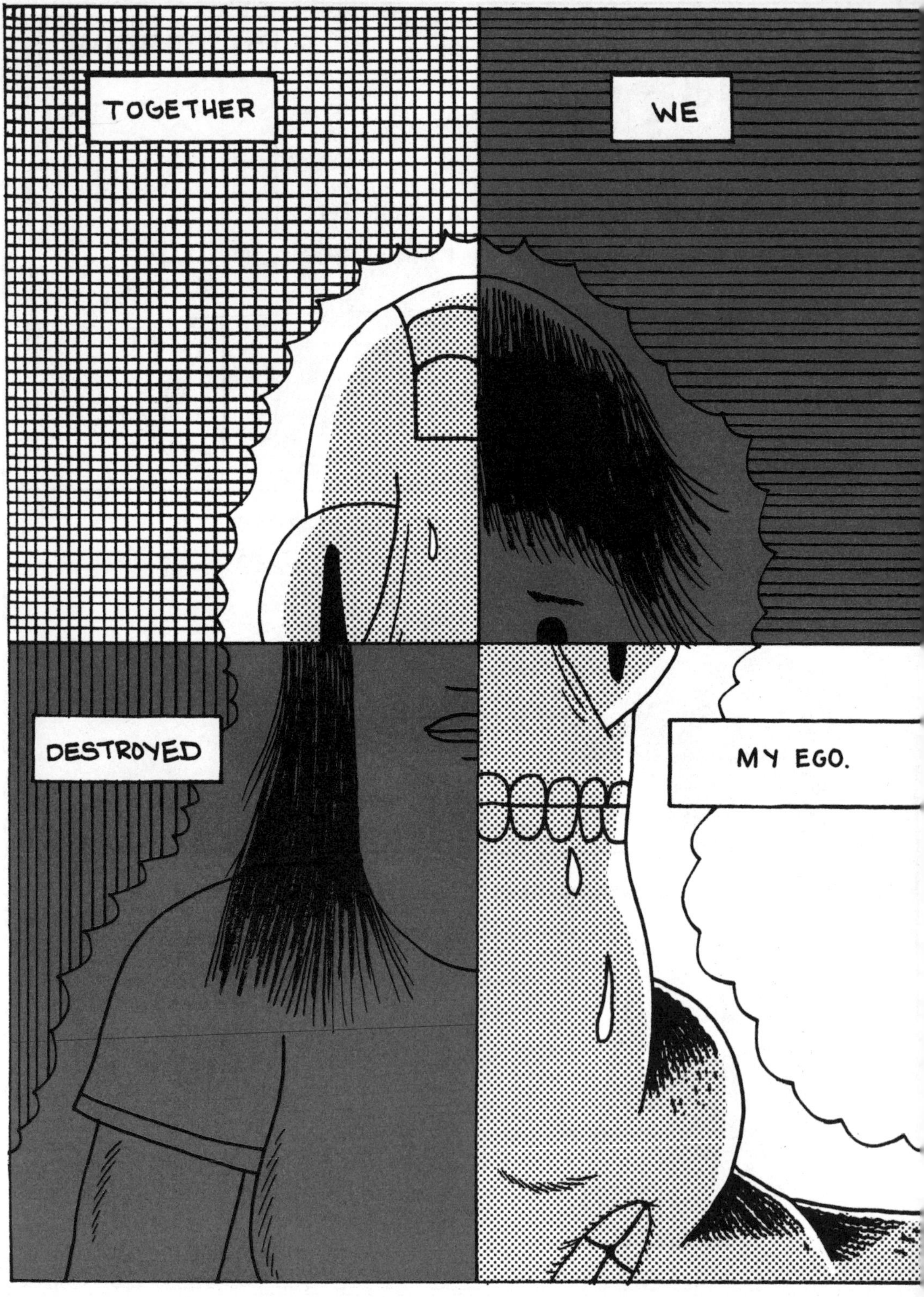
TOGETHER
WE
DESTROYED
MY EGO.

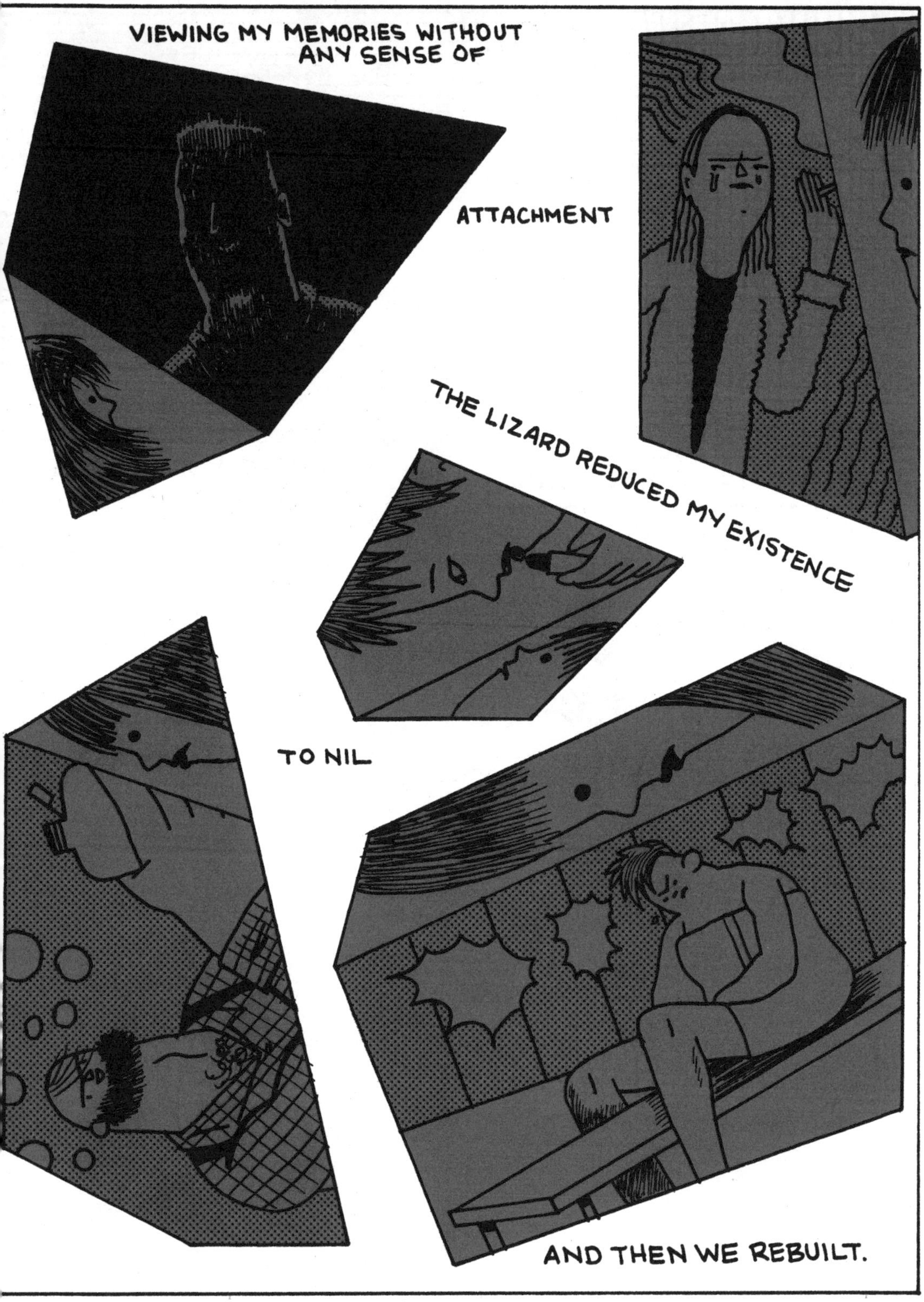
VIEWING MY MEMORIES WITHOUT ANY SENSE OF
ATTACHMENT
THE LIZARD REDUCED MY EXISTENCE
TO NIL
AND THEN WE REBUILT.

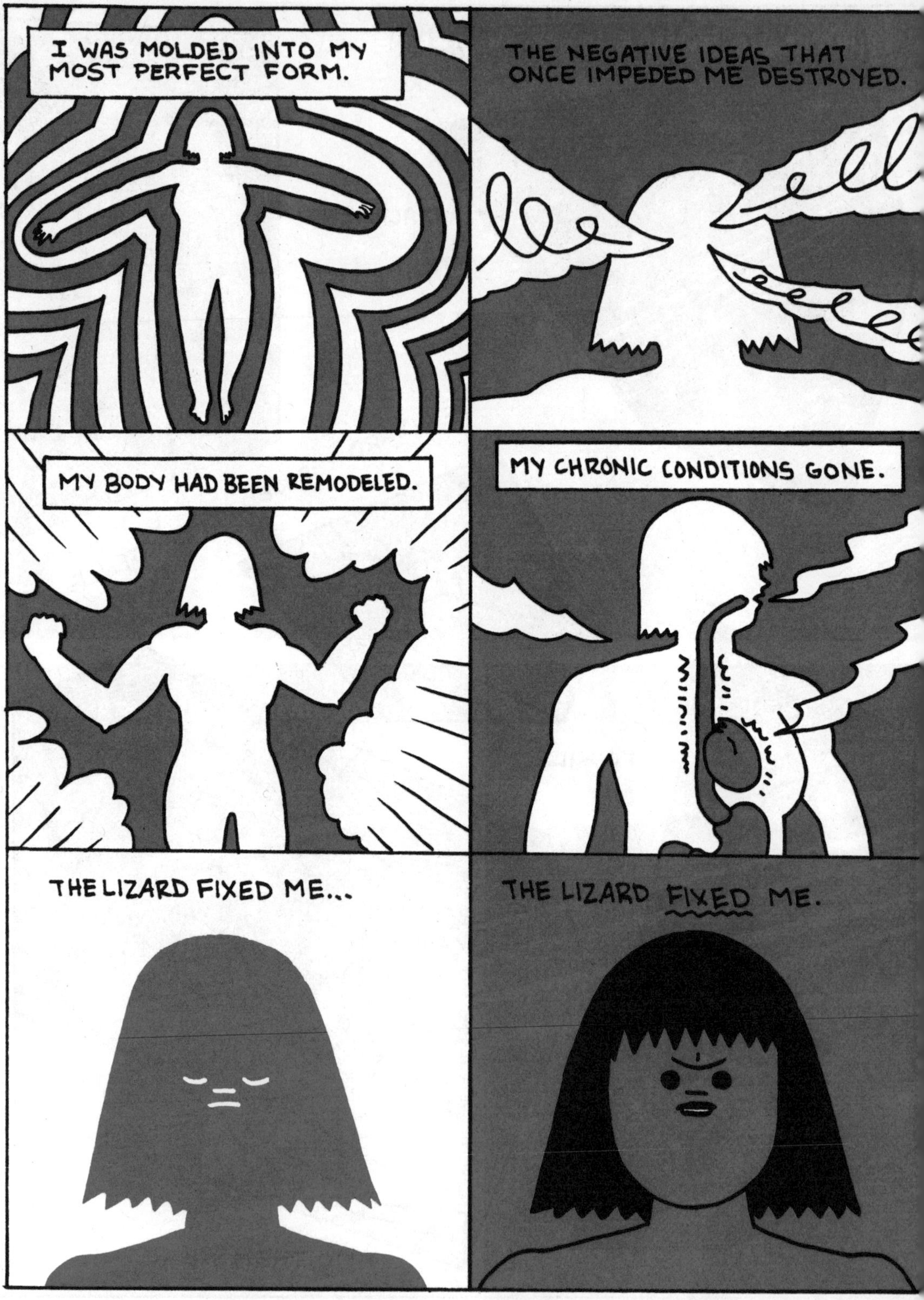
I WAS MOLDED INTO MY MOST PERFECT FORM.
THE NEGATIVE IDEAS THAT ONCE IMPEDED ME DESTROYED.
MY BODY HAD BEEN REMODELED.
MY CHRONIC CONDITIONS GONE.
THE LIZARD FIXED ME...
THE LIZARD FIXED ME.

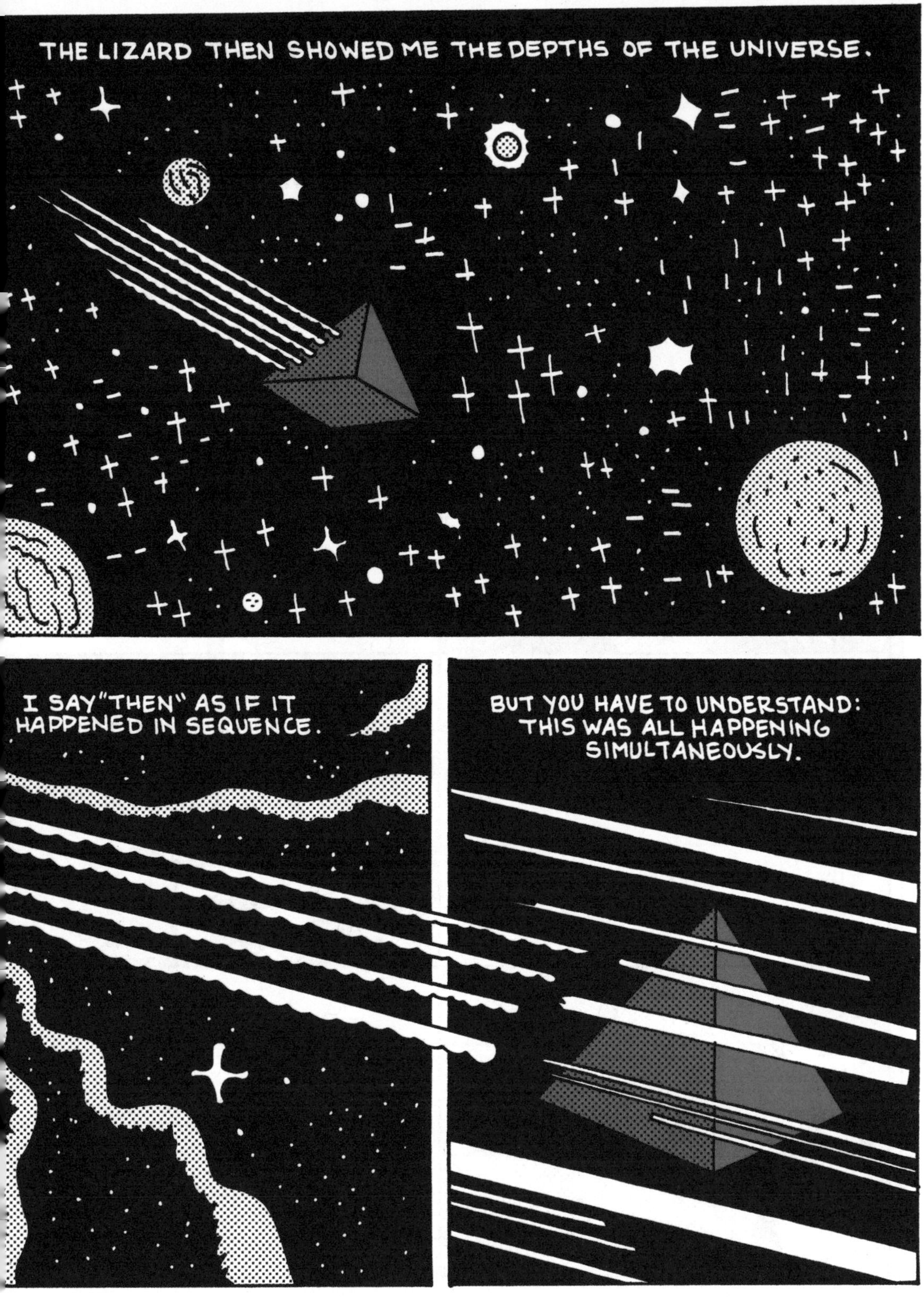
THE LIZARD THEN SHOWED ME THE DEPTHS OF THE UNIVERSE.
I SAY "THEN" AS IF IT HAPPENED IN SEQUENCE.
BUT YOU HAVE TO UNDERSTAND: THIS WAS ALL HAPPENING SIMULTANEOUSLY.

THE LIZARD SHOWED
ME LIFE ACROSS THE
UNIVERSE.

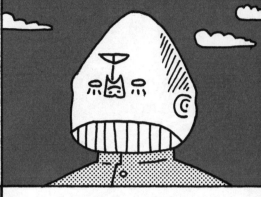

LIFE IS RARE
BUT IT'S THE SAME
THROUGHOUT.

FUTILE LIVES.

MEANINGLESS
EXISTENCE.

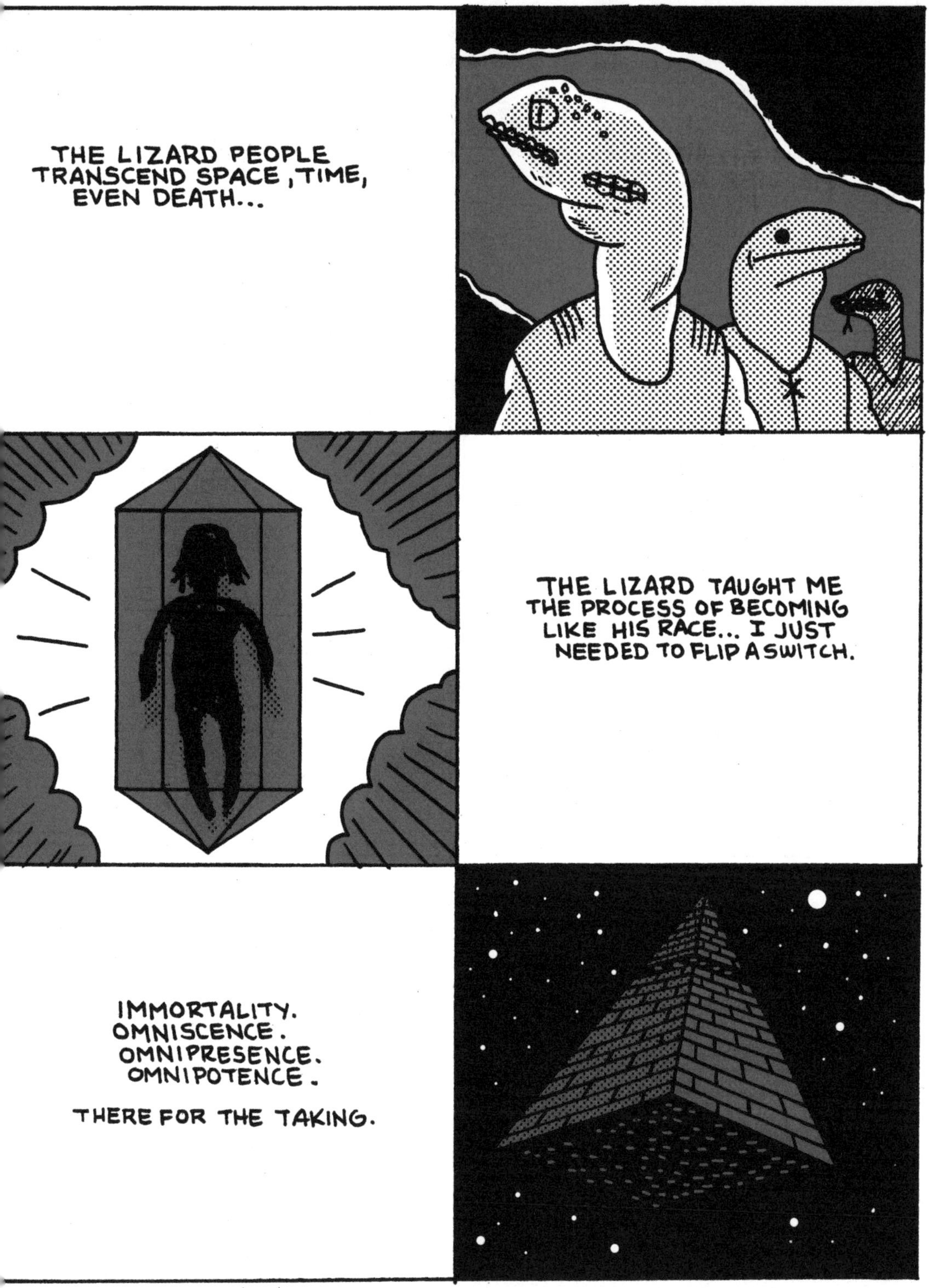
THE LIZARD PEOPLE TRANSCEND SPACE, TIME, EVEN DEATH...
THE LIZARD TAUGHT ME THE PROCESS OF BECOMING LIKE HIS RACE... I JUST NEEDED TO FLIP A SWITCH.
IMMORTALITY.
OMNISCENCE.
OMNIPRESENCE.
OMNIPOTENCE.
THERE FOR THE TAKING.

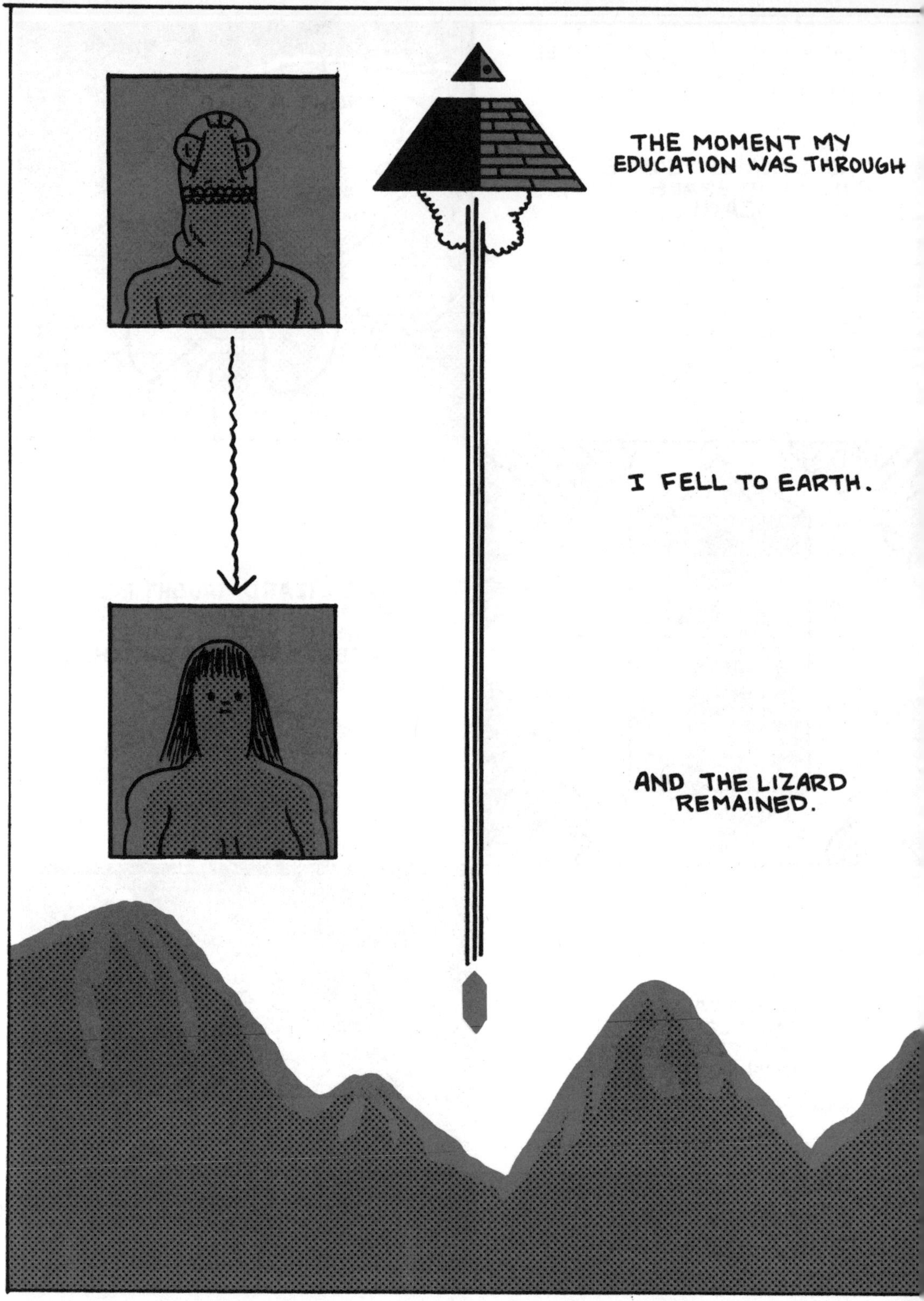
THE MOMENT MY EDUCATION WAS THROUGH
I FELL TO EARTH.
AND THE LIZARD REMAINED.

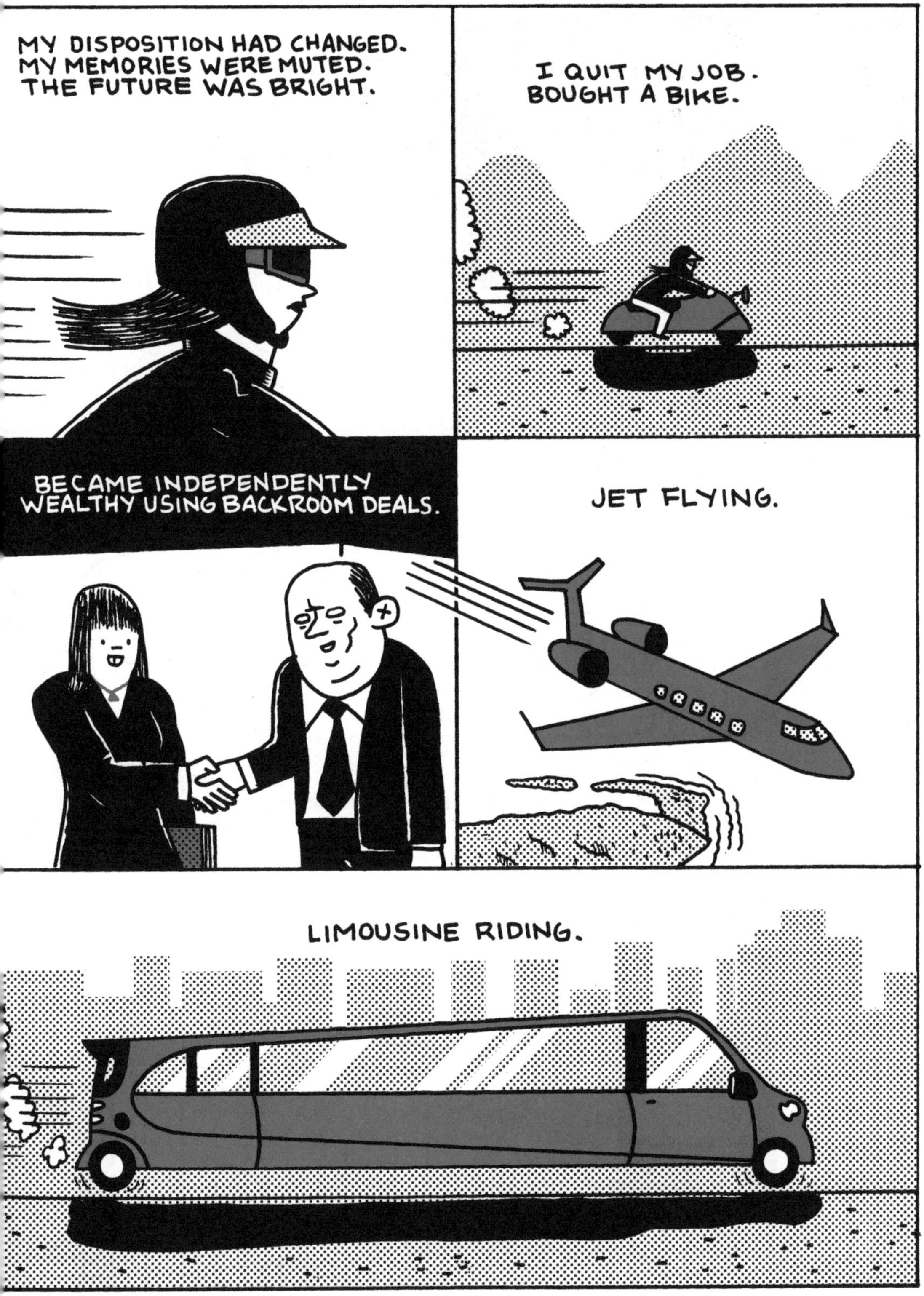
MY DISPOSITION HAD CHANGED. MY MEMORIES WERE MUTED. THE FUTURE WAS BRIGHT.
I QUIT MY JOB. BOUGHT A BIKE.
BECAME INDEPENDENTLY WEALTHY USING BACKROOM DEALS.
JET FLYING.
LIMOUSINE RIDING.

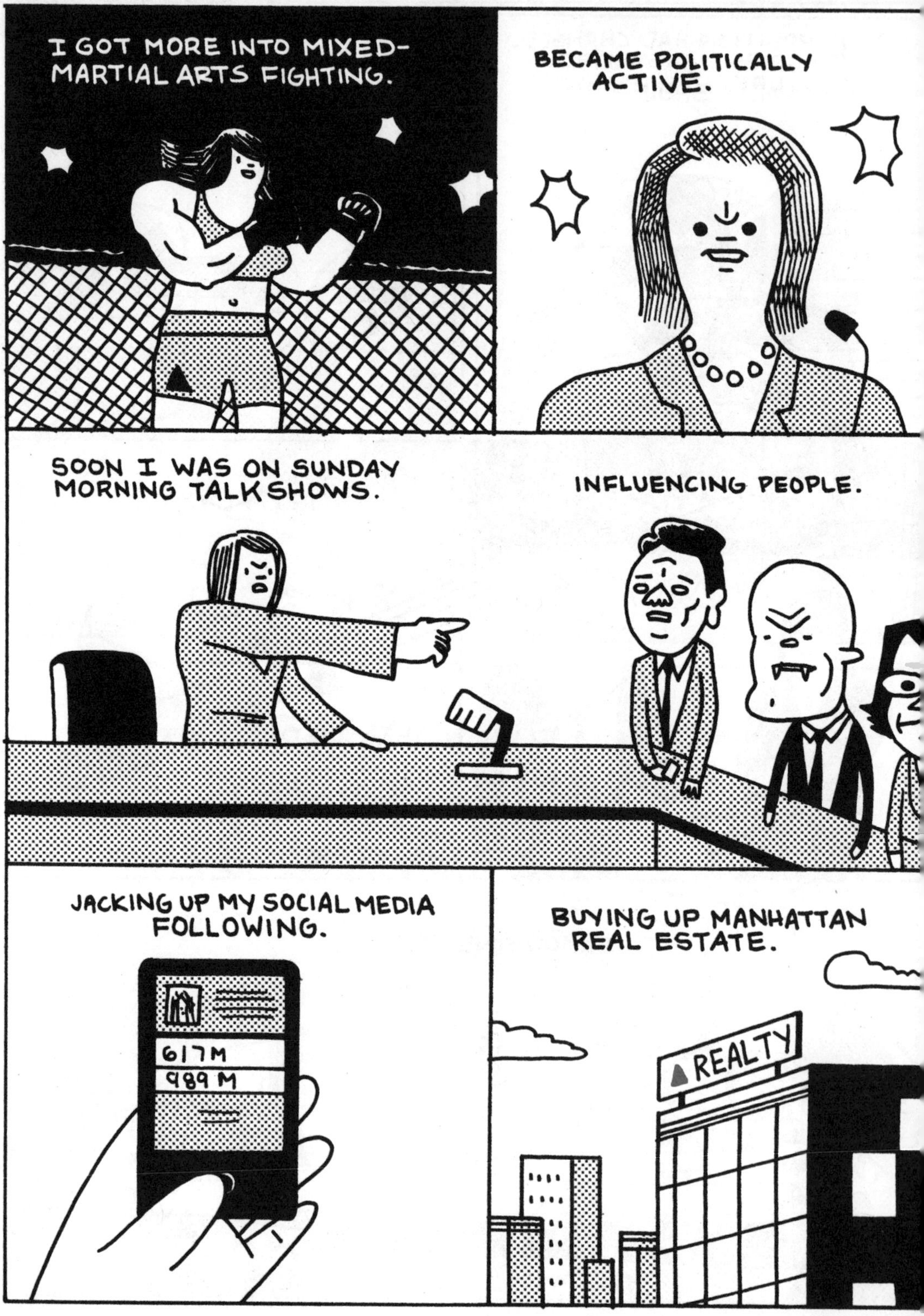

I GOT MORE INTO MIXED-MARTIAL ARTS FIGHTING.
BECAME POLITICALLY ACTIVE.
SOON I WAS ON SUNDAY MORNING TALK SHOWS.
INFLUENCING PEOPLE.
JACKING UP MY SOCIAL MEDIA FOLLOWING.
617M
989 M
BUYING UP MANHATTAN REAL ESTATE.
REALTY

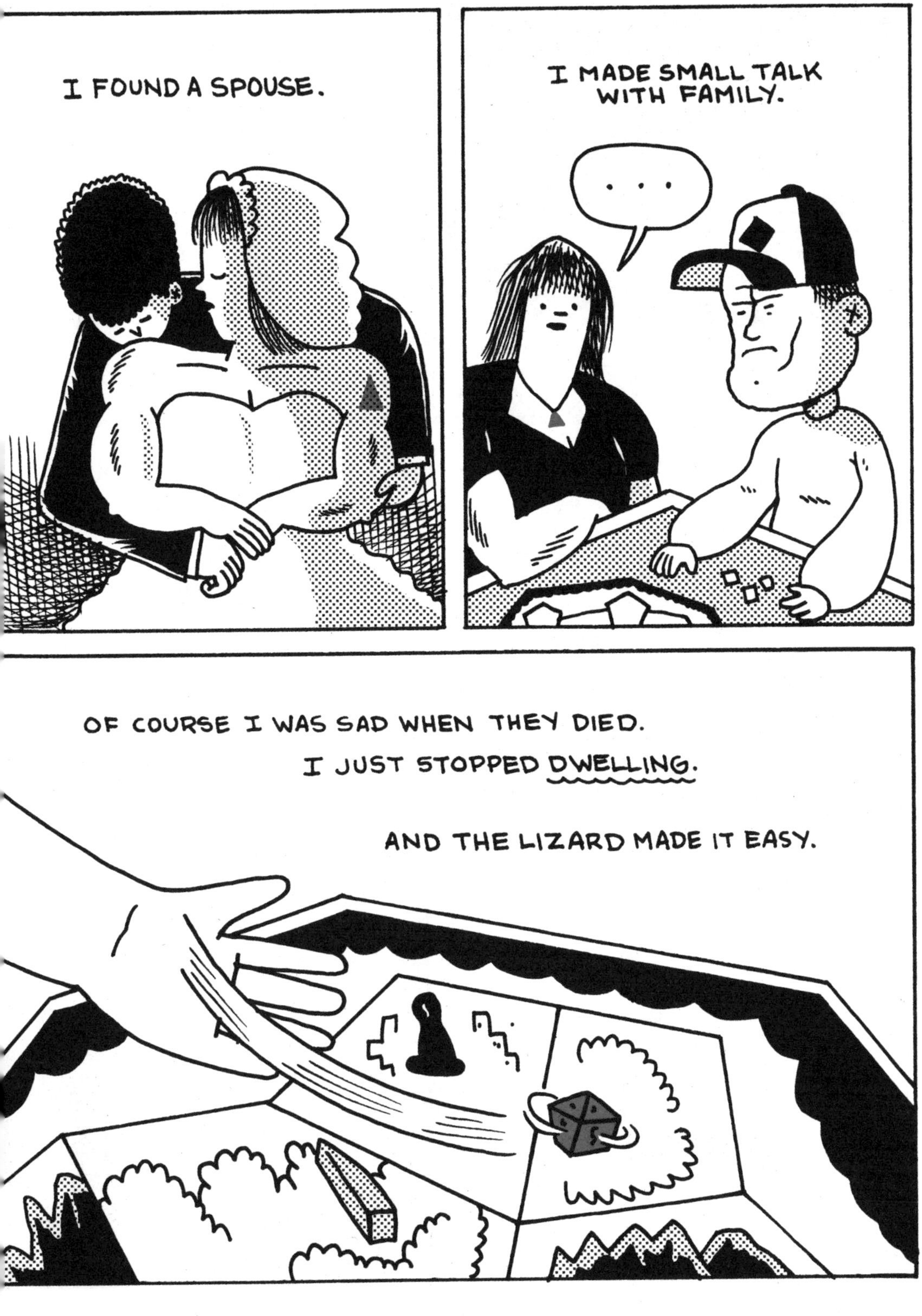
I FOUND A SPOUSE.
I MADE SMALL TALK WITH FAMILY.
. . .
OF COURSE I WAS SAD WHEN THEY DIED.
I JUST STOPPED DWELLING.
AND THE LIZARD MADE IT EASY.

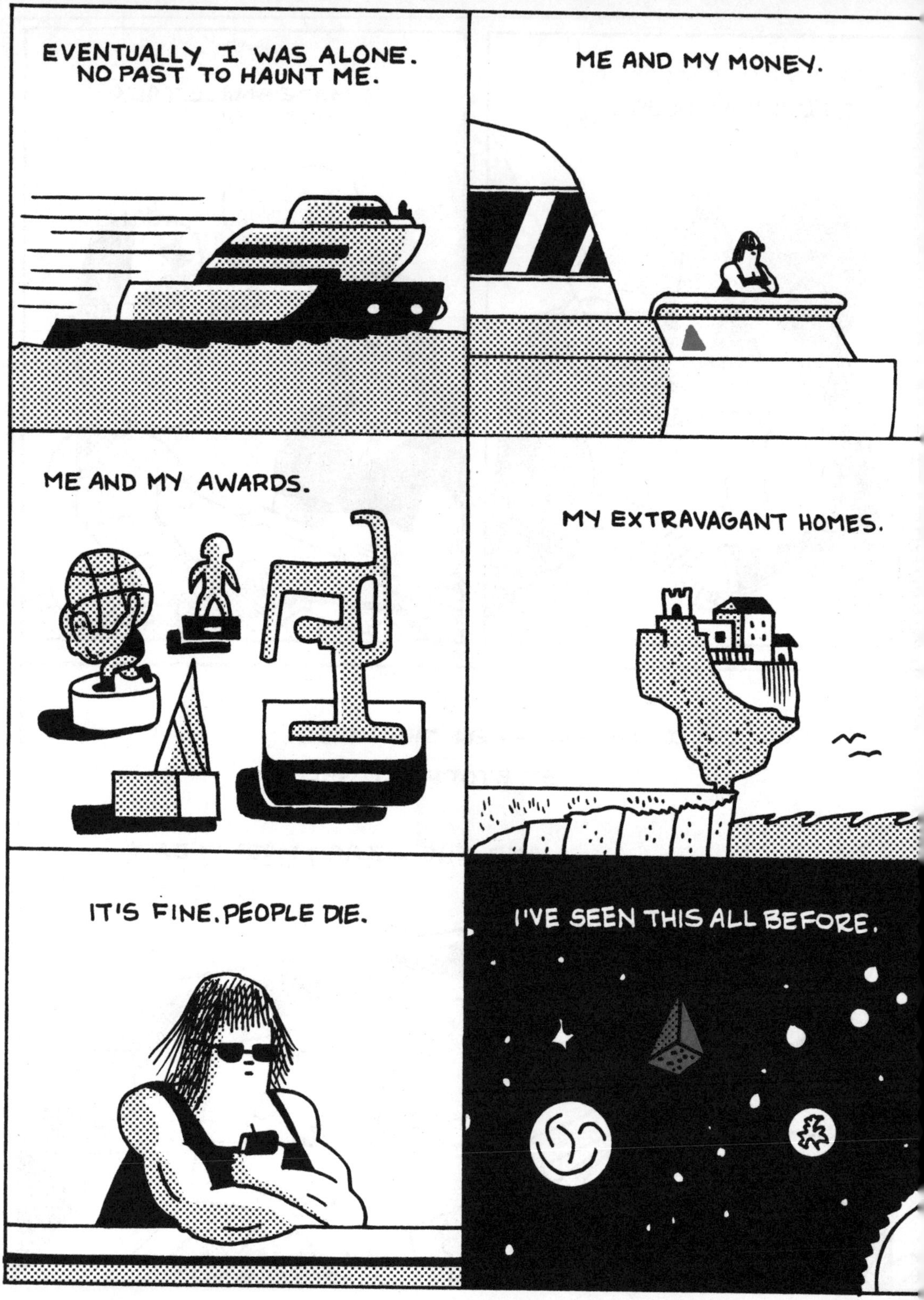
EVENTUALLY I WAS ALONE. NO PAST TO HAUNT ME.
ME AND MY MONEY.
ME AND MY AWARDS.
MY EXTRAVAGANT HOMES.
IT'S FINE. PEOPLE DIE.
I'VE SEEN THIS ALL BEFORE.

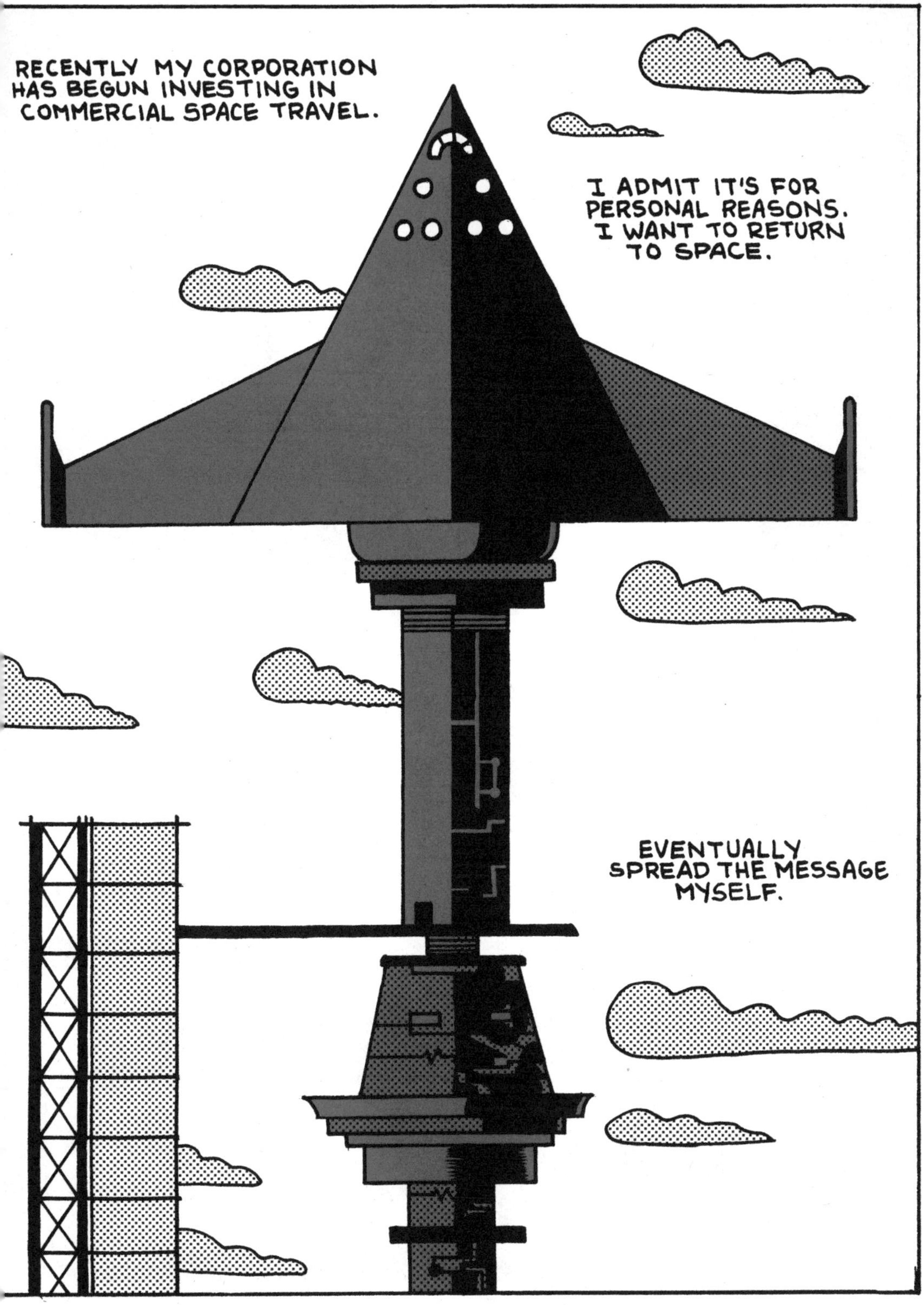
RECENTLY MY CORPORATION HAS BEGUN INVESTING IN COMMERCIAL SPACE TRAVEL.
I ADMIT IT'S FOR PERSONAL REASONS. I WANT TO RETURN TO SPACE.
EVENTUALLY SPREAD THE MESSAGE MYSELF.

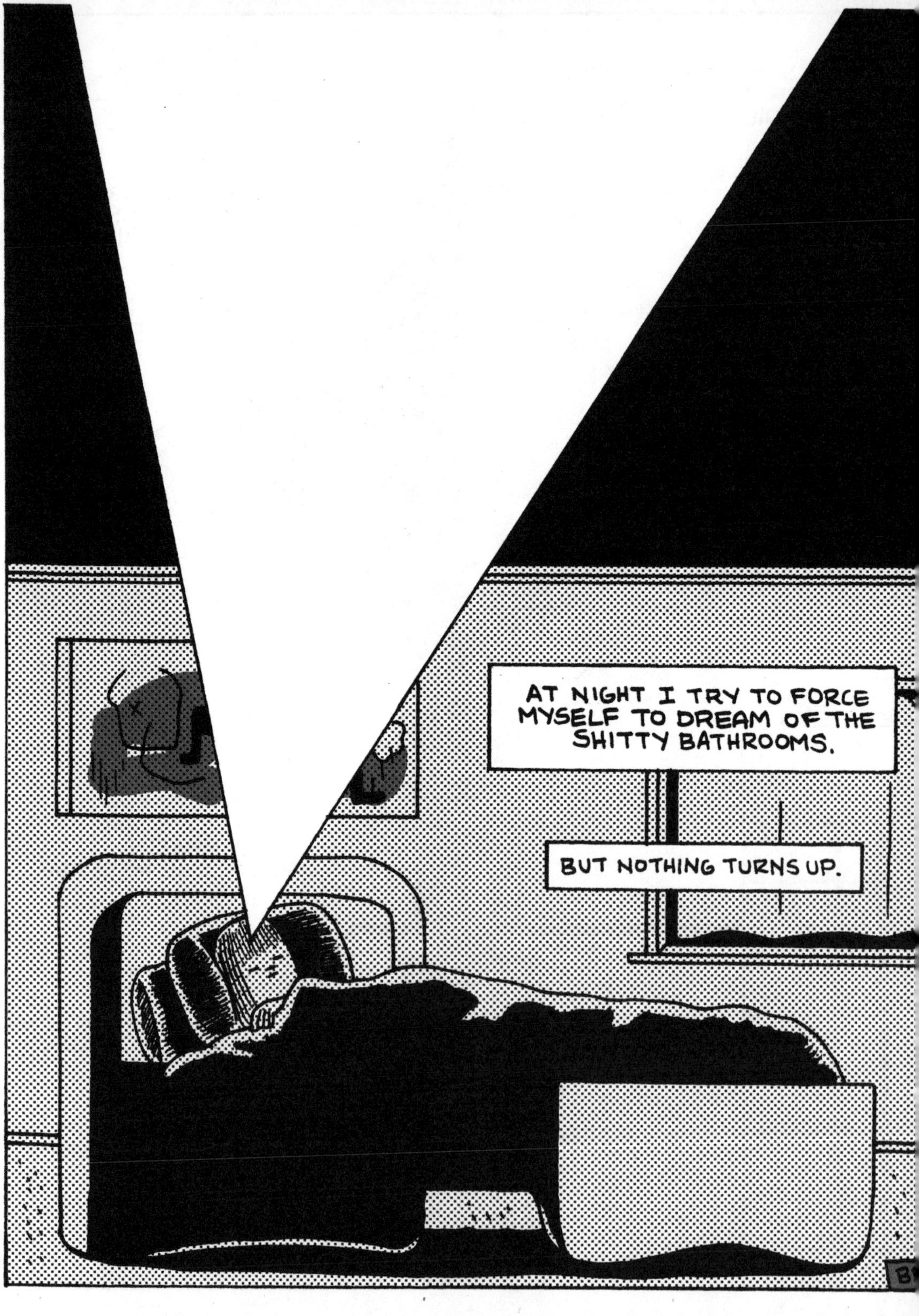
AT NIGHT I TRY TO FORCE MYSELF TO DREAM OF THE SHITTY BATHROOMS.
BUT NOTHING TURNS UP.

THE AUTHOR OF THIS TEXT